W9-APH-690

CROOKED CITY

Martin Preib

Copyright © 2014 Martin Preib
All rights reserved.
ISBN: 149-548531-5
ISBN-13: 978-149-548531-2
Cover Design: Candice Johnson

DEDICATION

This book is dedicated to Laurie Haight Keenan, an old friend who rescued me halfway through.

It is also dedicated to the patrolmen, detectives and supervisors of the Chicago Police Department, particularly those who worked the early 80s.

Finally, this book is dedicated to retired Detective Charles Salvatore, a lead detective on the Anthony Porter case. It was his dedication, integrity, and character that helped keep the case alive.

THE WAGON
AND OTHER STORIES
FROM THE CITY

University of Chicago Press, 2010
176 pages, Available on Amazon

From its aptly noirish title on, Martin Preib's *The Wagon* has rightness of authenticity about it. From the perspective of a cop he fashions a compelling view of the Chicago Algren once called 'the dark city.' There's a unique quality to his essays which manage to be broodingly meditative even as their narrative drive keeps you turning pages.

—Stuart Dybek, author of *I Sailed with Magellan*

Martin Preib worked as a bartender, a hotel doorman, a lowest-level cop (carrying out the dead). He filled his dresser drawers and his pockets and the patrol cars he drove with his scribblings, looking for his own form, his own voice. He believed he failed and he punished himself, but he kept on and the writing grew weightier, like the dead when they grow holy and sink into the earth. His language and thought escalated, he found a voice, and those fragments of street talk and cop-think took shape as comic or ugly but true stories of what Chicago does to its people. Now this inde-structible writer has fused his stories into a remarkable first book—an essay that is a memoir, and also something else that is very like a prayer.

—William Kennedy, author of *Ironweed*

[*The Wagon* is] about the real Chicago, the city of tribes, the city many of you know, not that fictional metropolis sometimes offered in magazines and TV shows. . . . So there are no blondes in red dresses. No detectives with cleft chins. It hooked me right there. And if there's a hero, the hero is an intelligent man trying to figure things out.

—John Kass, *Chicago Tribune*

The depiction of what it is really like to be a cop—in all its sadly hilarious glory—is what makes this book work so well."

—Sarah Weinman, Confessions of an Idiosyncratic Mind

CONTENTS

My most important problem was destroying the line of demarcation that separates what seems real from what seems fantastic.

—Gabriel García Márquez

Pausing, searching, receiving, contemplating.

Gently, but with undeniable will, divesting myself of the holds that would hold me.

—Walt Whitman

1. FOOT PATROL

I watch as the city winds arrive in the early afternoon. The gusts stir the trash lingering in curbs and doorways along Devon Avenue in Chicago, most of it tossed by gangbangers the day before. The plastic bags, candy wrappers, and cigarette butts rise up in large circles, then resettle. At the same time, the Black P-Stone and Latin King gangbangers stir in their apartments. They emerge north and south of Devon and gather in small groups on the corners. They seem at ease in the street, as if it is theirs, not mine. The floating debris adds to this feeling. Tossed on the ground the day before, it now rises up all around them. As they set up for a day of dope dealing, taking positions for lookouts, runners, sellers, I fight off the feeling of my insignificance and lack of authority on the street.

The trash generally hits people in the lower legs, but some rises up on a swirling gust, as high as any building on the street, then settles onto a car windshield or hits some pedestrian or shop owner in the ear or side of the face. They swat it away, keeping their attention on their business. The Black P-Stones are the most prolific. They talk loudly on their cell phones, especially when I am around, shouting "motherfucker" and "bitch" over and over. Some break out into dances on the sidewalk, as if their criminality gives them unbearable joy, and their fellow bangers yell and laugh in encouragement. Others linger for a moment outside a liquor store munching on some chips, then dart back in, come outside again, and cross the street in the middle of traffic right in front of me, causing cars to stop. The men wear their pants halfway down, exposing their underwear. As the summer day grows warmer, they will remove their shirts and let them hang from the back of their pants. Their bare skin reveals tattoos announcing gang affiliations, former girlfriends, mothers, and criminal intentions. The women push baby strollers up and down the drug alley. Cops learn early in their careers to check these strollers in an arrest. Likely there is dope hidden there. In a moment these women will break out into a shouting match as a way of distracting me, so other gang members can conduct a quick transaction or lift a computer from an unlocked car. Younger gang members on bikes, generally runners, ride on the sidewalks and the wrong side of the street. They turn in front of traffic, toss bikes in the middle of the sidewalk, and run into the store. No pedestrians or shop owners dare confront them. No one honks at them when they block traffic. No one ever makes contact with them. The Indian and Pakistani store owners who own the restaurants and small retail shops give the bangers a wide berth on the sidewalks.

I strap on my helmet, push the start button on the ATV, and move across the street before parking again. I technically work a foot post, but on warm summer days I take the ATV. This section of Devon lingers on a precipice. It is filled with ethnic restaurants—Indian, Pakistani—along with clothing and electronics stores. It is often bustling. But then there is this gang intrusion. No one is really certain what will happen, which direction it will go. When I first took the foot post, I had this notion I could help move it in the right direction. There were many ethnic areas in the city that were tourist and nightlife destinations: Greektown, Little Italy, Chinatown. Devon Avenue could join them, I figured, but there were too many restaurants and store owners that weren't taking care of the appearance of their businesses. Some never swept their storefronts. I walked up and down the avenue, enforcing the ordinance calling on merchants to keep their storefront free from litter. The owners got nervous when I walked in. They had been there for years and never seen a uniformed cop walk in. Most of them began sweeping up right away after I asked them. Only a handful I had to threaten with a ticket. Within months, I had most of Devon looking spiffy. Many people commented on the new look, and I took pride in it. But I could never get this section of Devon cleaned up, from Western to Damen, where the gangs had control. The store owners would never come out onto the street to encounter them. I couldn't ask them to do it. It would be too dangerous.

The gang members are angry because I started up my ATV and moved across the street. They thought I was leaving and they could go back to work. It is a trick I often play with them. Whenever I fire up the ATV, there is a slight relaxation in them. Now I turn the engine off and sit back, my feet raised up a little. From the rack on the front of the ATV, I grab my Starbucks latte and lean back. It's important I stay here as long as I can, maintain my presence on the street. I pull out my cell phone and check messages, dial a few numbers and chat with friends. In response, the gangbangers increase their shouting, riding bikes recklessly, having arguments that border on fights. Things always seem to be near a breaking point on Devon. One of these days things will get out of hand. I finger my radio, check to make sure it is on the right channel if I have to call for help. When I decide to leave, I turn the engine button on and press the starter. The engine turns but doesn't start. It's been happening more and more lately. I turn it off, act as if it's no big deal, then try again. No good. I check the choke, fire one more time, and give it more gas, knowing it may be flooded already. The gangbangers are watching carefully and start gathering around me. I pretend as if I have a message on my cell phone to buy some time in case the ATV is flooded. The gangbangers have circled me now and are talking shit.

"That motherfucking scooter ain't worth shit, Mr. Policeman," one says. "Let me ride it."

As he says this, he reaches out to touch the handlebar. I grab his hand, push it away, and curse him, but the others are smiling. I'm looking like a fool, sitting on an ATV that won't start. This time I press the starter button and hold it, give it plenty of gas. It shakes and rattles, and I hold on. The bangers are laughing but slowly the engine catches, and finally, with a thick plume of exhaust, it turns. I give it more gas to keep it revving and to spew exhaust on them as much as possible. They back off, waving the exhaust from their faces, and I leave. Farther west on Devon, I come to a stop again.

Foot patrol is an assignment that many cops work an entire career, a sign that they gave up on promotion and advancement for the steady routine of a daily job in a single neighborhood, alone on a busy street. They can be among the most knowledgeable cops in a district or the most clueless, depending on how they work their beat. Some spend their time getting information, taking plate numbers down, running the information in the computers, and developing theories. Others sit in cafés and read newspapers, flirt with women.

What attracts me about foot patrol is the imaginative freedom, the ability to walk or ride somewhat aimlessly about Devon Avenue as I ruminate on crimes and gather information about them. I am free from most calls for service; I just emerge on the street every afternoon. Sometimes I meet the store owners, trying to catch some gossip or listening to their complaints about what is happening in the neighborhood. Sometimes I arrest gang members for petty offenses, bringing them into the station, where I take my time doing the paperwork, trying to start a conversation with them. They tell me who their friends are, where they hang out, and I can run the information gathered in the computer and get a clearer picture of what is going on. Other times I wait on roofs of buildings or in someone's apartment, watching the drug dealing, climbing up the back stairs of the buildings in the dark, making as little noise as possible. There is plenty of idle time, plenty of pausing and chatting with people.

There is a change in my imagination from when I first arrived in the city to now, working foot patrol. It has become important for me to sort it out. More and more I am guided by images arising from crimes. One crime in particular has moved to the forefront. It occurred in 1982, when I was flunking out of school in Kalamazoo, traveling to Chicago every weekend. It has unfolded all the years I have been in the city. It seems as if it did not become clear to me until I was ready for it, as if it waited for me. It came to me from a story in the Sunday paper, describing a crime in which the offender from a gruesome quadruple murder in 1982 had been convicted, released on appeal, then re-offended.

At the time of these murders, I lived in Kalamazoo, Michigan. I was only eighteen, but I had taken my first few literature classes at Western Michigan University and they had set me on fire. I had friends in Chicago who called themselves writers, and I began hitchhiking into the city to meet them and hang out. This exposure to writers initiated my own first vague designs toward literature. After my first semester, I gave up on my classes, instead reading writers that interested me and those that my friends in Chicago talked about, the modernist writers like T. S. Eliot and Ezra Pound. I had this image of myself as becoming a university professor, attending conferences, writing papers, and traveling frequently to Europe, of writing poems that began with quotes in Latin or Greek. Yet in reality I was slowly dropping out of college, failing classes. There was a disconnect between my imagination and my circumstances. In those days, I never could have imagined that I would I become a police officer in Chicago, that I would one day be cruising city neighborhoods in a squad car.

One thing was true from those early years in Chicago until now: I gravitated toward writers who captured a specific place. They were called regional writers. In them there was a long germination before they finally found the images that gave life to a place. Then suddenly, the images were all around them. They had just failed to see them before. I look back at this murder case and see it slowly coming toward me, pushing away other things until it came to the forefront and took over everything else.

I pieced the story of this quadruple murder together from newspaper accounts, oftentimes pulling out the clippings from a folder I carried between my vest and shirt while on duty, taking notes and writing down questions. I would tell friends and coworkers about it as we stood at various corners of Devon or took a break in a café, asking their point of view, their interpretation. Then, after almost a year, I could not get away from it. I finally headed to the county court archives. I sat on the fourth floor in a building between the county jail and courthouses, entering the building with my police ID, but veering left instead of right, where most of the cops go to testify in felony trials. When I handed the clerk my police ID as the required deposit, she looked at me strangely, then handed over the cardboard box filled with transcripts and documents. The room was filled with offenders, their lawyers, or their relatives asking about documents related to their cases: bond slips, case reports, certificates. Very rarely had a cop come in to wade through transcripts in the corner of a room for several days. When I handed her the ID, I could feel her puzzlement as she looked at me. What was an off-duty patrolman doing looking into a case more than two decades old? If she asked me, what would I say? I hardly knew myself. I took the box, went to the corner, and began reading.

Even with these transcripts and the police reports, I had to reconstruct much of what happened that day. I had to use what knowledge I had of crime scenes. As best as I could piece it together, in August 1982 a cop arrived at the Rockwell Gardens, a housing project on the West Side of the city. At the building he met with paramedics assigned to an ambulance. They all proceeded to the Parker family's apartment on the seventh floor. Outside the apartment, a crowd had gathered. The officer entered and found the bodies of four Parkers dead inside, all apparently strangled to death: one female, Mary Ann Parker, fifteen, lying face-up in the bathroom with her feet on the toilet; a three-year-old boy, Jontae Parker, also in the bathroom, on his left side, facedown; another female, Cora Jean Parker, thirteen, facedown in a closet; and one female, pregnant, Christine Parker, thirty-three, lying in the bedroom face-up. Murders were common enough in those days, especially on the West Side. Crack cocaine had made its way into the city. I imagine the cop cursing to himself when the call of a death investigation came over the air, because any dead body could mean mandatory overtime. Since the door was open and the murders reported some time ago—the call came out as a death investigation—the officer was probably not too worried that the offender was still on scene, the way he would in an in-progress call. But no doubt he walked through each room carefully while the paramedics checked the bodies. As he found them one by one, he didn't know what the final tally would be. He also didn't know if he would find one still alive, gasping for breath, the eyes of a victim following him as he walked into the room.

I imagine the cop cursing again when he discovered the first body, overtime now certain. Perhaps he thought it was another gang or dope murder or a burglary gone bad. But when he discovered the other bodies, he knew he was into a much higher game, particularly when he saw a little boy, lying in his own pool of blood. Whoever did this must be caught, and he knew that his initial decisions and his report writing could have a bearing on this person's—or these persons'—capture and conviction. From the way he wrote the case report, I can tell he was a veteran officer. He knew that good report writing is based on the philosophy of less is more. The more he wrote, the more he left himself open on the stand to a defense lawyer. They pore over police reports looking for any contradiction, any factual error, and exploit it.

Shortly after the officer secured the crime scene, I imagine how the entrance of the apartment was filled with official sounds for many hours, the radios from cops and fire department officials, crime lab investigators, bosses arriving on scene and other cops. They remained at the entrance to preserve the crime scene for evidence. The responding officer was constantly interrupted, jotting down notes, facts, times, and phone numbers, before two wagons arrive and load the bodies for the morgue, two in each wagon. This was long before cell phones, so the responding officer likely had to use the phone in a nearby apartment. By then the entire scene would have been photographed, dusted for prints, and officers would have finished canvassing, knocking on doors throughout the complex to ask residents if they saw or heard anything. The canvass would come up negative, and the investigation would then fall upon the detectives. At some point it would have been made clear to all the cops at the scene that three-year-old Jontae had not only been strangled to death, but he had also been anally raped.

There was no sign of forced entry in the apartment, no kicked-out door or window frames that might lead to a theory about gangbangers stealing dope or valuables. Whoever had committed the crimes was welcomed there. This was the first lead for police. They later learned that five young men frequented the apartment, often late at night. These young men, they were told, arrived because the Parkers subscribed to a pay television station called ON TV, a precursor to cable television. Detectives divided up the names of the five regular visitors to the Parker household and began interviewing them, one by one. Four of them checked out. They all had alibis. When they arrived at the apartment of James Ealy, seventeen, the last one to be interviewed, he was playing basketball in front of the complex. They asked his younger brother to go get him. In the meantime, they spoke with his mother about James's activities in and around the time of the murders.

At this point in their investigation, James held no official status. He could be a witness, an offender, or nothing at all. But the detectives did learn that he once had a relationship with one of the Parkers, fifteen-year-old Mary Ann, who was found dead in the bathroom. The detectives talked with James's mother until James got there. When James arrived, the police asked him if he would come down to the station so they could interview him. James claimed he had a date that night, and the detectives assured him that he would be back in time for it. He agreed and left with them. At the station they asked James to give an account of his whereabouts at the time of the murders. His account conflicted with the story his mother had given, and they pointed this out to him. They asked his mother, who had arrived at the station, to speak to him, but, they said, James refused to talk to her.

In the hallway outside the interview room, another detective approached the two detectives conducting the interview. This new detective held the copy of a case report against James for first-degree rape six months earlier. That rape resembled the Parker crime scene so much that it almost looked like a prelude to the Parker murders. It held the same themes of violence with a sexual lust in it, strangling and humiliation of the victim. In the rape, Ealy had followed a woman up a flight of stairs from the eighth floor, grabbed her, and knocked her to the ground. He then dragged her to a stairway on the twelfth floor, where he began beating and choking her. Ealy dragged her again to the thirteenth floor and raped her as he choked her until she passed out. The woman's screams compelled a neighbor to call the police. There was a police unit in the building who responded. They gave chase to Ealy and apprehended him. Ealy was locked up for the crime, but was eventually granted bond and released.

This bond would be the first, strange instance of Ealy's liberation from his crimes. The bond was paid by Catholic Charities, an organization that often provided legal services to poor offenders. Catholic Charities also hired a prominent law firm to represent Ealy on the rape charge. Without this bond on the rape, Ealy would never have been free the night the Parkers were murdered. Why Catholic Charities had bonded out Ealy, why they didn't find the circumstances of the rape disturbing enough to leave him in custody, was never explained. At least one reporter covering the case seemed puzzled by this and wrote a story, confronting Catholic Charities. But the spokesperson was evasive. Nevertheless, many cops were shocked when they found out. They canceled their payroll deductions that gave money to the organization.

With this new information about the rape in hand, the detectives reentered the interview room and read Ealy his rights.

At the request of the detectives, James signed a consent-to-search form. Two detectives just starting their shift then went to Ealy's apartment to search his bedroom. Under his bed, they found several items, including lengths of material tied with knots in it, and a knife handle. They retrieved some of these and went to the home of another detective who had been at the crime scene. This detective told them that the material tied in knots resembled material around the neck of Mary Ann Parker, Ealy's former girlfriend. The detectives reentered the Parker apartment and matched the material to a raincoat where the belt was missing.

Confronting Ealy with the evidence back at the station, he changed his story, claiming he had seen a large black male leave the Parkers' apartment and drop the bundle. James said he picked it up and entered the Parkers' apartment and saw the bodies, checked their pulses to confirm they were dead, then returned home with the bundle, which he put under his bed. James would eventually claim he had played basketball with the bundle as he walked down the stairs, shooting it into trash cans on each floor. When asked why he didn't call the police, Ealy could not answer. The detectives asked James to sign another consent-to-search form, then returned to his apartment to gather the rest of the items in the bundle. When they got back to the interview room, they told James his story didn't hold up. At this point a vein in James's forehead was trembling, and he finally stated he would tell the truth. He confessed to the detectives, then to a state's attorney, who took his official statement. There is a picture of him in the court transcripts, sitting at the table where he signed the confession.

In his confession, Ealy claimed he had been drinking wine with friends all day, then told them he was going home, but instead headed to the Parkers' apartment. Cora Jean Parker, thirteen, and her mother, Christine, began teasing James about his red eyes, calling James a wine-head. James got mad, told them "not to worry about it," but Cora kept on teasing him, then slapped James on the back when she walked by him. James swung back and hit her. The mother, Christine, shouted from the bedroom for them to keep quiet. While James was watching TV, Cora Jean came into the room and continued teasing him. James chased her to the bedroom where Christine was.

"She was laughing. She thought I was playing," he said in his confession. "I guess you want to die or something," James said to her.

In Ealy's confession, he said that Cora Jean, unaware of the rage that was rising in Ealy's six-foot-one, muscular 205-pound frame, kept laughing. James grabbed Cora Jean in the bedroom and pushed her to the floor. He told her to put her head underneath the bed. He went and got the belt from the closet. He told Christine, who was still in the bedroom, to get on her knees facing away from him and wrapped the belt around her neck, forcing her to beg for her life before he strangled her to death. After she was dead, he placed her body on the bed. With some red socks, Ealy tied up Cora Jean, all the while kneeling on top of her to remain in control. Ealy claims someone knocked on the front door and Mary Ann, fifteen, his former girlfriend, got up from the couch in the living room to answer it. Perhaps hearing the commotion, Mary Ann walked toward the bedroom. Ealy slapped her, threw her down on the bed, and wrapped a belt around her neck, then led her into the bathroom. There he made her get on her knees and strangled her. Somehow part of the khaki material she was wearing was also used to strangle her. The cords around Mary Ann's neck were so tight that Ealy had to cut them off, but some of the khaki material remained. Ealy closed the door to the bathroom, saying he did not want Cora Jean to see Mary Ann's body. James claims three-year-old Jontae woke up in the living room and went toward the bedroom. This made him a witness, Ealy claims, and so he strangled the little boy near the entrance of the bathroom. He returned to Cora, still tied up in the bedroom, and strangled her, then threw her body into the closet.

I often reconsider the details of the murders, the sounds, the images. I think about Mary Ann found in the perverse position of her body on the floor but her legs draped over the toilet. The image betrays an intense, violent struggle, much flailing and kicking. Were any of the women alive to hear Jontae raped? What sounds does a three-year-old boy being raped and strangled make?

In his confession, Ealy never admitted raping Jontae, who hemorrhaged from his anus and lay in his blood in the bathroom. In the perverse logic of the criminal world, raping a child was the least manly crime imaginable, lower than the murders. Ealy wouldn't want a child rape hanging over his head in prison, and he probably would not want his mother to know what he had done to the boy. But how does the rape fit in among the other murders? Did Ealy truly rape Jontae after killing Christine and tying Cora Jean up in the bedroom? It seems strange to kill, then rape, then kill again. Why didn't he rape one of the women instead, especially Cora Jean while she was tied up? Perhaps he enjoyed making Cora Jean hear and see the other murders and the rape as a way to increase her terror and humiliation for teasing him. Surely after the other murders and the rape of Jontae, Cora Jean knew she would die as well. Inflicting that level of terror no doubt gave Ealy intense pleasure, just as he enjoyed beating and dragging from one destination to another the woman he raped six months earlier.

What I couldn't understand was how Ealy controlled the entire situation, how he murdered all four so brutally without more signs of struggle or without anyone fleeing the apartment. How did Ealy murder Christine while leaning on Cora Jean? Was Cora Jean, were all the Parkers, so paralyzed in terror that Ealy had his way with them? Why no screams from the bedroom by Christine or Cora Jean to alert Mary Ann in the living room what was happening, allowing Mary Ann to flee and call for help? I cannot get my mind around the crime scene. Criminals lie even when they don't have to. It's a way of maintaining some kind of control even when there is no point to it. Ealy's confession reeks of this, so much so that no one will likely ever know exactly what happened in the Parker apartment, a fact that probably still pleases Ealy.

I wonder if something else happened, if Ealy came to the house to have sex with Mary Ann but she refused. Perhaps this was the real source of his rage. Or perhaps he raped Jontae first. Then, as the Parker women discovered what he was doing, he killed them one by one. Maybe he came to the apartment from the outset to rape and murder. This makes great sense to me. I can see the hours of drinking wine awaking his sociopathic rage. He lied to his friends about going home, then sneaked over to the Parkers' apartment. The rape arrest six months earlier was still hanging over his head. The trial was approaching. He tasted the first ecstasy of raping the woman in the stairwell. How many more chances would he get in life? A long prison term was likely from the rape arrest. How many years? I can imagine Ealy came to the apartment drunk, with nothing more to lose, hell-bent on rape and murder from the outset.

I turn over Ealy's crimes again in my mind. After the slaughter of the Parkers, I could imagine Ealy was exhausted. I've reconstructed enough crime scenes to know this. He must have been breathing hard and dripping sweat. It was a hot August night. It's not easy to strangle four victims, adding a rape into the slaughter. No doubt the sweat from the victims mingled with Ealy's sweat as he murdered and raped. At some point he stood in the Parker apartment surveying his work. He had wrapped many incriminating items, including the belts, together in a sheet, then wiped the apartment down for fingerprints. For some reason, it seems important for me to know whether he turned the television off at some point. I have this image that he wanted some quiet after the deed. He had to pause and make sure he covered up everything. How silent the apartment must have seemed. What a moment of self-insight for Ealy. He was only seventeen and had just murdered a family of four; Christine, the mother; Cora Jean, thirteen; Mary Ann, fifteen, and her son, Jontae, three.

Ealy told detectives that he picked up the phone and called his mother in their apartment three floors below. His mother would later corroborate the phone call. Ealy told the detectives he made the call because he didn't have his apartment key and he didn't want to be stuck outside in the hallway holding the bundle of evidence, waiting. He said he made the phone call from a downstairs pay phone, but I believe that was another lie. I think he made the call from the Parkers' apartment. He would not make the call from a public place carrying a bundle of evidence from the murders. Even so, calling his apartment from the crime scene only increased the evidence against him. It provided more proof that he was at the crime scene. I could see a prosecuting attorney confronting him with the evidence of the call.

"We have records, James, that someone made a phone call to your apartment from the Parkers' around the time of the murders . . ."

Ealy should never have taken the evidence into his apartment to begin with. He should have gotten rid of it right away. He could have thrown it down the trash chute, tossed it into a dumpster somewhere, set it on fire in a trash can. But it was clear to me it was some kind of trophy for him now. I know from some research into killers like Ealy, ones who kill with a sexual lust, that such trophies are a way to relive the murders in their sexual fantasies. I think about the phone call to his mother. I think he needed to hear her voice. What a moment in his life to clutch the phone tightly to his cheek while he waited for his mother to answer, standing among the four Parker bodies. He never broke down and confessed to her in the phone call. He did not sob or ask for her forgiveness.

After the call, Ealy carried the bundle home, lied to his mother about what it was, and placed it under his bed. Then he reviewed his witless alibi throughout the night.

With the evidence and the confessions, Ealy was charged with four counts of first-degree murder. Because he was only seventeen, he could not receive the death penalty. During the trial, his attorneys slowly paved the way for the appeal. There was so much evidence against him, including his confession, that there was little else they could argue. They tested out the theories of their appeal on the judge, submitting motions that Ealy was unlawfully arrested. The trial judge refused all of it and upheld the prosecutor's case. The trial went forward. Ealy was convicted for all the murders. Ealy was only one month shy of his eighteenth birthday at the time of the murders, a certain death sentence if the murders had occurred one month later. After his trial, Ealy's lawyers went forward with their appeal, arguing that the police had acted unlawfully when they came to his apartment and asked him to come to the station so they could talk to him. They claimed that this constituted an arrest and, at that point in their investigation, the detectives lacked probable cause to arrest Ealy. Ealy also argued that he was tortured into confessing, saying that police came into the interview room and beat him until he agreed to confess. Such claims of torture would become common in Ealy's era. But why would the detectives torture him when they had recovered so much evidence right under his bed? There was no evidence of torture at all, no marks, no complaints, nothing. The torture accusations went nowhere. But the claim that the cops had no probable cause was upheld. As a result, all evidence they had gathered as a result of that interview, including the confessions and the bundle of sheets under his bed, was tossed, and Ealy was remanded for another trial. The cops, prosecutors, and trial judge were furious. The same judge and lawyers met to retry Ealy, but the prosecutor said that without the evidence they had no case and could not move forward. The judge made an impassioned speech, saying that the criminal justice system had completely failed and that billboards should be constructed throughout the city announcing that a predator would soon be roaming free. He then dismissed the case. Ealy wasn't let loose right away. He was sentenced to twenty-three years on the rape charge against the woman in the stairwell six months earlier, but was out after ten years, free again.

As I recalled the Ealy murders that day and many others while working on Devon Avenue, I concluded that crimes hold a special power in Chicago. It is through them, and only them, that the city fuses the fantastic and the mundane. These crimes are variously crafted in their patterns of deceit, compelling in their arrangement. They tie the city together and give life to its mysteries. Without them, little exists with which to imagine the city. Without them, all metaphors falter, then fall away. Alone, on foot patrol, I conclude that a vast imaginative life is rooted in city crimes. I do not believe they have had their proper say, their proper perspective. I hold out hope that, when arranged appropriately, these crimes will serve a higher purpose, that the deceptions, lies, and brutality in them will rise to something akin to the power of art: that they will suddenly, as Picasso says, "enable us to see the truth." I believe the city is desperate for the illumination they can provide. In saying so, I am aware of my own responsibility, that there is a preparatory condition of mind, without which it is useless to imagine them. I hold out some fading hope that, in this right state of mind, these crimes will hold some deliverance in them.

What proves inevitable in this preparation is a picking and choosing of crimes for their illuminative power, the mysterious ways they touch upon one's own life, in one's own time and place, so that even the most forgotten crime—and Ealy's story was certainly forgotten, buried in the city's judicial archives until he himself brought them back to life—can suddenly take on a heightened significance, rising to the level of metaphor, allegory, paradigm, or worldview. What is required is confronting that which seems compelling in these crimes, sensing that what arises might hold a larger value, be the stuff of a better vision. In doing so, one is free to wander through them in one's own way, according to their own meaning, and there, for a moment, is the first tantalizing liberation in them. This, I tell myself on foot patrol, is the reason the Parker murders call out to me.

2. INFESTATION

At Rockwell Street, I come out of a café to write some rush hour parking tickets. Across the street I spot two Black P-Stone gang-bangers, suspected of committing almost a dozen burglaries in the district. I fold up the transcripts of the Ealy trial I was reading in the café and place them inside my vest. The transcripts are the testimony of the pathologist who did the autopsies on the Parker homicides. I don't know why the Ealy case has come to consume me, why I spend more and more time reviewing the transcripts. Coworkers joke about how much I have come to talk about the case. I see something in the murders.

The two thugs weave in and out of the store owners and shoppers on the sidewalk. Our eyes meet. I see them whisper to each other that I am across the street. As I walk westbound keeping an eye on them, I admit that there once seemed to me nothing that might constitute a common vision of the city. Such a conclusion is understandable, because the path to the city's real mystery is a treacherous imaginative leap, bridged and illuminated only by its crimes. I joined the police department when I was much older than the rest of my academy class. I had been thirty-eight, and I fancied myself a worldly person, having traveled much, worked in the service industry, attended several colleges, and fought union battles in the hotel industry. But nothing prepared me for what I encountered on the South Side of Chicago, in the city's worst neighborhoods.

It is difficult to be certain, to know if one has the right perspective on the city's crimes. In the Ealy murder trial, for example, all the parties involved simply got up and left in a bitter anger, never to agree or reconvene, the entire enterprise abandoned. The trial judge ruled that Ealy's arrest was entirely reasonable, with the appeals court saying that the detectives had unlawfully arrested Ealy. It's as if everyone forgot the reason why they assembled to begin with and got lost along the way. Ealy

15

sneaked out during the bickering. Nevertheless, I believe the right perspective on the city's crimes is possible. I think this is one reason why the Ealy case has come to consume me.

I never worked the Rockwell Gardens Housing Projects on the West Side of Chicago where Ealy lived. I spent a great deal of time hunting down cops who did. These cops wore their tenure there as a badge of honor because the Rockwell Gardens were considered among the most cruel and violent housing projects in the city. I had worked a few projects, the Ickes on the Near South Side and the Altgeld Gardens on the Far South Side, but only for a short time. These veterans told me that the early 1980s were particularly violent. They would park their cars close to the entrance of the buildings so as not to be struck by the soiled diapers, rotten fruits and vegetables, bowling balls, and metal objects that were hurled down upon them. Residents used high-powered water-pump guns, half-filled with urine that they shot down at the cops. Inside the apartments were weapons, often trained on the officers as they moved in and out responding to calls. Every veteran officer recalled getting shot at, the bullet holes left in squad cars. Cops refrained from taking the elevators because they reeked of urine and were smeared with excrement and afforded easy opportunity for incapacitation and ambush. On the occasions they had to use the elevators, cops always went one floor above or below their target floor to avoid walking into a well-orchestrated attack. Offenders, once they gained access to the buildings, disappeared like roaches behind the walls and stairwells, getting cooperation from the entire population, few of whom would ever snitch, and would never, ever testify, even for such things as murders and rapes. Cooperation was so implicit in the buildings that many apartment dwellers had partially knocked-out cinder-block walls so drugs, weapons, and offenders could easily move about and avoid searches. There was more than cooperation. In the projects the residents would turn on the cops at every opportunity, even the people who had called them to settle a domestic dispute or report some crime. When a fight broke out, residents would rain down blows and projectiles on the cops, who then shouted for help into their radios. Officers from the entire district flooded the building, knowing the risks involved.

Some projects lingered in remote ghettos on the Far South and West Sides. There they could be dismissed as some outland aberration, some other place, disconnected from the city's center. But some projects, like Ealy's Rockwell Gardens and Cabrini Green, were situated closer to thriving, bustling neighborhoods. They were two worlds so utterly apart, so utterly unable to imagine each other, yet coexisting within the same municipal system. The sociopath's mind is similarly divided into contrary factions, much like the city's schizophrenic landscape. One minute, the sociopath is engaging and charming, like the city's downtown. The next, he is violent and cruel, like Ealy's West Side. What images to trust in this landscape? Which ones illuminate and which ones deceive? When a sociopath tells you a story, which part of it do you believe? Only the crimes will tell. Crime scenes are crucial, the sole repository of anything authentic. A sign of their power is the mesmerizing accounts of them in restaurants, squad cars, and district parking lots, fellow cops nodding their heads. Often it is the most absurd, the most fantastic images that generate the greatest response. Even I, an aging, mediocre North Side cop, have learned their power, have learned to move toward what seems compelling in them, without subservience to official accounts or schools of thought.

I was as much a part of this schizophrenic landscape as anyone. In 1982, when Ealy murdered the Parkers, I can see myself sitting with friends in cafés and restaurants on the North Side, talking literature. I was as far removed from the mentality of the projects as anyone could be. If some cop had sat down in the restaurant, we would have eyed him for signs that he was power-hungry and racist. We would have thought of him as ignorant. We would have rejected his descriptions of the projects as jaded. I can see myself sitting at Aphrodite's restaurant on Sheridan Avenue with a group of friends, talking about modernism, talking about "The Love Song of J. Alfred Prufrock." One could walk for hours along the side streets of Rogers Park, the old brick two-flats and imagine the line "in the room the women come and go / talking of Michelangelo." I smile at the memory. Now I walk Devon Avenue in my policeman's uniform, watching two gangbangers carefully.

I was never present at the Parker crime scene, never saw the remains of any Ealy crimes, but I re-create them with my limited eye. I find my own images there, like the "old and recent" bite marks on Jontae, Mary Ann, and Cora Jean Parker, bites that the pathologist testified were consistent with rats or cockroaches. I imagined the bite marks even before seeing them cited in the pathologist's reports. I had worked in a few projects, but several fellow cops told me how bad the rat and roach infestation was at the Rockwell Gardens. Anytime you walked down the hallways, you would see them, they said. They were in many apartments. It was reassuring to see something I had imagined confirmed in official reports. The bites were mentioned in the trial only to establish cause of death, then dropped altogether when it was determined they were not related.

"That's what you think," I muttered to myself when I read the transcripts in the county building.

I had been in the projects enough to see apartments so infested that their residents were regularly attacked. I had arrested people who had scars from rat bites from when they were growing up. I can imagine how they crawled on the Parkers when they slept, especially at night when the only light was the glow of the TV. I've refused to enter an apartment because the walls were moving with roaches. But sometimes you have no choice, like the Parker crime scene, where their four bodies littered the apartment. I could see the roaches flashing across the TV screen in the apartment. I imagine that when the cops were processing the crime scene, they were constantly checking their shoes and pants, conscious never to set anything down in the apartment. It's possible that the rat bites were made while the four dead family members were alive, particularly those on the children, gotten while they slept. Rats seem to sense the vulnerability of children. Infants and toddlers won't necessarily flinch or cry out when the creatures crawl up to them in their beds or cribs. The children might have fought them off earlier in their lives, but in time, when their outcries generated no reaction, they just got used to them and slept soundly as the rats and roaches crawled about, much as you get used to a dog or cat crawling into your bed. When the vermin bit into them, they would have learned to swat them away or just lay there and wait for it to end, or to just cry quietly.

There was no mention of whether the TV was on when the police responded around noon to the call of a death investigation at the Parker apartment. A group of residents gathered around the door of the Parkers' apartment on the seventh floor. If the TV was off, the only sounds emanating within the apartment for much of the twelve hours between the murders and the discovery might have been the scurrying movement of the rats over garbage and dirty clothes gathered in random piles and, perhaps, the sound of their eating. Sometimes, if there are enough of them, roaches give off a kind of buzz and the smell of molasses. These would have been the sounds through much of the night, and perhaps even into the early morning, but in time these sounds would be mixed with those of the children, Lavelle, three, and Torrence, two, the only Parker family members not murdered. For some reason, they did not attract Ealy's lustful rage. There was an account that the two children were eventually discovered wandering the halls on the seventh floor in the late morning. Since the call came out as a death investigation, these neighbors likely peered into the apartment and saw at least a few of the bodies before calling 911. There was no record or comment describing how long Lavelle and Torrence had wandered about the crime scene before going into the hallway. But there was quite a while between the murders and their discovery. An account said that Torrence was too young to remember the murders, but Lavelle had a memory of them. What happened to these two children between the murders and the discovery? I have this image of them sidling up to the bodies, trying to wake them up and let them know they were hungry or bored or they wanted to watch cartoons. Or I wondered if they just sat next to the bodies wailing, their sounds drowned out by the morning TVs and stereos blaring throughout the complex. It was never indicated whether they had rat and cockroach bite marks on their bodies, but it's likely. The other bodies did. How could they have avoided them? Perhaps the children were bitten more than normal that night and the next morning, since the dead bodies gave the vermin unbridled access, so they flooded the apartment. Or perhaps instead that night there was a reprieve for Lavelle and Torrence, the four bodies and the unusual quiet and stillness providing ample sustenance for all the vermin, who instinctively moved toward motionless, silent bodies, as opposed to live ones. Perhaps the two children even slept that night, an unfettered slumber. Perhaps that night was the deepest sleep of their lives.

The bite marks on the Parkers obliterate any easy distinctions between criminal and victim, a primary truth of the city. No doubt the Parkers were victims of the most heinous crimes, some of them forced to witness these acts before they themselves were done in. It's quite likely at least one of the Parkers witnessed her relative strangled to death or the youngest victim of the family, Jontae, raped before being strangled.

But at the same time the prevalence of vermin hinted at the Parkers' own sins, their own criminality. For how could a man, a teen really, on bond for a brutal rape bordering on attempted murder be welcomed into a dwelling late in the night among young women and children? How could he be left alone night after night to watch TV with the children and teenage girls? Only in an apartment where roaches and rats run free. What kind of matriarch would allow fifteen-year-old Mary Ann Parker to have so many "boyfriends"? And what exactly was meant by the term "boyfriend"? I suspected that the prosecutors, cops, and officials were being charitable. Ealy had "dated" Mary Ann, so did another frequent visitor to the apartment. It was the five frequent visitors to the Parker apartment, all young men, who led detectives to James Ealy to begin with. It was more than just pay TV that drew these "boyfriends" in. Mary Ann was fifteen and Jontae was her three-year-old son. That meant she was twelve when she bore Jontae, probably eleven when she got pregnant. The truth is that these frequent visitors, these "boyfriends," likely came to have sex with Mary Ann on a regular basis, arriving late at night, stoned, and Christine, the mother, let them in and left them alone. Why? Why did she allow this to happen to her own daughter? Why did she let a sociopathic predator into her home late at night? Was there something she got in return? I wondered if the visitors gave her something—money, dope, information.

In my mind, the vermin also undermine many of the arguments by the defense to throw out the case, arguments that it was unfair, cruel even, for the police to leave Ealy in an interview room for as long as eighteen hours while they investigated the case, returning time and again to confront Ealy with a new piece of evidence. First it was the rape. The detectives learned about it when a colleague approached them in the hallway and showed them the case report: sexual assault, strangling, rage—all the themes of the Parker homicides. They returned to the interview room. *What about this, James? Why,* they would ask him after securing a consent-to-search form, *are there rope and other artifacts of the murder under your bed? Why are there sheets?* Ealy tried to concoct different stories in a floundering, half-witted attempt to throw the suspicion on someone else. But the eighteen hours he remained in custody was hammered by Ealy's attorneys, then picked up by the papers, none of them seeming to see how painstakingly the detectives had investigated exactly to avoid accusations of misconduct. Ealy could be sentenced as an adult when he killed the Parkers. The detectives had no obligation to bring his mother into the interview. He had been repeatedly Mirandized and had not asked for a lawyer. The detectives made two trips to his apartment to gather evidence. They could have gathered all the evidence the first trip, but they were making every attempt to follow the law unambiguously. The second trip added another few hours onto the time Ealy had to wait in a clean, quiet room. But eighteen hours is nothing. Suspects often wait this long. But, really, the vermin dismiss the entire argument, for how traumatic could a clean, quiet room be for a guy who made regular forays into a roach-infested apartment in the projects to routinely rape an underage woman, a man who can rape a woman on a public stairwell, among the syringes, the urine, and the excrement that always lingers there?

I mean, really, what the fuck?

Here, too, the vermin put the Chicago Housing Authority on full display—its sociopathic lie that these projects would provide inexpensive shelter and opportunity for the weak and oppressed. But the bite marks indicate otherwise, point to a more sinister way of life operating in the "Housing Authority," a strange, bellicose name for a public institution. What kind of community allows James to walk around freely unshunned for a rape he had committed, to hang around with the same friends at the basketball courts? When Ealy approached the basketball courts, why didn't mothers and fathers come down from their apartments and lead their children away? Why didn't a collection of residents come to his bond hearing to demand that he not be released into their community again? Instead, some people attended his bond hearing, testifying that Ealy should get out of jail and return home. Ealy had status and power in the Rockwell Gardens. Ealy said to the victim moments after the rape that he had friends in a gang and that if she told on him, Ealy would unleash them on her . . .

All the light on Devon Avenue is artificial now. The two gangbangers slipped down a side street, then an alley. I couldn't keep up and wouldn't have stopped them anyway, unable to contrive any probable cause.

I worked in the projects a short time when I first got out of the academy, entered many homes suffused with roaches and rats. Once, a medium-size rat climbed out of a trash can where I was standing and ran past my right leg. I jumped backward when I saw it, then spied two others standing in the corner. My veteran partner was trying to subdue her laughter. Now on foot patrol, I deal less directly with crime. I go to fewer calls, and I like it. I wonder if there is a retreat in me, a resignation, itself a roach-like, rat-like tendency. I am a representative of the same city that built and maintained the projects; I myself have patrolled them. There is a line connecting the vermin to me as well. I know it. I am no innocent. I find imaginative possibilities in the roaches that inhabit the city's crime scenes. I wonder what have I become in the city, what is my imagination.

I look at the timing between Ealy's rape and his quadruple murders, only six months apart. The rage had already taken him over. I wonder how many other victims were in the Gardens but didn't come forward, ones lost, hopelessly lost, in the city's public housing system, the way the Parkers were, living, then dying, among roaches and rats. There could be victims before the first rape, ones in between the rape and the murders and others after Ealy was liberated. I read the transcripts of his rape trial in two days at the Daley Center downtown, in the archives room. By attacking the woman out in the open, there was a witness, one who called the police because the victim fought and screamed the entire time Ealy beat and choked her, then dragged her down the stairwell and hallway of the twelfth floor. She tried to kick at apartment doors as they passed them, and she even screamed out the name of a friend as they passed by his apartment, but he wasn't home. The screaming reached one tenant. (Just one, in a high-rise? What does it mean that only one person seemed to call about the rape? Why were there no sounds emanating from the Parker household that compelled anyone to call for help? Were there screams and shouts that were simply ignored?)

The tenant called 911, then looked out the window and saw Ealy on top of the victim. He called again. During the rape, there were cops nearby, West Side cops, among the best I have ever seen. Sometimes I am embarrassed to hang around them because I only worked the busiest neighborhoods for two years before I opted for the ease and security of the North Side, with its cafés, restaurants, bustling activity. These cops heard the radio call and gave instant chase, hearing Ealy's fleeing footsteps after they found the twenty-year-old woman on the stairs barely conscious, her shirt ripped open, breasts bared, vomit all over herself because Ealy had forced himself into her mouth twice before raping her, strangling her when she initially refused to receive it. Probably Ealy would have killed her had the cops not arrived. The Parkers are proof of that.

"Speak up, please. I can't hear you," the defense attorney said to the rape victim during her testimony. But she remained strong. She endured the investigation, the trial preparation, the trial itself, the inevitable rumors and innuendo and perhaps even the threats from Ealy's fellow gang members at the Rockwell Gardens. I wonder where she was when she learned that Ealy only served less than half his twenty-three-year sentence for the rape, even though everyone knew he murdered the four Parkers, including the appeals court. In the archives building, I make a note to myself to retrieve the records, if they still exist, of the parole board hearing that freed Ealy so early. As soon as the detectives in the murder case learned of Ealy's rape, they knew they had their man. But it didn't really matter in the end, anyway. Ealy got out of the murders. I make a note to myself to call the Cold Case detectives and remind them to look for any unsolved murders where the victim was raped and strangled, anywhere around Cook County. I would tell them to look particularly at victims in the Rockwell Gardens when Ealy lived there. A part of me wants to also advise them to look at crime scenes that were unusually infested with rats and roaches. But of course, I don't.

It's just an image I can't shake.

3. MAGICAL REALISM

The Parker crime scene wouldn't leave me. I forced myself to put it into some context with my own gestation. I compared, contrasted. While Ealy was still in prison for the rape, I was working as a doorman, living in a studio apartment on the Far North Side. Why a college graduate was stuck in the service industry working as a doorman, I couldn't really explain, except that I was lost. I had no idea what to do with my life, so I lived the day-to-day existence of a service worker. In these years I knew nothing about the Ealy case, had never heard of it. I had also never been near the projects where he lived. I do remember one summer afternoon I was washing dishes right before I headed out to my doorman job. As I stood over the sink, I noticed two small bugs run from under a dish to the back of the counter, where they disappeared. They were so small I wasn't sure what they were, but thought they might have been roaches, so I grabbed the pesticide I had under the sink from an invasion of ants a few years earlier in another apartment. I shot jets of poison behind the sink and counters where they had scattered, forgot about them, and went to the shower to get ready for work. When I got out of the shower in a towel, the phone rang in the kitchen and I ran to get it. While I talked, pacing back and forth, my gaze turned to the floor, and I froze. There was a roach upside down, easily three inches long. His feet were flailing, as if he had some chance of turning himself over and finding refuge under a nearby counter. I hung up in someone's midsentence and stood over him.

We stared at each other, my left arm holding the towel around me. Otherwise I was naked and still dripping. I didn't know roaches could get so big. He was a granddad, more the size of a pet than a pest. I had seen them before in other apartments, but never like this. In Lansing, Michigan, I had found them in the cupboard and the shower, but could

24

control them with regular cleaning and pesticides, so too with an apartment in Kalamazoo, Michigan. In my sleep, I imagined this giant could get to me, possibly even kill me by crawling onto my neck and biting into my carotid artery. Someone told me that for every roach you see, there are at least a thousand others, a statistic often true with crimes as well: For every robbery a guy gets pinched for, how many others did he get away with? And murders, what about murders? Only about half of them are solved. I suddenly felt vulnerable and gazed up to the ceiling, then along the walls and to the floor, imagining all the places they could be hiding. They were likely watching me right then, knowing my schedule and that I was leaving for work soon. They were angry about the spray; no doubt they had lost several comrades, including this giant before me. What if he wasn't the giant? What if there were others bigger, stronger? I wonder now what roaches watched Ealy murder the Parkers, how many were on the walls. I wonder how many rats were hiding behind furniture, under kitchen counters. I wonder if they froze at the sounds of homicides, the wrestling, the gasps for air, then slowly and cautiously emerged after Ealy left.

In my own kitchen, I could not face the crunch of stepping on this roach. He was too big. It would be like breaking bones. A familiar feeling arose that perhaps I didn't belong in the city, that I could not imagine it, that I could not deal with it on its own terms. My family hailed from Chicago, but I had grown up in the suburbs outside of Detroit. I had moved back in my late twenties. The roach brought an eeriness into my apartment, an eeriness that increased over time, even as I struggled to manage the roach invasion in the following months. The eeriness brought to mind the fact that two men had been shot the week before a few blocks away. It brought to mind coming home drunk on the train late one night a few weeks earlier. Walking home from the train station, I stopped singing a song to myself in my drunken levity because I sensed something was wrong. As I turned around, I reached into my jacket where I kept a large knife. There was the guy standing behind me, just a few steps away. His hand was in his own dark trench coat, but it was summer.

"Hey, brother, didn't mean to scare you. I just wanted to know if you had a cigarette," he said.

"One step closer and that's it," I bluffed, holding my hand on the knife, hoping he would think it was a gun.

He walked away, down the alley.

The roach in my kitchen could have been female, the queen that some errant shot of insecticide somehow struck dead on, but I thought of him as the male. He had grown comfortable and careless, only to be wiped out by some unlucky, unexpected burst of Raid. How long had he been hovering around the apartment, avoiding my lazy and untrained gaze? I stared at him some more, my towel wrapped around me. I didn't want him to see me naked. I felt vulnerable in his gaze. Our meeting seemed fateful and prophetic, but I didn't know what fate, what prophecy. I sat down in the kitchen chair and faced him awhile longer. Sometimes his legs went still, probably from fatigue. But if I moved at all, they resumed. Certainly he knew what was coming. He was most vulnerable in this position and so was I, almost completely naked.

After some time I stood and went to the bookshelf next to the entrance of the kitchen and searched out my heaviest hardcover as a means of quick execution, a way to kill him without touching or feeling his death. It would have to be a hardcover I could sacrifice. No way would I keep a book that was covered with roach juices. As I moved toward the bookshelf, I kept one eye trained on him. Then I glanced at the books. Scanning across the titles, I set on the weighty compendium of Plato's complete dialogues, my favorite book during my freshman year of college in New Mexico. I had loved it, followed Socrates all through *The Republic*, marveling at Plato's artistry, weeping when Socrates drank the hemlock, refusing to leave his beloved Athens. Socrates, it was said, faced the laws no matter what. Certainly the unexamined life was not worth living, he said, and I agreed with him that year of college in the mountains. Every other student had reached the same conclusion. None of us wanted anything at all to do with an unexamined life. What could be worse? But in Chicago, Plato's dialogues fell away. The Socratic method was of no use. City residents did not enjoy its irony or its con-descension. They did not like their ignorance exposed through question and answer by a lowly tradesman. To get people to listen, you had to be connected, have some clout. It was a difficult place to analyze one's life anyway, to know when it was fully examined or under what model or paradigm to consider it, so the book remained on the shelf for several years. Before moving into this apartment, I had even considered selling it to a used bookstore, but I had written so many notes in the margins with exclamation points: *Yes! Yes! Exactly. The soul is immortal!!!*

I was reading Walt Whitman now and the Magical Realists. These writers seemed to need only the stuff around them, the stuff of their daily lives, to build the most gorgeous symbolic worlds. I would not sacrifice these books. They were mostly in paperback anyhow. I carried them in my pocket so I could read them on the trains or in cafés and restaurants. They could not kill the roach. The roach might survive their falling on him, might even carry the books away with the assistance of other roaches. It could be dangerous if they got ahold of them. It would be me who would have to move out. Now, suddenly and unexpectedly, I found some use for Plato's dialogues. In order to use both hands to hold the book, I had to let go of the towel. I could have left the room and gotten dressed, but what if I came back and the roach was gone? Certainly I was being watched. The other roaches could seize this opportunity. What if his comrades sneaked him away? I held the hardcover with two hands high in the air, trying to keep it level with the floor so it would fall evenly on the roach. For a moment the whole scene seemed entirely appropriate, Plato's dialogues dropped upon what must be the ideal city roach. But what a disaster if the book fell sideways and somehow scooted the roach in a manner where it could regain its uprightness and scurry back behind a baseboard. It could regain its strength, shed the effects of the poison, nurse itself back to health. Then where would I be? Philosophy can jam you up like that if you're not careful.

As I stood over him, naked, both of us were fully exposed, him on his back, his legs flailing. I stood straight, my hands in the air holding the book, unable to cover my freshly scrubbed privates. I had this sneaking feeling that he would somehow leap up in a burst of desperate, vengeful energy and burrow into my pubic hair, then latch on to my balls and begin biting and secreting some deadly bacteria or eggs into them, or climb into my ass so deep I could never get him out. Dialectical roaches. Platonic vermin. But he didn't. He just kept flailing away. So I let go of the book, both hands at exactly the same moment—a perfect hit, straight and level. There was a long silence afterward. The book on the ground would have to be thrown away after I got dressed, Socrates sacrificed once for Athens, now for Chicago. I lifted an edge of the book, keeping it at arm's length, and threw it into the trash, then covered it with other debris before I took it to the dumpster, and washed my hands. From that day forward, there were roaches in my apartment. When I came home at night and turned on the light in the kitchen, they ran behind counters, under the sink. Watching TV, I would see them run across the floor and I would give chase, sometimes catching them.

4. HOOPS

What kind of man, I often wondered, murders four people and a day and a half later is out playing basketball? Some offenders would take flight. Others would behave so desperately that people closest to them would know something was wrong. Some might even turn themselves in out of guilt and remorse. But Ealy returned to the basketball courts, almost as if nothing had happened. It was one seemingly insignificant detail about Ealy's crimes that took on great meaning for me.

Basketball arose in several areas of Ealy's story, in both the facts of his crimes and his lies about them. There was the fact that when detectives came to Ealy's apartment to ask him questions about his relationship to Mary Ann and the number of times Ealy frequented the Parker apartment, Ealy was at the basketball courts. It also arose in Ealy's subsequent lie in the interview room after the detectives had found incriminating evidence of the murders under Ealy's bed, then confronted him about it. Ealy claimed that he had found the bundle of evidence outside the Parker apartment. He said he took the bundle and began shooting baskets into the trash cans with it. Where did that notion of a story involving shooting baskets with artifacts used in a quadruple homicide come from? Clearly basketball was deep in Ealy's imagination. People close to the case told me that Ealy spent hours at the basketball courts outside his building, was considered one of the best players there. Everyone who ever encountered him commented on his size and strength, his intimidating presence.

Ealy served about ten years for the rape of the woman on the stairwell, his quadruple murder case falling apart along the way. When Ealy was set free, I had left the city for a short while and was living in northern Michigan, working as a journalist for a small-town paper. This would be in the late 1990s, I figured, still a long time from when I would consider being a cop in Chicago. I still coveted some connection to literature and writing, and I figured journalism was an appropriate start, so I sent résumés throughout the Midwest, finally getting a job in Manistee, Michigan. Basketball was a powerful factor in my imagination as well, even in this small town. After work each day I went to the basketball courts. I parked my beat-up Nissan next to the court, popped the trunk where my shoes and basketball were tucked in a gym bag, sat in the grass while I put on my sneakers, then walked onto the court with the ball. It was soothing and distracting to shoot baskets after a day of writing crime stories for the local newspaper. The basketball courts in this small town were guarded by a phalanx of large conifers, which blocked the wind coming off Lake Michigan. Sometimes a group of local kids would arrive in beat-up student cars and pickups, having just smoked some weed, and we would get in a game or two. They were too stoned to play intensely. Defense, and passing in general, was out of the question. But mostly I just shot alone for a few hours before taking a swim in the lake, the stories I had labored under all day already forgotten.

I had been covering the courts and crimes beat for about six months. At first I had protested taking the crime beat when the other reporter walked off the job, but then took advantage of its simplicity: People were either arrested or they weren't, charged or not, guilty or not guilty. The leads were easy, the description right there in the reports and transcripts. A few quotes from the prosecutor and a victim, and there you were. I would find the worst cases, the ones I knew would titillate readers, and write the obligatory lead, body, wind it up. Most of the time I could gather the stories from the court files and make the necessary phone calls from the newsroom, never even visiting the crime scene or the people involved. The stories became well regarded in the little town because I doled them out steadily with a good eye for the juiciest ones. There were no night meetings to cover as there were on other beats, so I was finished by five every afternoon. By five thirty I'd be shooting baskets in the summer sun.

Earlier that week I had finally obtained permission from the prison leaders to tour the city's biggest employer, the maximum-security state prison. It had taken months to get the approval. I figured if I was going to cover the courts and crime beat, I should at least visit the state prison. It was on the edge of town, cut out from a section of the Manistee National Forest, soothingly called The Oaks. A level-five facility, it took

in the worst of the worst criminals, those inmates that couldn't make it
in other state prisons. I had to fill out a bunch of paperwork about liability in case something went wrong and sat through a briefing where I
learned what to do and what not to do. The guy who gave the tour was
named Earl. He had worked his way up from corrections officer to media
liaison. Earl was cautious around me, choosing his words carefully, not
sure what I would write about the place. Clearly he had been burned by
journalists before. Our last stop was the tier called Administrative
Segregation, where the most depraved criminals in the system were
housed. These inmates were not allowed contact with other prisoners.
They got an hour each day out in the yard, but it was fenced off, in an
outdoor cage. We walked slowly down the corridor, the inmates taunting
us from behind the thick glass windows of their cells. Earl whispered
some of their crimes to me after we walked away.

"Raped two women in his neighborhood. Raped his child . . . then strangled her . . . Shot a guy during a drug deal . . . Not sure about him . . . he
just got here."

"Come in here, young man, and I'll show you a good time," one said
from behind the door.

"You white motherfucking pussy. I'll tear your fucking head off," said
another.

In one cell an inmate was shadowboxing, his arms flying faster than
I could follow him, his body cut like an Olympic athlete's. Our eyes met
for a moment. One-on-one with him, I thought, I'd have no chance. In
another cell, the inmate was doing one-armed push-ups with his legs on
his bed and his arms on the floor. He did about fifteen while I watched
and admitted to myself I could probably not do one. The inmates came
from all over the state, many from Detroit, others from rural areas like
Manistee, and represented the whole spectrum of crime. A collection of
strictly enforced rules, laws they could be called, determined their conduct toward one another and toward the staff in the prison. Earl filled
me in on these laws and how the staff worked around them, manipulated them to keep order, how effective, for example, or dangerous it
could be to take a television away from an unruly inmate and how crucial it was to develop snitches. We walked out onto the yard and came
upon two officers taking a smoking break. I started asking them questions, how long they worked there, what it was like.

"Look at these guys," said one officer, who looked like a homegrown
Manistee native, a fisherman and hunter, pointing his thumb back inside

the hallway. "There's not one guy here who wouldn't cut your throat in a second if he had the chance. They're fucking animals." The other officer nodded his head as he spoke. Earl shifted uncomfortably on either foot and moved us on, not sure if I would write down their comments. He could already see the headlines: "Prison Staffer Calls Inmates Animals." Near the end of our tour, we came to the gymnasium where the prisoners worked out. There was a small basketball court. A basketball sat on the court. I picked it up and walked to the free-throw line.

"If I miss it, I have to stay in a cell. If I make it, I'm free," I joked.

"If you miss it, you're staying," Earl agreed, laughing, finally the ice breaking between us.

I reviewed my fundamentals, tried to fight off the uncomfortable notion of one shot separating me from this place. I felt the weight lift when the ball just barely rolled in. For me, basketball was an extension of my delusional life, the façade I was living. But not for Ealy. To him, basketball was a central expression of his will and his trade. I can only see it clearly now as a cop. It makes sense that Ealy could go and play basketball a day and a half after he had strangled four people to death. Ealy's crimes required great physical strength and domination. Six months earlier, Ealy had held down the woman he raped, dragged her to various locations in the building, an expression of his intense need to dominate her, as much as the rape itself. So, too, with the manner in which he strangled the four Parkers, wrestling them down as he pulled the cords tighter. The defense at one point argued that one man could not have killed all four Parkers. That theory was shot down, but it did illuminate Ealy's mysterious power in the apartment that night, for no one knows for certain how Ealy killed all four Parkers. I can see the complexities of leveraging a rebound on the court serving him in his murders, the pushing and shoving. And not just the skills and strength he gathered there. It was the setting as well: Ealy mastered the game not at some boys' club or organized league, but in the worst projects, surrounding by armed gangbangers, where any petty disagreement on the court could erupt into fights or gunfire. I could see that Ealy relished his strength and balance on the courts not simply for the game itself, but for the crucial lessons in control they offered, control under the most intense circumstances, when everything was on the line. Control was the theme of all of Ealy's crimes, so that when the moment finally came to be close to his victims, to place his face right in front of theirs as he stared at them intensely and pulled the cords tighter, the terror itself became the joy, Ealy relishing the fact that it was his own breath that would be the victims' last memories. Every game Ealy played was a preparation for this, and, when finished, Ealy would instinctively return to the courts until opportunity and inspiration merged once again.

On the courts outside after work, in the solitude of shooting baskets, I acknowledged that my daily crime stories captured little of the worlds they described. My problem was, and always had been, my imagination. I was unwilling to do the hard and courageous work of knowing a place, and then corresponding with it. That in itself was a great crime. The empty ritual of shooting baskets was a frail, cowardly substitute for such correspondence. The significance of hitting ten shots in a row was exactly what, I asked myself in a rare moment of honesty. I huffed and puffed about the court, overweight after laboring for months at a desk on deceptive stories. To remain as a journalist, would I always need to construct such stories? It seemed as if I would. The ball struck a rock at the edge of the court after another terrible shot and bounced into the conifers. I waddled after it, lifting large branches. Then I crawled inside after it.

I could hear some sounds of the outside world, the buzz of a motorboat on the lake, a car on the road, but could see only inside the tree from the little sunlight that made it in. It was private, quiet, and the smell of pine was pleasant, like a freshly cleaned apartment. I paused, because it felt so comfortable there. I couldn't fight off the feeling that this was a place where I could exist, where I should exist, far from Chicago on the edge of Lake Michigan. In this tree, there was natural shelter. I could make a bed of fallen branches. I could hang things easily. There was food in the trash containers left over from picnics, salmon in the lake, water from a pump, public restrooms. As I thought about my new life, a gust of wind suddenly hit the branches and pine needles swatted me, snapping me out of my reverie. When I finally reached for the ball near the trunk, I stepped back, jamming my leg into a broken branch jutting out, which penetrated my skin. I began bleeding. I caught my shirt on another branch, tearing it. Stepping back, I tripped over still another lower branch and fell backward. Several lower branches caught me and broke my fall, but they sank under my immense weight and rolled me out of the tree onto the grass away from the court, as if I were being delivered. Somehow the ball followed and rolled to a stop next to me. I stood up and walked heavily back toward the court, emerging, a man in his thirties, bloodied, with splotches of sticky sap all over me and pine needles in my hair.

As I rounded the tree where I had recovered the ball, there was the sound of another basketball bouncing. Brushing the pine needles out of my hair, I nodded to this other person, older, but in good shape and joined in the solitude of shooting baskets. If his ball bounced my way, I stooped and passed it back to him. He returned the favor. We both waited politely on our own shots until the other's cleared the rim. It's rude when your basketball smacks the other guy's back into the bushes. I monitored his speed, the skill of his shooting form, his apparent right hand dominance, as I moved about the half court launching shots with unspoken fantasies behind them. In my mind, each shot was hoisted with only two seconds left in a game. When they fell, I was a hero. When they missed, there was a foul or a problem with the clock and I always got another chance, or I got the rebound and tipped it in. Like my crime stories, I knew my shots were all false, but I craved both the adulation of my imagined crowd just as I craved titillating the local readers, who stopped me and asked me about my crime stories; most of all, I wanted so much to be the hero of the game.

"Play some Twenty-One?" I asked this guy.

"Sure," he said.

What Tom (that was his name) lacked in skills, he made up for in strength and wind. He was almost seven years older than me, too. He used his body, forcing me to push and lean, draining my weak legs so that I quickly lost the advantage of a better shot, for no one shoots accurately on wobbly legs. Most of all Tom forced me away from my fantasy life and into the true requirements of playing ball. Our games were generally split, me winning the early ones until my endurance faded, then Tom taking the final games. We began meeting frequently in the late afternoons, playing intensely with no animosity. About the third time we met, we got to know each other better while shooting around. Tom was the prison psychologist at The Oaks, the only one for some five hundred inmates. He conducted group therapy meetings, was called late at night for the attempted suicides and other mental health problems. In his dealings with these sociopaths, he could not afford to portray them incorrectly in the narrative reports that were required. He could not fudge his assessments or be too cavalier; it was too dangerous to get them wrong, and he couldn't bullshit the inmates. If they caught him on it, his life was in danger.

Looking back, I mark these afternoons as the origins of a worldview, one that would finally provide me my own correspondence with the world, even as it tossed me forever into the arena of the criminal. In the lull between games, I confessed my shortcomings as a journalist and asked Tom sincerely if there were some way he could help me out, if he could provide me a psychological paradigm that described criminals, some profile by which they might be better understood, apart from the usual claims of poverty, class divisions, and historical forces. He nodded. Criminals, he said, quoting some elementary psychology that had somehow escaped me, have a five-point personality profile. They feel no remorse for their crimes, no matter how cruel. They see themselves as victims regardless of what they have done. They believe their own lies. They are manipulative and narcissistic, and they have a need to control. I paused, because so many of the crimes I covered—the sexual abuse against children in the small towns, the robbers and burglars, and the men who showed up every Tuesday at family court for simply refusing to pay a paltry child-support payment—now held a common identity, a common mind, and I began to see the outlines of it. Later, this paradigm became even more illuminating, the rants and lies of offenders instantly touching on these themes, and, as a cop, I knew instantly what I was dealing with.

Tom tossed the ball back to me at the top of the key. I leaned back and launched one, and it went right in. I head-faked him on the next one and he bought it, so I drove it to the hole.

"It's just truth, Tom, just truth," I said.

Each successful shot afterward I whispered "truth," until I perceived Tom fighting for every loose ball, battling for every inch of ground to the hoop, and I knew I had pushed it too far. I had pissed him off. Soon I was sucking oxygen, and Tom was moving me down low and hitting bunny shots until I collapsed in the grass next to the court.

"Truth that," he said after putting in the winning lay-up. He took his ball and began shooting solo on the court. I remained on the grass huffing and puffing, aware of what a smartass I was. Tom existed in the center of his world. I lived in mine secondhand. My goal as a journalist at the papers had always been to be clever and entertaining. If Tom missed a shot, as he did now, he burst toward the basket, rebounded it, and put it in, while I remained in the lush grass. I stood up for another game, certain a good ass-whipping was exactly what the doctor ordered.

5. TRIAL DATES

An African American man in his forties cuts in the line one spot ahead of me in the hallway of the federal court building. He sets down a small manila file folder on the floor, creating a kind of barrier between us. Turning his back to me, he embraces the woman who has been standing in front of me. They begin chattering away, clearly old acquaintances. He's wearing a wrinkled and dirty polyester suit. The tie hangs down too low and it looks as if his shirt is too tight around the neck to fasten the top button. The woman is dressed fashionably in professional attire, a long skirt and a scarf. They hold hands while they speak, and, as they do so, the man moves closer to the wall where we are lined up, transforming himself from a guy who just stopped by to talk into a bona fide person in line. It is a bold, slick move. To get around him, I would have to step over the envelope and past him at the same time, an awkward, difficult, and aggressive gesture. There is no slowly inching my way around him. Looking down at his folder, I can see there are two newspapers stories sticking out of the side it. They are copies of stories about police torture along with some illegible sentences scribbled on the front.

When I walked into the Dirksen Federal Building earlier, the lobby was packed with news media on the first floor. Their vans were lined up on the street. I made my way to the elevator then out to a well-lit hallway, with security posted outside the courtroom and several officers standing by. The hallway was crowded. There were many African Americans there, gathered in groups, along with professional-looking whites. There was an excitement about them, and they spoke loudly as if they didn't care who heard them.

This man's boldness presents a problem to me in a delicate place. I desperately need to get into this hearing. In ways I cannot yet articulate, the Ealy case has drawn me to this proceeding, the final day of the Burge trial: June 28, 2010, the day Jon Burge, a former police commander, would be sentenced to prison for allegedly lying about torturing suspects. I am drawn to this hearing, even though the Ealy case is not connected to Burge. The Ealy case took place on the West Side. Burge and his men worked the South Side. Burge's men, therefore, had nothing to do with the investigation that collared Ealy for the Parker homicides. But there are common themes: men accused of murder beating their cases, allegations of torture against the police, the time period. After reading the Ealy files, I had come to believe even more that the police had done nothing wrong. In fact, they had conducted a solid investigation, clearly with the intent of getting an evil man off the streets. The detectives were clearly motivated by justice. I was beginning to think that the Ealy case wasn't the only instance of the police being the fall guys. This feeling led me to the Burge cases. It seemed that any allegation of police misconduct always found its way back to Burge. There was such immense propaganda that Burge was a monster. Even when I contacted lawyers, academics, and activists about the Ealy case, the first question they would ask me was "Do you think Burge is guilty?" The truth was that I didn't know for certain, and part of me didn't want to. The accusations were so dark. So it was with a strong sense of dread that I had arrived at the federal building that morning. I had to sort out my feelings. I just had to. But, I wonder, what am I getting myself into?

I had watched the man get off the elevator, saw the panic on his face when he observed the line stretching down the main hallway and turning down another, smaller hallway. He walked back and forth eyeing an opening before he finally spotted the woman, who never saw him because she was immersed in a legal discussion with someone ahead of her. I was, as far as I could tell, the only Chicago Police Officer in the hallway. Other cops, friends and supporters of Burge, sat with Burge behind his defense team. They were let in and out of the proceedings as a group and were not forced to wait in line. I had never met Burge. I eye myself. I look like a cop: short hair, jeans, a T-shirt covered with a sweatshirt, gym shoes. My belt is standard police issue, strong enough to carry a gun holster, cuffs, and pepper spray. I resemble a plainclothes tactical officer.

I stand in the line considering what to do about the man who has just cut in front of me, watching and listening to the crowds in the long hallway. They mingle in various groups, openly calling police racists, torturers, and criminals, in particular officers from the Chicago Police Department. So do the man and the lawyer in front of me. In the media, there is always the prefatory disclaimer by these groups that not all cops are bad—it was only a few rogue cops, they said, who were brutal and racist—but in the hallway, where media interviews are not allowed, the disclaimer is tossed. Here, we are all thugs. We are all racists and cannot be trusted. I knew this vocal condemnation of the police was coming and had prepared myself as I drove down Lake Shore Drive that morning. This was the second day of the sentencing hearing. The first day I had arrived too late and was forced to sit in another courtroom, where the proceedings were broadcast. In this secondary chamber, attendees were free to talk over the trial, and I sat through several hours of commentary on what a monster I was as a Chicago Police Officer. I kept my mouth shut, thought about leaving a few times. Now, staring at the back of this man's head—the man who cut in front of me—my eyes adjust to a group beyond him, holding hands and praying loudly, swaying back and forth in unison, talking about overcoming police brutality.

This sentencing day marks the culmination of a thirty-year quest by these activists to get Burge convicted. Burge, who had risen through the ranks of the department swiftly because of his ability to solve crimes in the worst neighborhoods on the South Side, faced accusations of brutality; the pivotal brutality cases were in 1982, the same year as Ealy's quadruple homicide. He had been through two civil trials over the torture allegations and survived both of them, the juries refusing to convict him. But these losses in court did not deter the activists, who mounted an intense, unrelenting campaign against Burge and his men. Eventually they took their claims that Burge and his men regularly beat, electrocuted, and threatened to murder suspects to the Police Board hearings. This board, comprised of civilians, ruled that Burge and his men did engage in abuse. In response to this ruling and the intense public relations campaign by the anti-Burge activists, Mayor Daley fired Burge. Once Burge was terminated, the claims of abuse by inmates increased, with one inmate after another claiming they were innocent and that Burge and his men had tortured them into confessing. Burge dodged criminal charges, partly because of the statute of limitations. Then, in a civil deposition, Burge, on the advice of his lawyer, denied torturing suspects rather than simply demanding his Fifth Amendment right to remain silent. That was all that federal prosecutors needed to indict him for perjury. And so after thirty years of pursuing Burge, lawyers were finally able to get him prosecuted.

I wanted nothing to do with the Burge cases. When I was in the academy, we were lectured constantly on ethics and maintaining our moral code on the job. We were warned about trying to steal money from dope dealers, from setting people up. These lectures didn't mean much to me, because I could care less about making extra money and I had no antipathy toward anyone. I was not a violent person. Such behavior would disgust me. The Burge saga played out in my first decade on the job. I listened to it, read about it, but kept it at a distance. Working as a cop was already dark enough without entering a world like this. My first year on the job, I was transferred to Area 2. The media attention on Burge was so prolific that the phrase "Area 2" became a kind of buzzword. The allegations arose in your mind when you drove to work, forcing you to wonder what had happened. You wondered what would happen to you working there. Off duty, there was a momentary pause whenever someone asked where you worked and you said, "Area 2." Some people would come right out and ask, "Burge's district?" There was so much coverage against him, so many claims of malfeasance, that I had assumed something had gone terribly wrong when he and his men worked there. Now I am not so sure.

The night before this hearing, I started my research about Burge by tracking down the case with the greatest evidence of torture against him. It occurred, to my astonishment, in February 1982, the same month Ealy had raped the woman on the stairwell, six months before Ealy would strangle the Parkers. It was a fertile year, I was seeing, for city sociopaths, particularly those who claimed police abuse and misconduct. I was sitting at my desk when I called a journalist who spearheaded the investigations against Burge. I introduced myself and asked him why he thought Burge had tortured this prisoner, a career criminal named Andrew Wilson, who had killed two policemen during a traffic stop. I sat and listened, expecting some bomb to be dropped, some irrefutable evidence that Burge had beaten a confession out of him. I expected this journalist to tell me of witnesses who had come forward to say they saw Burge commit these acts. I expected other cops to testify that they had evidence he did it. I figured the case against him was rock solid, given all the media fanfare and his recent conviction. But the journalist told me only about the physical evidence of Andrew Wilson's wounds the night after he was picked up for the murder of two cops.

There were, the journalist said, cuts and bruises and some marks he claimed were burns on Wilson's body. He also said there were marks on Andrew Wilson indicating where clips had been applied to his ears and genitals as part of an electrocution using a torture device. I always had such immense doubts about this claim. How would Burge pull this off in a crowded police station, with cops walking around, the media saturating the building? I figured the accusation arose because someone had actually witnessed Burge using this machine. There must have been witnesses. But there weren't any. These marks could have gotten there a million different ways, including using a roach clip. Wilson knew he just murdered two cops and would likely get the death penalty.

The journalist got mad when, after a long pause I asked, "That's it? That's all you've got?" and he quickly got off the phone.

It was the same reaction I had when I read the specific allegations of malfeasance against the detectives in the Ealy case. They asked Ealy to come to the station? That was why the appeals court tossed the conviction? My mind went back to every arrest I had made where the offender claimed that I had hit him or abused his rights, the offenders who had threatened to sue me, all the arrests where the offender had smashed his head against the wall in order to create injuries, particularly offenders facing felony crimes.

I tied this suspicion I had about the Ealy case and now the allegations against Burge to my own experience. One recent crime in particular rose up. In late autumn I was working the wagon when a tactical unit got on the air to announce a car had taken off at a high rate of speed from a traffic stop. The car had been parked in front of a liquor store on Howard Street, the driver sitting in it with the engine running. When the unmarked car pulled up, the driver suddenly fled southbound, right around rush hour as people were coming home. A woman and her son had just gotten off a bus and were crossing the street when the driver approached at around eighty miles per hour on the small side street. They had no chance. Both were hit head-on, their bodies caving in the entire windshield and frame of the car, mother and son catapulted almost half a block into the air before they were tossed like rag dolls onto the pavement. The woman died immediately, but the boy was still alive with severe head trauma.

I saw none of this, just heard it come across the radio in the broken, desperate narrative of emergency calls. But I was on Devon and the offender was heading straight our way. I pulled up to the cross street of Devon and Glenwood, along with several squad cars, as the radio announced that the offender's car was no longer drivable. The offender had smashed into several cars before abandoning it and was now on foot, running almost straight into us. We grabbed him and he began resisting, asking what was going on, as if he were just walking down the street and we had accosted him. Already he knew to deny everything and lie. When he wouldn't comply to get on the ground and we began forcing him to do so, he began shouting out, "Police brutality," at the top of his lungs. As we placed him in the rear of the wagon, he kept up his denials and accusations. By the time we got him to the station, he was demanding a lawyer, saying we had violated his rights. We were North Side cops, not facing the daily chaos of the South and West Sides, but we all knew not to talk to him, to leave it to the detectives. We stayed at the district for a while. While we waited in the hallway, more information came back: the woman dead, the boy gravely injured and going in for emergency surgery on his brain. Apparently the father of the boy, who was in a wheelchair, watched the whole scene unfold. He and the son had gone to meet the woman, his wife, at the bus stop there. The offender railed and railed in the interview room, cursed us out every time we walked by. After a while we took him to the area for the detectives. It took all my patience not to grab him about the neck and choke him, saying, "You fucking son of a bitch, you might have killed that little boy and he's got brain damage now. You killed his mother, you worthless piece of shit, and you don't even fucking care."

Eventually he admitted he had been driving the car, but not once did he ask about the woman or the boy. You could tell it never even crossed his mind. Sometime later we were called to the crime scene, a whole block long. I had to drop off some paperwork to a car on scene. It was nighttime now, late autumn, and the streetlamps created all kinds of shadows. I walked under the crime scene tape, toward the squad car, when an officer got on their speaker and announced, "Look out." I stopped, looked down. There at my feet were the woman's brains. A little bit farther over were her shoes and her purse. There was a line of other fluids and tissue, and the cops pointed out where she had eventually landed half a block down.

As I stand in the line at the federal building listening to the man talk to the woman in front of me, it becomes clear to me that the man is one of the exonerated criminals who has claimed torture at the hands of Burge, and the woman is a lawyer/professor who has worked on his case. My anger rises up. I am fed up with hiding my identity, as if I were some kind of criminal. All the shit you have to deal with as a cop. Here I am in the halls of a justice building in the center of downtown. But I know if I confront the exonerated man about cutting in, he has nothing to lose by becoming bellicose. Perhaps he can sense I am a cop by my haircut and silence, and he realizes this would be an ideal environment to challenge me. In any other context, I could have tapped him on the shoulder and told him to move. But here is different. He has nothing to lose, whereas I would face all kinds of consequences for getting into a squabble with him. He could turn any altercation against me and say I was the aggressor. Would I get witnesses in this group? Hardly. It would be pointless and unfair to involve the sheriff's deputies who are providing security for the hearing. They have enough on their hands. The woman lawyer has already let him cut in without saying a word. What if the exonerated guy refused to obey the sheriffs' command to get out of line and became combative? What if he started cursing us all out? What if it got so out of hand, they were forced to arrest him?

I can see the headlines: "Victim Harassed by Police Again." "Cop Initiates Brawl at Corruption Trial." "All Suspended Pending Investigation."

What if, on the other hand, the ex-con refused to go to the end of the line and they took no action? That would be a bitter dose of humiliation for all of us. If I were going to do anything, it would have to be on my own. My heart rate increases. This visit to the courthouse could all go completely haywire. I can see myself being escorted out from the building, the dozens of cameras set up in the lobby capturing the escort, my supervisors at work notified.

"What the fuck were you fucking doing, causing a fucking disturbance at the fucking Burge trial?" I could hear my supervisor asking me in a disciplinary meeting as he holds up the headline. "What the fuck were you fucking doing there in the first motherfucking place?"

"You weren't there. You didn't hear what was said. Besides, he cut in line."

"You're damn right I wasn't there. Why didn't you just stay home? Leave it alone."

"But he cut in line. I wanted to see the sentencing."

"What the fuck were you doing there to begin with?"

"I need to sort out these crimes, get the right take on them. It has become crucial to me."

"You want to what?"

"Sort out these crimes. You see, there was this guy on the West Side in 1982 who murdered a family of four. He was tried and convicted, then released after an appeal . . ."

"Who gives a flying fuck about 1982? What the fuck is wrong with you? What the hell am I supposed to do with this?"

"I'm sorry, but I couldn't see another way. He did cut in front of me."

"Who gives a fuck? Let him cut in, Goddamnit. Now I have to take some action against you."

"It's all right. I understand. It's my own fault. I know it."

The problem for me was that I perceived a great possibility in the Ealy murders, as if they had introduced me into a new world, even though Ealy's murders were largely forgotten in the city. I had dredged them up myself. This feeling intensified as I read the court transcripts and hunted down detectives who had worked the case and then other detectives who worked this era in Chicago. My heartbeat increased when I drove to the building where Ealy's apartment, and the apartment of the Parkers he murdered, once existed on West Jackson. I stopped the car with a veteran cop who worked there for years, knowing that if we just sat there, the stories would start flowing. I needed to hear them. The Ealy murders now merged into others in the same year—each murder becoming part of what I sensed was a larger, unacknowledged tapestry. There were common themes, the fact that these other murderers claimed they were tortured into confessing, just as James Ealy had done in his case, claiming at his trial that a cop came into the interview room and beat him, telling him what to say in his confession. But such accusations were obviously untrue. There were no marks on Ealy at all, no signs of any abuse whatsoever. There is a photo of him after he signed his confession, looking perfectly composed. He never made a complaint of abuse to the state's attorney, nor to the stenographer. More so, his accusation of torture was not very feasible. The detectives already had all the evidence they needed, an overwhelming amount against Ealy. They had collected this evidence of the strangulations from under his bed. He had admitted being at the Parker apartment, admitted he had brought the evidence back to his apartment. Why would the officers jeopardize their case with needless abuse? Neither the trial judge nor the appeals court in the Ealy case upheld the complaints of torture.

The doors to a nearly empty courtroom open. Everyone straightens up. The sheriff's deputies wave the people in front to a table where they will surrender their bags for inspection. I feel as if I am moving into a mystery introduced by the James Ealy case, the liberation of a man who killed four people, confessed to it, and got out. Part of me dreads it. It is a vitriolic, brutal world. I can't help it. I am guided by the sense that what holds these crime scenes together, and what is most valuable about them, is how they move deeper and deeper into the fantastic, yet are entirely real. I think about Ealy getting out of the murders, then look at this scene in this hallway where the people are chanting and cursing the Chicago police. They are cursing me. There are many pitfalls and dead ends in wandering these murders, many instances where I would be the buffoon, like standing in this line or getting the story entirely wrong. But I arose early that morning and made my way down to the hearing because I had this sense that these murders are the source of something original and vital.

With all this in my mind, I still don't know what to do about this exonerated man who has cut in line in front of me. But finally, I say fuck it and step over the manila envelope, suddenly in front of him, standing inches away. I can feel his silent glare, but he says nothing.

The line inches forward. So much is at stake. For me, I risk defending police torturers, men who are accused of electrocuting suspects, putting guns to their mouths, and beating them senseless. Some of these suspects, it was claimed, were innocent of any crimes and would spend decades in prison for crimes they did not commit. I look at myself in the hallway: What have I become? How low can I sink? Yet I perceive an anxiety in the activists as well, for all their celebration in the hallway. I know well the kind of people they had liberated from prison. These exonerated men are wandering the city again, just like James Ealy was eventually released after his quadruple murder conviction was struck down. Now that the fanfare of the Burge scandal is coming to an end, many of these criminals would return to their ways. In this regard, James Ealy is a kind of guiding light.

After the sentencing of Jon Burge for perjury that day, whenever the activists or the exonerated murderers or the media talked about Burge, they can call him a torturer without the word "alleged" and cite the "long history of police abuse." Armed with such authority, they could re-create so much. They could re-create me. Intoxicated by such power, they act as if the story were now concluded and consider the sentencing to be a celebration of their achievement. Dozens of inmates had been freed, tens of millions of dollars paid in restitution. Cameras and reporters on the first floor wait for their comments. I watch them later flood onto the elevators and head downstairs after Burge got four and a half years, after Burge maintained in his speech to the judge that he had never even met—let alone abused—one of the men who accused him of torture. That man had been convicted of setting a fire that killed seven people. Would Burge risk another perjury conviction by lying to the judge, saying he had never even met the guy? It struck me as odd.

But in this insistence on claiming that their narrative was official and complete, the wrongful conviction advocates, in my mind, revealed a dangerous bias. I know the activists and the lawyers could not admit, at least not yet, that nothing had ended at all. They are still ignorant of the subtle ways that the sociopath's fate turns and turns, and turns again.

6. LIGHTS AND SIRENS

A train finally moves out of the Howard Station. I stand on the train platform just south, staring at it. I use the trick of watching it with one eye closed, seeing its headlight flicker behind a barrier, a sign that it is moving. Howard is the end of the line, so the train can only be moving toward me, not away. As I watch it approach, I form a conclusion that what ties the city together, what illuminates the fact that we are merely artifices in a larger, more powerful creation, is the irony haunting the city, particularly its crime scenes. This irony is the city's preferred creative device, surpassing all others in its intensity. The police became aware that they were trapped in this irony long before anyone else. It came to them in a blinding, violent illumination, as if they were characters in a tragic play. If the rest of the city had paused and listened—if I had, for example—we might have observed two decades earlier that the condition of the police had the force of the universal about it. But that isn't feasible. It is the nature of irony to arrive too late, past the point of altering the course of things, revealing itself, say, in the moments during or after a murder, but not before.

The train pulls up, the doors open, and I step in. I once rode the trains every day. When I first came to the city, I was captivated by them. They would take you anywhere in the city for a dollar. They cut through neighborhoods, giving you a vivid, intimate look at the people and the buildings. They were filled with every manner of person. Now, I rarely get on them. There's too great a chance of meeting some gangbanger I've arrested. If things got out of control, how would I call for help? How could I defend myself against a pack of them? What would it be like, firing a gun on a train? Even if an altercation or a shooting broke out and I was entirely justified in my actions, would I get a witness? There is a good chance I wouldn't. But today and the rest of the week, I have to go downtown to the city archives building and gather transcripts from murder cases. It would too expensive to park all week and the bus takes way too long, so I am on the trains again for the first time in a long while.

There are only a few riders. I sit with my right side against the wall so that no one can sit next to me and rub against my gun. As the train takes the slow curve before Morse, I admit to myself that this irony holds a vision. Three police officers had been shot in just a few weeks, two of them fatally. In that year, 1982, these police murders were hanging over the heads of every officer, not just as reminders to be careful and events of aching sorrow, but as indications that something fundamental had changed. There was some shift in power they could not fully measure, as if some fate in the city now operated on behalf of the sociopaths, giving them more power. It was not a transient shift, or a temporary one, but a shift for all time. The cops could not necessarily describe it so. They merely perceived with their trained eyes the slight changes in time and movement that afforded the crucial advantage to the sociopaths, which gave their ascendance a more ominous, otherworldly aspect.

Then on February 9, 1982, these suspicions took vivid focus in the daring, decisive movements of Andrew Wilson when he lunged for the gun of Officer William Fahey during a traffic stop near the intersection of Eighty-First and Morgan. The two men, the officer and Wilson, were standing on the passenger side of Wilson's car. They wrestled, and, as they did so, they moved toward the rear of Wilson's car. That's when Wilson pulled Officer Fahey's gun from its holster after the two men slipped wrestling for control of the weapon. Wilson aimed the pistol at the back of Fahey's head and fired once, striking Fahey in the back of the head. Wilson then cunningly crouched behind the rear passenger side of the car and shot at Officer Richard O'Brien across the trunk of the Chevrolet, hitting O'Brien in the chest as the doomed officer tried to take position and return fire. The ironies came alive now, even to Fahey and O'Brien—an unarmed man wrestling a gun from a seasoned South Side Chicago cop, then firing and hitting O'Brien before he could get a shot off. These ironies were a source of final horror and sorrow for Fahey and O'Brien, intoxicating and joyful for the likes of Andrew Wilson, that stinking motherfucker, who climbed atop the trunk of the Chevy after Andrew's brother Jackie informed him that O'Brien was still alive, loomed over O'Brien, and pumped three more rounds into his chest.

Now the ironies exploded, wrapping the cops in a web they couldn't escape and never have. After Fahey and O'Brien were shot and the Wilson brothers fled, the wagon arrived on scene quickly, its officers facing the dire image of O'Brien alive and trying to speak, but unable to do so, as well as the delicate but brute task of collecting the two officers, lifting them off the street into the rear of their lumbering vehicle. The cop on the passenger side screamed into the radio updates on what streets to block, what route they were taking, so other officers could block traffic along the way. The officers transporting Fahey and O'Brien would have to live with the burden of choosing the wrong route, delaying any arrival by seconds in the frantic drive to the hospital. The dispatcher would have to keep control on the radio, a nightmarish responsibility. The cops would have to live with the decisions they made. At the crime scene, everyone remaining would have to remember their duties, to remain focused and establish the crime scene, gather information and send out messages and begin the paperwork. How difficult it would be to keep a steady hand on the paper, to write the names and numbers legibly. Don't fuck it up. Don't write a wrong address that could lose the offenders. Don't write the wrong name of a witness who might have knowledge that could find the offenders. They had to keep working as they heard O'Brien was declared dead at the hospital. Fahey would linger for a day before he died.

The train approaches Uptown. I realize my mind is trapped in these ironies as well. Officers Fahey and O'Brien had just returned from the funeral of a murdered police officer when they stopped the Wilsons. They were still wearing their dress uniforms. I believe that as the crime unfolded, when Andrew Wilson began wrestling with Officer Fahey, both officers must have been struck in a momentary epiphany at how strange, how unlikely such a turn of events would be, that they should get into a shooting the same day they came back from the funeral of a murdered cop. When Andrew Wilson came up with the gun, I wonder if there was a moment when Fahey sensed this irony, then O'Brien, too, when the gun went off a moment later and Fahey slumped to the ground, how incredible that they should get in a shooting right after the funeral of another murdered cop. How incredible to get shot while still mired in the sadness and weight of a police funeral.

Irony.

The train pulls up to Argyle; the smell of Asian restaurants and markets invades the car when the doors open. I wonder at the force that pulled Fahey and O'Brien to Wilson's car. It seems otherworldly to me. One account claimed that Fahey and O'Brien stopped the car because it matched the description of a vehicle used in a holdup a few hours earlier. Another theory was that Jackie, who was driving, blew off the stop sign at the intersection, and still another theory was that one of the Wilson brothers threw a whiskey bottle out the window. Many cops would have let the Wilson's Chevy pass by for any of the transgressions cited, laying low for a few days to let the shock and sorrow of the police funeral subside. The intuition of Fahey and O'Brien was dead-on. There was something dreadfully wrong about the car. They were veteran officers who had learned to sense such things and to trust these senses. One of the officers may have pointed at the car casually as the Chevy drove by and said, "That motherfucker is dirty." Veteran cops say this to each other every day. The partner nods and says, "Yeah," acknowledging that he agrees to stop the vehicle by reaching forward to activate the lights, then says, "He blew off the stop sign," or, "He just threw a bottle out the window," as legal justification for making the stop.

But when the tide turned on them, when Andrew Wilson came up with the gun, they knew by the irony of it that they were trapped. The problem is that it has never stopped. A tapestry expanded at the crime scene, came alive for the rest of the officers who responded, who heard the radio call for the second time in a week that an officer was down, this time two officers. The voice that announced it was irregular, not the sound of a familiar dispatcher or even a police officer, but the panicked voice of a civilian who came on scene right after the Wilsons pulled away, blurting out a call for help in the normally calm dispatches. It was the voice of one of the first witnesses on scene, who picked up the radio in the car. (This was when radios were still in cars.) *What? Again? It can't be*, the cops thought. Many of them had just returned from the funeral that day as well. Many were no doubt still talking about it when the voice came over the radio.

The officer who had been murdered four days before Fahey and O'Brien—the one whose funeral they had attended—was James Doyle, a rookie. He and his partner, Robert Mantia, were parked in a squad car on the South Side when they were approached by a witness who claimed he had been robbed at gunpoint a few months earlier. The offender, he said, was on a bus that just pulled away. The witness said he had a warrant for the offender, Edgar Hope, and showed it to them. The officers told the witness to get in the squad car. They pulled in front of the bus. Doyle and Mantia got on and walked toward the rear. Edgar Hope was sitting with another man. Mantia watched the man sitting with Hope while Doyle searched Hope. The rookie officer found drug paraphernalia but missed the two guns Hope was hiding in his winter clothes. Doyle escorted Hope to the front of the bus, Hope in front. As they walked toward the entrance, Hope suddenly reached for the gun, spun around on Doyle, and fatally shot him in the chest. Hope fired more shots, grazing a woman in the head and another in the finger.

Doyle's partner exited the rear. The gunfight continued outside. Mantia fired from behind a CTA bus shelter, striking Hope, who collapsed on the ground. Mantia ran over and handcuffed him. Doyle died from the single shot to the chest. Hope, shot several times, recovered to one day request clemency from the governor.

The ironies expanded another degree, encircling the cops. Detectives later learned that Andrew Wilson and Edgar Hope were friends. They had also pulled jobs together. When the Wilson brothers drove past Fahey and O'Brien, they were on their way to the Cook County Hospital to try to break Edgar Hope out of custody. Hope was at the county hospital recovering from his wounds in the gunfight on the bus. It would be the easiest way to break Hope out. There would only be one or two cops guarding Hope. Jackie Wilson would later admit they were willing to shoot their way out of the hospital. Just before they drove past Fahey and O'Brien, the Wilsons had committed a burglary, thinking the owner of the building they had broken into was a cop. They wanted more guns and ammunition and possibly some police uniforms for the breakout. But they came up empty, only getting a little money and some other items, like a jar filled with coins, some of which they took with them in the car. They planned on dressing in hospital uniforms instead, and they had the disguises in their car.

The chaos they could have created at the county hospital if they had made it there, had they not encountered Fahey and O'Brien. Likely they would have killed the cops at the hospital and taken their guns, would likely have killed hospital workers or security staff as well. They would kill anyone. Fahey and O'Brien deflected the Wilsons' sociopathic plots onto themselves and saved the patients, nurses, doctors, and fellow cops at the county hospital. I wonder if it ever crossed the minds of the hospital workers what could have happened to them that day. I wonder if they ever imagined their own coworkers lying bleeding on the hospital floors, the Wilson brothers at large, and Edgar Hope free again. Then, with Hope on the outside, how many other people would the three men have killed in their efforts to remain free? How many more cops killed, cars stolen, home invasions? How much more chaos? Did people in the city ever stop to think of the lives Fahey and O'Brien saved that day?

Cops throughout the city were desperate for the ironies to end here, desperate for some reprieve, but investigators traced the two guns recovered from Edgar Hope at the bus shooting. One gun came back to a police officer murdered several weeks earlier at a McDonald's restaurant on the Far South Side. Hope had entered the McDonald's causing a disturbance. Two off-duty sheriff's department officers walked over to him. At that moment, Hope's accomplice burst into the McDonald's and fatally shot one of the officers in the chest with a shotgun. Hope knocked the other officer to the ground. He raised a gun to the cop's head. The cop begged for the lives of the workers—not his own life—and put his hand in front of this face just as Hope pulled the trigger. The cop testified that Hope was smiling right before he shot, but the cop blocked the bullet with his arm and the bullet bounced off his tooth. He faked his own death until Hope and his accomplice fled.

Between Andrew Wilson and Edgar Hope, the tally now stood at five officers shot in one month, four of them fatally. It could have been worse had Andrew and Jackie Wilson made it to the county hospital.

I look from my seat in the train as we head out from the Sheridan stop, my mind moving into that hopeless place that tries to explain the thinking behind these killings. Why were Hope and Wilson so hell-bent on slaughtering cops? Could Hope truly have believed he would get away with shooting two cops in the McDonald's? Could Andrew Wilson believe he and his brother would shoot Fahey and O'Brien and then what—lay low for a while and it would be forgotten? Did he think he and his brother could go to the county hospital, shoot it up, free Hope, and the three of them would somehow get away with it and never be apprehended, that they would spend the rest of their days stealing and getting high? Did James Ealy think he would get away with the quadruple murder of the Parkers? Did he think no one would ever find the evidence under his bed, wrapped in the sheets? There was no sense to it. It seemed as if the sociopaths didn't care, or, worse, all the killers somehow sensed that this was their time and it gave them inspiration.

From the moment Andrew Wilson murdered Fahey and O'Brien, the ironies exploded in complexity and darkness, then moved into other crime scenes. They have never stopped. Looking out the train window south of Sheridan, I realize that I, too, had fallen under the spell of the vision these ironies unfold. I sense the bare outlines of it in Ealy's quadruple murder of the Parker family, his appeal from this conviction, then his complete liberation when prosecutors declined to try him again after all the evidence was tossed. The Wilson murders of Fahey and O'Brien took place a few weeks before Ealy raped the woman on the stairwell, six months before Ealy strangled the four Parkers, the rape of three-year-old Jontae in the course of those strangulations a kind of finishing atrocity. One of the first witnesses who pulled up as the Wilsons drove away from the murders of Fahey and O'Brien stated that Andrew Wilson was smiling as he got into the Chevy and fled. To me, Wilson acted not as if he had just ruined his life, but that he knew this was his time and his place and that his crimes, far from condemning him, would be the source of his liberation, his own deliverance into psychotic glory. And they would be. Wilson would avoid the death penalty and become a celebrity, a kind of godfather in the prison system, a counselor to every killer in the joint who strove to get out. Certainly he had some influence on James Ealy, who adopted Wilson's torture allegations. They were, after all, in the county jail at the same time. But for the cops, it was Wilson's smiling face after the murders: here was a vision of the crooked city, one where only the sociopaths were truly free.

The train picks up speed. The city's ironies are so dark and cruel, it is painful to see how one is wrapped up in them, how they hold us. It seems as if one goal in the city is finding a way to avoid them. I'm as guilty as anyone else. I see myself sitting in cafés on the North Side talking literature at the exact moment the Wilson shootings took place. I see myself hitchhiking to the city from Kalamazoo, Michigan, right by the district station where the Wilson brothers were held a few days later when they were caught. To avoid these ironies appears to me now hopeless and naïve. The ironies are all there is. A tension between prison and liberation lays at their core. In them, one constantly sees the world a certain way only to have it revealed as the opposite, the way the detectives in the Ealy case went from capturing and prosecuting Ealy to being blamed for his release. It is a kind of captivity. But there was something else in it. These ironies are their own creative device, their own means of seeing and arranging the city. I admit on the train that I would let them guide me, perceiving simultaneously the dark threats abounding in them, as well as letting the vision they unfolded take shape, the way, for example, they tied one murder into another.

I don't know it then on the train, but I had already taken a giant step into my own sociopathic design, embezzling the cruel works of predators like James Ealy and Andrew Wilson into my own vision. There was no other way. I had to.

It is a crooked city.

7. THE MEDICAL SECTION

A pain shoots down my leg. I lean forward, trying to find a position that won't aggravate the disk pinching the nerve, but I am having trouble finding one. My legs are twisted and my back bent to the right, an absurd position. The seats are metal in the medical section of the police department, where you wait until a nurse comes out to the lobby and calls your name. I've been waiting for more than an hour and am wondering if they have forgotten about me. I am here to set up my second surgery for herniated disks in my back.

My disks herniated from a melee some five years earlier. Every weekend, one car from our district was sent to the West Side to deal with the surge in crime there. It was an assignment nobody wanted. The reason is that you don't know the streets, the watch commander, the sergeants, or most of the other cops. You don't know the gangs. The West Side is much busier and more dangerous than the North Side. But it was our turn that weekend, so we met a bunch of cops who were sent over from their districts and began patrolling Garfield Park. We drove a squad car and were assigned to a sergeant we didn't know. We were supposed to patrol the park, but we could also be called away to other cars. While in the park, a call came over the radio of a large noise disturbance farther west. Our sergeant told the dispatcher that we were on our way. We got in our squad cars and followed him, none of us knowing exactly where we were. We pulled up in front of a house on a corner packed with partygoers. There were large speakers set in the windows blaring rap music so loud it could be heard for several blocks. The bass pounding seemed to make the ground shake. The sergeant began talking to a woman who looked as if she was the resident of the house. He had to lean into her ear and shout. Soon she was shaking her head and he was pointing his finger when he turned to me and shouted in my ear, "Arrest this woman."

There were hundreds of people running around the home and the yard. An arrest might kick off a larger disturbance.

"Arrest her," he ordered me again.

I leaned over to my partner's ear and shouted, "This night is quickly turning to shit," then I pulled out my handcuffs and the woman bolted. I made a halfhearted move to pursue her into the hostile crowd. That's when things kicked off. Bottles started flying, rocks were thrown. The sergeant was pursuing a guy in his twenties. This guy threw something at us from the stairs on the side of the building. Now I was pissed. Whatever he threw had all his strength behind it. It could have killed one of us. I took a few steps up the stairs. When I reached him near the top, I felt something from behind. Some guys had grabbed me. They pulled me backward as they tripped me, and I rolled down the stairs onto the grass below. Still dazed, I sat up, feeling my legs and back to see if I was okay, when I looked up on the balcony and there were five or six men, one the guy I had tried to arrest, picking up a large potted plant, more like a tree, and they were heaving it at me as I lay on the ground. As I moved out of the way, I felt the first twinge of pain. The tree came down right where I had been sitting. I looked at my partner and said, "I think my back is fucked up for good," and it was. The guy I had been chasing, who threw the plant, got misdemeanor battery and was out the next day.

It was one back episode after another from that day on, including surgeries. When I drove down Lake Shore Drive to get to the medical section this morning, I could feel the familiar tightening, knew it would be a long walk from my car to the headquarters building at Thirty-Fifth and Michigan. I found a spot two blocks away. It was winter and there were snow drifts at the edge of Michigan Avenue, so I parked some distance from the curb on the one-way street, enough to open the car door and squeeze out. But I had been sitting so long, my back wouldn't stretch out and wouldn't support me. I collapsed, holding myself up only with one arm on the car door and another on the roof of the car. The waves of pain, spasms they are called, subsided, and after a few minutes I took my first few steps, gingerly extending my right leg.

A collection of officers lingers in the waiting area, back injuries, shoulders, stitches, broken bones, a few colds and flu. They sit in their own twisted shapes. I turn my gaze to the rack of pamphlets urging regular prostate examination, colonoscopies, and a poster warning against faking injuries to get off work. On the way down that morning, I had drunk some coffee and eaten a bran muffin. It wasn't a good move, because now the thought of using the public restroom in my condition terrifies me. I would have to stand up again, limp to the other side of the building to the bathroom, and enter one of the stalls. The groans and heavy breaths that arise every time I try to sit down could attract attention.

Worse would be a total collapse of my back in the bathroom, like the night when they hauled me out in an ambulance. I went to bed that night with some expanding stiffness after slipping on some stairs on a domestic battery call. There was that dreaded twinge. When I got up early the next morning to hit the bathroom—before the sun rose—I felt an electric shock roll through my body, and I collapsed on the floor. My two cats stared at me, waiting for me to get up, but there was no way. I waited about a half hour, but the pain shot through me every time I tried to move. It's strange to lie on the floor of your own bedroom, unable to move. *Perhaps I should have gotten married when I had the chance*, I thought to myself. Eventually I realized there was no choice but to call an ambulance, but where was my cell phone? Slowly I reconstructed my movements the night before from the floor of my bedroom, concluding that the phone was on the table near the front door. I began crawling in that direction, wearing only my underwear. I moved slowly out of the bedroom, into the small hallway, making frequent stops. It helped to sometimes grab doors or door frames to pull and twist. Sometimes it was best to just roll onto my side and inch my way along. There was much cursing, sighing, and heaving breaths. When I got to the front door, I grabbed a rag and flung it up at the counter where I hoped my phone was. Everything came tumbling down, my wallet, keys, change, and the phone.

"Yes, I'm an off-duty police officer and I need an ambulance," I said to the 911 operator.

"What is your injury?" she said.

"I injured my back at work tonight, and when I woke up just now I couldn't walk. I'm on the floor. I did an Injury on Duty Report."

"You did a report?"

"Yes."

"Okay. I need you to get the door open. Otherwise, the Fire Department will have to make a forced entry."

My heart sank. How could I crawl up the three stairs to my front door, reach the lock, and open it? There was no way. But have the fire department break open my door, my neighbors coming out and seeing me on my floor in only my underwear? No way. I would have to find a way to get it open.

"Okay, I'll get it unlocked," I said. "Wait a minute. Are you sending cops as well?"

"Yes, we have to when an officer is injured."

"Well, I'm in my underwear. Can you send male officers?"

"Well, I don't think so. We have to send who is available, and I can't say who will show up there once it goes over the radio."

It was hard to imagine my female coworkers seeing me on my own floor in my underwear. But there was no way around it.

"I understand," I said to the operator. "You might want to send a message to any female officers, tell them Christmas is coming a little early," I said. I turned my head and saw myself, liked a beached whale, in the reflection of a glass window on the door that separated the living room from the kitchen.

"I'll do that," the dispatcher said, laughing.

There is a profound solitude in the moments between calling 911 while on the floor in your underwear and the time when the fire engines pull up outside your building, the red siren lights flashing in your window. It forces an accounting, how exactly one ended up on one's floor waiting almost naked for one's coworkers to arrive. I looked around my condo. Been meaning to clean it for a long time. I would have stayed there on the floor, but I had to open the door. I rallied my resolve, inching my body as close as possible to the three stairs at my front door. There were two locks, the deadbolt and the door handle. That meant an extra moment spent upright turning both of them. I tried to move upward toward the door, but the electric pain zapped and I fell to the floor. One of my cats sat on the arm of the couch watching me. Cats, unlike dogs, are rarely any help. I couldn't say to my cat, "Run, Frances, run. Go outside the open window and get the extra key from the maintenance guy, then show the firemen where I am. Go on, boy, you can do it." Instead, we just stared at each other. I crawled up the three stairs slowly, got my body as close to the door as possible, then put my left hand on the wooden floor and pushed up, turning the deadbolt as I yelled out in pain, held myself up a moment longer, and turned open the doorknob lock. Then I fell back to the floor, breathing heavily, sweating, when I realized the paramedics would have to be buzzed in. Just then I heard the siren approaching, the red lights waving around my windows.

The nurses at the medical section are also police officers. My regular nurse is beautiful. She is Latina, with big brown eyes and a soft voice. She's a few pounds overweight, which only adds to her sensuality. It's not just her beauty. She also looks out for me, explains in detail how the medical section works when I have questions, takes care of all the paperwork. She likes to kid around, too, and I tease her about how lucky her boyfriend is. All the while we banter, she riffles through the paperwork like an old pro, sets up the appointment. I'm anxious to see her again today and then get out of the place, get back home. I wonder if she is perhaps off today, and that is the reason for the delay. I look again to see if she is coming, but the hallway is empty.

I turn my body in the opposite direction, seeking relief. There is only a muted television playing in the room, no magazines to read. I should have brought some transcripts from home, some case reports on the Ealy murders to go over. It was stupid to come empty-handed. That way I could review the central claim in the appeal that got Ealy off, the one that said the detectives violated Ealy's rights. Sitting in the waiting room, the question comes back: Exactly what did the defense attorneys and appeals court judges expect of the detectives in the Ealy case? The defense claimed that when the detectives asked Ealy to come to the station to answer some questions, this constituted an arrest. The judge who oversaw the original trial rejected these claims and went forward with the trial. Ealy was eventually found guilty of the murders. But when the appeals court took up the case, they agreed with the defense and tossed the arrest, as well as all the evidence obtained from it, including the evidence wrapped in a sheet under Ealy's bed and his confession. Without the evidence, prosecutors declined to retry Ealy. But I ask myself again in the waiting room, just what did the defense lawyers and the appeals court expect of the detectives? In this crime there was a level of rage that indicated the most brutal kind of homicide, one wherein the offender kills for the sexual pleasure of it. The fact that the cords were embedded in the necks of one victim and that there was the rape of a three-year-old boy were proof of that. Any detective familiar with such killers knows there is often an escalation after the first few crimes. Look at Ealy: he went from the rape of one woman to a quadruple murder plus the rape of a child in less than six months. What would be his next venture?

What if the detectives had followed the dictums of the defense attorneys and the appeals court? What if they concluded that asking Ealy to come to the station was a kind of arrest and therefore abandoned the idea of taking him there? What if they somehow concluded this despite the fact that they had made this request in dozens of other investigations? What if it were standard practice? Instead, the detectives would have had to question Ealy in front of his mother. Rule number one in any investigation is never question someone in the presence of another person who has already provided a story. If Ealy started saying something contradicting what his mother had just stated, she would cut off the interview. Ealy would not talk in front of his mother in any case. He would not talk about his relationship with Mary Ann in front of her. If Ealy knew something about the offender, he might be less likely to say something in front of his mother and his younger brother. For all these reasons, it was best to speak to him alone. The detectives could easily be looking at the advent of a serial killer.

Ealy had raped a woman six months earlier, would likely have murdered her if the police hadn't shown up. There was a chance now that he could go out and kill again that very evening. The detectives would have to live with that, live with the fact that they were at his home and let him go, didn't try to get him somewhere alone where they could speak to him. Even if he didn't go out and kill someone, Ealy could take the opportunity to steal the evidence hidden under his bed and drop it in a dumpster several blocks away or hide it somewhere where it could never be tied to him, or burn it and it would be gone forever. It is fine for the lawyers and judges to pass judgment on the detectives' methods, but they were the ones actually conducting the investigation. A huge responsibility was in their hands, life and death.

Every step of the detectives' investigation was run by supervisors, colleagues, and prosecutors, many with decades of experience, and none of them told the detectives to let Ealy go. I could find nothing on the record of anyone criticizing the move, anyone who raised any red flags about it. After speaking to Ealy for a while, they were called out to the hallway and another detective showed them the case report about Ealy raping the woman six months earlier. They went back in and read him his rights. Now he's a suspect. Many times, I pulled out the appeals court ruling and read it again, wholly unable to see what the judges were getting at.

Ealy would remain in the room for about eighteen hours as the detectives searched his apartment twice, gathered evidence, briefed detectives and supervisors coming on from other shifts. Much was made of the time period. The accusation was repeated over and over that investigators kept him there without bathroom breaks or food or water or sleep. But the real reason Ealy was there so long was that the detectives were painstakingly reviewing every step of their investigation, making sure everything was legitimate. That was one reason they searched Ealy's bedroom twice. The first time they took only a few items, then they returned to gather more as the evidence mounted against Ealy. If they were crooked detectives who didn't care about procedures and ethics, why were they so careful in obtaining the evidence? Ealy could have slept all he wanted in the long intervals between interviews, putting his head down on the table or crawling onto the floor. Offenders go to sleep during investigations and during processing all the time. A seventeen-year-old knowing he is about to be charged with a quadruple homicide and rape, along with a pending rape charge hanging over his head, might not have much of an appetite. Maybe his stomach was knotted up from the thought of a lifetime of prison awaiting him. Ealy couldn't know yet that his appeal would fly. That the defense would end up dropping the case. At this point, the case was solid. It was good police work, a gift-wrapped case by seasoned detectives, complete with a written confession.

The appeals court decision brought back the first memories I had on the job, when I was sent to the Far South Side of the city, Roseland and Pullman. Eager to learn the job and be proactive, I made steady arrests, most of them misdemeanor. I read statutes over and over, memorizing the elements that comprised them, then pored over arrest and case reports, singling out the ones I thought were the best. Then I imitated them in my own report writing. The artistic process went through my mind as I adopted this method of report writing: imitate, assimilate, originate. Each arrest was hours and hours of work. But no matter how well I wrote the reports, my cases were routinely rejected by the judge in this district. These were reports that were accepted in other courtrooms when I worked in other districts. No matter how I wrote them, how I covered the elements, I could not get this judge to convict on my cases. Why bother, I decided after a while, many of the veteran cops explaining that my experience was typical. The truth is that judges and appeals courts are comprised of people with their own biases and ideologies. A cop learns early on that some cases fly in front of one judge, are squashed in front of another. Police know that judgeships are like little fiefdoms, where cases can find strikingly different interpretations, one case going forward in one courtroom, the same one shot down in another. So it was in the Ealy case, the trial judge rejecting the claims that the police unlawfully arrested Ealy, the appeals court coming back and asserting they did. Would another appeals court have made a different decision?

I glance up from my ruminations, take a long look around the room, which is filled now with many injured officers. My torso twists one way, my legs another. I look around and see others in the room. I imagine the contortions of the Parker bodies strangled to death, can see the detectives wandering in, taking notes, pointing out evidence, pulling the cord embedded from the neck of Mary Ann Parker. I can see the tightening of the detectives' core muscles when Ealy's attorneys allowed Ealy to claim he was beaten into confessing. The allegations of racism simmer in the claims of the defense.

This twistedness, this is the city. Soon, I conclude, there would be a full separation into parts. A vast, undiscovered vision lingered in the city. This collection of murders in 1982 mattered because they gave form to it, and, as it took shape, everything one knew or became in the city seemed tested. This vision relied upon one's ability to recognize a crime scene and interpret it. Here the police presented the most educated mind. It wasn't simply justice that was at stake, nor ideology. It was our humanity. When Ealy was in jail awaiting trial for rape, his first crime as an adult, he came up for bond three times. The first two times, he was denied because of the brutality of the rape. But when he came up a third time, Catholic Charities bonded him out. After Ealy murdered the four Parkers, Catholic Charities continued to support him. Catholic Charities retained the same law firm for Ealy in the murder cases. One would think the charity would demure from further representation after they freed their client and he went out and killed four people. But they didn't. They continued paying for Ealy's representation and they got him free again. Why? What crazy fate always worked on freeing Ealy? What force in the city was working so hard to free him? Why not just let him stay in the county jail until his trial for the rape came up?

A noise breaks my concentration. A cop with a broken leg dropped his crutch against the wall. The waiting room is full now; some people are standing because there are no chairs. I look down the hallway and see my nurse finally coming, walking all the way up to my seat to help me stand up, looking beautiful as ever, and smiling.

8. DOWNWARD DOG

I feel trapped in the corner of the yoga class at the Evanston YMCA, far from the entrance. There is no quiet way out. I want to leave, though I'm not exactly certain why. Just opening the door will spoil the focus of the other students with the light and noise from the hall-way. The room is mostly dark and quiet save for the music and occasional direction from the instructor. There are four rows of people, mostly women, lined up in the yoga room, the instructor in front facing them. The instructor claimed she was in her fifties, but she looked more in her thirties, with perfect posture and elegant curves. Each student has her own mat, towels, and water bottles next to her. The lights are off and the instructor has put on a tape of soothing New Age music, as if it came from somewhere deep in the ocean and many creatures, like dolphins and whales, moved in harmony with it. Leaving the room will require walking around and over people in their various positions, my voice repeating "excuse me." I'm afraid I will trip over someone in the darkness as they get up from downward dog, or will step on their hand. What if I accidentally kick their water bottle, the liquid spraying people and the bottle hitting someone in pose? What if I step on some-one's iPod?

"Jesus Christ, what are you doing?" one of the meditating students might lash out.

Just the movement of me standing up and gathering my iPod, shoes, and socks off the windowsill next to me will be a distraction. Even so, I cannot remain. I cannot abide by the ritual of it, the easy embrace of prayer and the presumptions of spirituality that attend the class. When everyone put their hands together and said "Namaste" at the beginning, my heart started racing. Rather than relax, I became anxious. I wanted out. I did a few halfhearted downward dogs, but gave up before cobra, sitting against the wall in the dark room, the teacher steeling me with an icy stare.

Evanston is the first suburb north of Chicago along Lake Michigan. I live just south of its border and travel to the YMCA here because the one near me in the city is not safe. The YMCA in my neighborhood has gang-bangers hanging out, particularly in the basketball courts. If any of them recognized me, I'm sure they would have broken into my locker, spied my car and slashed its tires. Evanston's YMCA is more affluent than the neighborhood one. It is filled with professionals and professors at Northwestern University, which sits on the lake. The downtown is crowded with cafés, restaurants, and bookstores. I have been coming to this Evanston Y for years. It has two pools, a sauna and a steam room, two complete basketball courts with a track above. You can have as many towels as you want. There is a full-time locker room attendant, so the locker room is always clean. Even though I come there every day, I have always felt like an outsider, as if I don't belong and I can't say why exactly.

As I lean against the wall in the far corner of the room, a tingling and numbness move down my right leg. I have had two surgeries now. My spinal disks are failing again, lending me into my own crookedness. One disk in particular has broken through and sticks out, pinching nerves that go down my back to my leg. The doctor showed it to me on my MRI, saying it was herniated to an above-average degree, above average to extreme, he said. It was a common ailment among police officers, a common reason for ending up on disability. The weight of the belts, sitting for long periods in cars, then jumping out into an altercation or to chase someone all lead to cracked and herniated disks that pushed on the sciatic nerve. It seemed to be getting worse. The next step is fusing the disks with metal and screws, to be artificially straightened out. I dreaded the notion, and many people had warned me against it, said I would never be the same. The surgery, they said, was irreversible.

I walk bent over much of the time, leaning on things. Getting out of a squad car means standing for a while before walking, as if my back needs to unfold from one position to another. I spent hours researching back treatments, weighing the ups and downs of fusion surgery. Friends and personal trainers had been nagging me about yoga classes for years, so I had grudgingly signed up for the class and attended a few of them, impressed with the health and straight backs of the fellow students, none of whom struggle in their movements as I do. I felt inadequate in the room, crooked in the presence of so many straight people. They all seemed so healthy, such good posture and flexibility. Why, then, could I not follow through on the classes? Why could I not mold body and spirit, chakra and other life forces into a new upright me?

I get up and walk across the room. There are nasty glances, people breaking pose to put their hand on a water bottle or iPod so I won't step on it. I don't make eye contact with the instructor. Leaving the yoga room and emerging in the large well-lit work-out area, a familiar isolation comes over me. I had really hoped yoga would work for me, that I might even embrace the group there. But clearly that isn't going to happen now.

In my research of Ealy's criminal history, I was coming to a point when Ealy was released on parole for his rape. He was sentenced to twenty-three years for the rape, but did just about ten years, which struck me as strange, because everyone, including the appeals court that struck down his conviction for the quadruple murder, admitted there was little doubt he strangled the four Parkers to death. Why didn't they keep him longer in prison? All he had to do was serve his remaining term for rape. I imagine what it was like for him the day he found out about the appeals court decision, going from guaranteed life in prison to eventual freedom. Where was he when he found out? I wonder what it was like when the news floated through the prison. It must have spread like wildfire, another convicted murderer getting out by claiming police misconduct. If Ealy could get off, anything was possible. I could see the creative juices of even the most doomed inmate flowing. They met and talked about their cases, compared notes on what arguments worked and which didn't. Torture? That worked. Unlawful arrest? That worked too. Merely by the detectives asking Ealy to come to the station, Ealy and his lawyers found grounds to get him off from a quadruple slaying.

I began thinking about Ealy being back out on the street after he was paroled for the rape. Ealy listed a North Side address at the time of his next arrest two years later in 1993. He had moved to the border of Rogers Park and Edgewater, just a few miles from where I was living, just a few miles from the border of Evanston. He was moving closer into my life. I could see it clearly in retrospect. Ealy and I had possibly passed by each other on the sidewalk or the CTA platform, perhaps even ridden in the same train together. Perhaps I sat in the seat across from him. I often rode my bike right by his address in the summer, to and from the lakefront path. Perhaps I had ridden by him more than once.

While on the North Side, something clicked. Ealy was arrested in the neighboring district for solicitation of prostitution. According to records, Ealy was fined $95 for that offense and he was on his way again, the legal system once again catastrophically failing to deal with him.

In these years, I have this image of Ealy floating through the city, scouring corners with prostitutes, eyeing the right one at the right time and place. I wonder how many times he walked the streets of the North Side, eyeing each woman who walked by him, looking into apartment buildings with poor lighting, watching woman get off buses and walk out onto the street. I wonder if he followed them on foot or in his car, looking for a woman who wasn't paying attention. I wonder, too, if he ever headed up to Evanston, lurked around downtown or near the Northwestern campus. There are so many young women there.

Two years later Ealy was back on the South Side and struck again. Two officers only a year or so out of the academy waited at a red light in a squad car on Thirty-Fifth Street. They saw a car make a turn then suddenly veer out of control and crash into a building right in front of them. As they pulled up to the vehicle, a small woman jumped out, shouting, "He got a gun. He got a gun." The officers pulled out their weapons and approached the car. James Ealy, imposing in his size and strength, emerged. Both officers, a male and female, were leery of him, anxious he would fight. They were relieved when he followed their instructions. They placed him in custody, then searched the car and found the gun. The victim, a prostitute and lifelong drug addict with a long criminal history, said Ealy had picked her up a short distance away. While they were in the car, Ealy reached over, calmly grabbed her by the neck, and told her this was the last day of her life. The woman began struggling.

How long had it been for Ealy? How long since he felt the ecstasy of strangling a woman to death? And to think he almost got four life terms and would never get to do it again. I wonder if Ealy realized in the car at the moment she began to fight back that he should have waited, wondered whether he blew it by revealing his sociopathic intentions too early. He could have played like a legitimate john (a legitimate john?) until they parked somewhere and she was trapped. But he betrayed himself. The woman reacted quickly, directly. She had probably known many men like Ealy in her day, knew what they could do. So intensely did she struggle with Ealy that, even with her small frame, she made an impression in the dashboard with her foot, a measure of her terror and willingness to fight. The two cops later noted it. Then she saw out of the corner of her eye the squad car waiting at the intersection while she struggled with Ealy, and she lunged for the steering wheel, crashing the car into the building. She survived.

The officers took Ealy to the station and began the long process of categorizing and processing his crimes. Kidnapping, unlawful restraint, unlawful use of a weapon by a felon—there were so many to consider. The officers might have had some skepticism about the case before they ran Ealy's rap sheet. The woman might have made up the story because Ealy didn't pay for sex, or she might have tried to rob him and that was how they began fighting. There were a million scenarios. But the indentation on the dashboard, Ealy's menacing presence, the woman's genuine terror at the crime scene, the gun, and now the rap sheet showing the quadruple murders and the previous rapes. Was there any doubt? Ealy's rap sheet gave them pause. There wasn't enough evidence to charge him with what Ealy was really doing to the woman: attempted murder.

Look what we got, the arresting officers said to other cops in the station. Then they retold the other cops the story of the accident right in front of their eyes.

The cops eventually made their call to the state's attorney's office. I could find no record of the conversation, but I have experienced enough of these calls to imagine how weak the case was against Ealy. The victim and sole complaining witness was a whore and drug addict with a long criminal history. The crime took place in the context of a prostitute and her john. There was a good chance the woman would fade away and never show up for court. What began then was the negotiating that initiates almost every felony case. Charges are either approved or disproved by the state's attorney, the prosecutors often dismissing charges based upon the quality of witnesses and the likelihood of winning the case. Then afterward, the attorneys on both sides wheel and deal like merchants in a marketplace, murders becoming manslaughters; armed robberies, thefts; aggravated batteries, simple batteries. Charges almost always go down, not up. They eventually settled on unlawful restraint and unlawful use of a weapon. That was it. Ealy was sent to prison for another ten years but served less than four, another attempted murder whittled down to—to what, a weapons charge and felony restraint?

Then Ealy was out again, his résumé now four murders, two attempted murders, and two rapes. That is, the ones that were known.

As I think about Ealy being loose again on the street after this assault on the prostitute, I acknowledge there was still a long way to go on his rap sheet, more of his crimes I have to investigate. Why, I wonder, am I so obsessed with his criminal career? Why am I carrying around transcripts of his case everywhere, digging every day for more information? Why does his case pull me to so many others, like Andrew Wilson's? The answer is becoming clearer. The Ealy murders give form to my own doubt, a doubt that is unbearably dark and isolating. This is one reason I had to leave the yoga class, why I naturally gravitate to the solitude of the work-out room. It isn't just that the Ealy case is connected in compelling details to so many other murders, in the timing of his murders, the brutality of his crimes, and the strategies of his liberation. It is that the themes and circumstances of the Ealy case, taken together, reject much of the orthodoxy surrounding the police and crime in the city, surrounding the claims on exactly what makes the city so crooked. This orthodoxy has become known as the wrongful conviction movement. At the same time as Ealy's criminal life took shape, so did this movement. Ealy's murders and the first claims that many police were racist thugs and torturers started in 1982, the same year I came to the city. It felt as if I were moving toward Ealy's crimes all my years in the city. His brutal crimes and his recurring liberation from them remained in relative obscurity, the notion that his murders and rapes revealed more perfectly than any others a city conspiring with its sociopaths in some magical way largely ignored. But this is what I saw. This is the fantastical city I perceive. My own evolution in the city, therefore, placed me on a path wholly contrary to my own times, made me a heretic. That's why Ealy's narrative calls out to me, why it guides me. It is the reason I found myself attending the Burge trial after reading the Ealy murder transcripts. It is the reason I dug into the Wilson murders and into Edgar Hope's murders. I do not see any of these men as victims of anything significant at all. Instead, I see these killers as paradigms of the city's crooked power, men transformed from what they truly were into something else completely. This is the crookedness. They are heroes only of the city's corruption, icons of its most insane violence and brutality. I know now at the Y that I will continue to dig into these murders and others until I can articulate clearly where I stand with them. I let the Ealy murders take me wherever I need to go. I know in doing so the loneliness would increase, as would the anger. But I feel there is little choice now. I smile. So be it.

A few days earlier I was in a spinning class. There were about twelve people, all pouring sweat, right after one of those long intervals at maximum tension on the bike when the instructor has to yell at you to keep going. The instructor turned down the music to engage everyone in conversation, the only instructor who did this. I hated it, wanted in no way to reveal myself in any way, so I let other people chatter away. I had this feeling that it was dangerous for anyone to truly know me at this Y. Somehow the subject of the police came up and the other spinners jumped on it. A few members began talking about racial profiling, how endemic it was, how terrible. I guess they assumed no police officers were in the class or that it didn't matter. I let it go for a while, but the woman next to me wouldn't let up. She was raising her voice, talking about how we just go after people because of their race, the vision of cops as marauding racists clearly part of her worldview. Many of the other attendees, male and female, leaned forward on their bikes nodding their heads in agreement. I looked over at the woman when she momentarily paused in her diatribe.

"Lady, with all due respect, you don't know what the hell you are talking about," I said, and everyone stared at me.

This greatest burden of this doubt is that it forced me to confront my own humanity, to try and understand what I have become in the crooked city. Inevitably, it led me back to the Andrew Wilson case, the one with the greatest evidence against the police department, particularly Burge and his men. More than any other, this case gave shape to the wrongful conviction movement, a movement in which inmates, like Ealy, claimed torture, police misconduct, and cruelty. They claimed police racism. Some, like Ealy, got out. Others, like Andrew Wilson, went from death row to life in prison. They became heroes in the prisons, godfathers. Several days after Andrew and Jackie Wilson murdered Officers Fahey and O'Brien, Burge and his men captured Andrew Wilson in a basement apartment and brought him back to the district. He spent most of the day there, save for one trip to another building where he was identified in a lineup. Later that night, two wagon men brought Andrew Wilson to central detention, where the lockup keeper refused to accept him because Wilson had so many bruises on him. The next day, when he arrived at the county jail, the doctor listed his bruises and wrote a letter to the superintendent of police about them. This was the origin of torture claims against Burge. The former commander and his men were twice sued over Wilson's injuries in civil court, both times the juries unwilling to convict Burge and his men. Nevertheless, a flood of similar allegations poured out of the prison system. In my mind, Ealy's claims were part of that flood. Based on these sorts of allegations, many inmates gained their release. The complaints alleged that not only did Burge and his men torture suspects, but they often got the wrong guy and knowingly conspired to convict him. The complaints alleged these actions by Burge and his men were racially motivated.

There was in my doubt an essential, horrifying moral consequence, one that haunted me from the first few moments I read about the Ealy case. What if one had city murders wrong? If you sided with the appeals court in the Ealy case, you would let out a murderer. He could murder again. Already Ealy had tried to kill a prostitute. If you sided with the accused cops in some of the Burge cases, it could turn out they were torturing inmates. In either scenario, if you were wrong, then you were an agent of the corruption, a part of the evil in the most corrupt city. Nevertheless, at some point I knew I would have to make some pivotal choice concerning these murders, act upon my sense that Ealy was riding a wave of false claims about police misconduct, my sense that Burge and his men didn't torture confessions from suspects, and my strong conviction that they were not racists. But once again, what if I was wrong? What did that mean I had become? Inmates and their lawyers claimed the suspects were strapped across radiators and burned by Burge and his men until they confessed, wires connected to their genitals and currents zapped into them. Some of them were not even guilty, they said.

My back hurts. I sit down in a chair next to the blood pressure machine at the Y. I eye it. Better not, I think, and let my mind range freely from the Ealy murder to Andrew Wilson's, the image, for example, of Wilson's smiling, ecstatic face in his flight from the scene where he shot Fahey and O'Brien and stole their guns. The doubt takes life again, paralyzes me. Then there was the image of Wilson's tears in court as he repeated his claims of being tortured by Burge and his men. Which one? Which one, Goddamnit?

I walk into the gymnasium and begin shooting at a corner basket, gingerly at first, seeing if my back can endure the movements. Okay, no problem. Sometimes the rhythm of my shot finds a balance with the music on my iPod. Sometimes the ball falls far away and I am forced to walk after it. I can no longer run. I am all alone in the gym. There isn't even anyone on the track above me. I have this image that everyone in the building has left. They somehow knew my doubts about these murders, about the wrongful conviction movement, and they couldn't stand it, so they went home. I have this feeling they all hoped I won't return to Evanston, that I will stay in the city, a ranting, raving lunatic Chicago cop. With this image in mind, I want to make as many shots as possible, to demonstrate that, for all my crookedness, all my corruption, I am capable of something straight and elegant, like hitting several shots from eighteen feet out. I wonder if James Ealy felt a parallel sociopathic grace in his years at the Rockwell Gardens Housing Project, particularly in the brief time between the murders of the Parkers and his apprehension by the police. Perhaps he played some of the best basketball of his life then, played with an intensity and focus that caught the attention of the gang-bangers and everyone watching. I have this image of him dominating the entire afternoon, no one coming close to guarding him, Ealy stalking the court like a hawk, leaping up and grabbing a rebound before anyone else. His game would be that of a man who had found himself, who knew at seventeen clearly what he was. I am forty-five, crooked, not even able to run after an errant shot. I am a man who can't understand the world, can't figure it out, who is paralyzed by doubt, who cannot even endure a yoga class that very well might help me. Not only do I lack any faith, I lack the clarity of mind to discern it.

I stand on the free-throw line, trying to make five in a row. I do so not simply trying to make the shot, but doing it so perfectly that the ball actually swishes as it goes through the net, never touching the rim, with just enough backspin so that the ball comes back toward me after it bounces. In this fashion, I have to take only one step forward to retrieve it, then reassume my former position for another shot. It means nothing if the shot just goes in. It has to come back to me, full circle. In my life I have actually gotten to the point where I can make a couple dozen of these in row, but I am out of practice, hoping for just one or two today.

After Andrew Wilson arrived at the county jail bruised and beaten, lawyers began their thirty-year crusade against Burge, claiming that Burge and his men routinely used torture devices on prisoners. A line of battle was drawn over the Wilson accusations. Many cops, including the police union, backed Burge, saying there was no torture, that the abuse against Wilson was from a few cops overwrought in frustration and anger at five police officers gunned down in a month, four fatally. More and more my mind moves in this direction. It seems impossible to me that no one turned Burge and his men in if they were torturing Wilson or other suspects, no cop, no state's attorney handling his cases. None of the supervisors demoted him or transferred him or initiated an investigation on their own. And this went on for years? What a bunch of sick sons of bitches we all are. I shake my head. Burge was held in the highest esteem by working cops, considered one of the best cops in the department. Every aspiring cop considered it a badge of honor to be on his team, and he was nothing but a racist torturer? One fact arises in my mind: James Ealy, Andrew Wilson, Jackie Wilson, and Edgar Hope were all in the county jail at the same time. They were all conspiring.

Alone in the gym, I recall what the detectives, none of whom worked with Burge or in Area 2, went through in the Ealy case, accused of allowing torture, of beating a confession out of Ealy, willfully depriving him of food, not letting him use the bathroom. I don't believe a word of it. Yet isn't what they were really trying to do was stop a mass murderer in the black community? Who else was pursuing justice for the Parkers? Who combed through the crime scene, amidst the roaches and rats? Who brought the Parker bodies to the morgue?

The lawyers?

Burge was tried twice in civil court by Andrew Wilson's attorneys. Both times they failed to convict him. The activists went to Vietnam. They claimed Burge learned how to use electrocution devices for torture when Burge was a soldier there. (A strange commentary on the armed forces, particularly a highly decorated soldier like Burge. Deep down, were American soldiers also sadistic, racist criminals in the minds of these activists?) One of the activists had a replica of the electrocution device constructed by the maintenance man at his office building. His supporters took the replica into court and tried to introduce it as evidence, arguing that this was what the electrocution device would look like. The judge, furious at such high jinks, threw it out. Even after allegations of torture arose against Burge, the lawyers argued in the media that Burge used this device. Where, I wonder. It's hard to imagine that a cop would keep such a device handy even after allegations arose that he was using it, a charge that, if proven, could get him decades in prison. Where would Burge keep it? In his locker, car, or apartment, where any prosecutor with a warrant would find it? In his office? In what manner would he carry it into the interview rooms?

"There goes Commander Burge into the interview room with his bowling bag," one cop working the desk would say. "It's the damnedest thing. Every time he talks to a suspect about bowling, the suspect confesses. Burge is just amazing. He gets them so worked up about bowling, they're just screaming about it."

In my doubt, I often come back to the night when Andrew Wilson arrived downtown after he was interrogated and confessed, the lockup keeper refusing to accept him because of his wounds. The wagon men took him to the hospital, where their rage against Wilson was witnessed by several staff members. I worked the wagon for years. I wonder if after it was all said and done, if after Wilson confessed and the case was completed and I was called to transport him, and on the way out of the station toward the wagon Wilson walked that familiar sociopathic shuffle that betrays not only no regret for the murders, but a deep and fulfilling joy in them. I wonder if at that point, as many cops told me, Wilson looked up at the wagon cops and said, "I should have killed more of you fucking pigs," I wonder, in the solitude of the gym, if I would have whaled on his ass, too.

9. STRAIGHT MAN

This lunch in the diner is starting to look like a big mistake. The periods of silence are growing longer and longer. There was a long conversation on the best manicotti in the city, then the best steakhouses, but soon that train of thought fizzled out too. Now there is complete silence. Some guys are checking their cell phones, looking for an excuse to leave, I figure. I am probably the most anxious because I set up this meeting, trying for months to get everyone together for the first time. Our condition seems palpable. The waitress is annoyed we haven't ordered yet. The busboy left a water pitcher at the table and doesn't come back, even though it is empty. The menus are still stacked in the center of the table. My eyes look around the table, at the seven of us: a couple of retired detectives, lawyers, a private investigator, a journalist, and me.

This meeting has come together after months of talking on the phone and meeting individually with each person about various wrongful conviction cases, including the Wilson murders. I told people what I was doing with the Ealy case, and they told me about other murders from 1982. We identified common themes among these cases: claims of police torture without physical evidence, allegations of other misconduct, killers freed, the careers of good detectives ruined. We all expressed our grave misgivings about the liberation of these offenders. We discovered that there were many people in the city who shared our suspicions— lawyers, a few journalists, private investigators, and just interested citizens—but they were cut off from one another. The year 1982 had great significance for us. Many people, particularly detectives throughout the city, were reluctant to meet. They had been burned badly in their careers. Now the silence at this table gives me doubts. Maybe I rushed things. Maybe I had not planned things well enough. Maybe this whole thing was just doomed from the outset.

A few hours earlier I had gathered up my computer bag and walked to the street parking outside my condo building. There stood my scooter next to my car, a difficult choice. On the one hand it was a beautiful summer day and the notion of riding down Lake Shore Drive on my new scooter was hard to resist. It was also much easier to get on and off a scooter with a bad back than it was to climb in and out of a car. On the other hand, I felt self-conscious pulling up to the diner on a scooter. Scooters and cops just didn't go together. A few years earlier I was working patrol when I saw someone get on a scooter parked tightly between two cars and ride down the street. That was the first time I thought about getting one myself, the idea of no longer searching for parking spots for twenty minutes, of riding along the lake on a summer day, excited me. The next day I went and bought one, the smallest model. When I pulled into my district parking lot the first time on this scooter, everyone standing outside stopped talking and stared at me. I took a lot of ribbing. But eventually, many cops asked me about buying one. Now standing outside my condo, staring at my new, larger scooter and my car, I thought about driving around looking for a parking spot. No way, I thought. I put my bag in the rear storage compartment, strapped on my helmet, and started the scooter up. But even as I did so, I worried it was a bad move. This meeting was tense enough. I should look as regular an off-duty cop as I could. Looking like some bohemian, some urban artsy type, I was not likely to win the trust of anyone so easily.

Lake Shore Drive was wide open, the pavement recently resurfaced, black and smooth. I pulled onto it from the Bryn Mawr ramp. The scooter was 500 cc's, the same as many motorcycles. I opened up the throttle a little and pulled into a left lane, closest to the lake. It was so peaceful and beautiful, the blue of the lake and all the people strolling along or riding bikes. I got off at Randolph to go across the river into the Near West Side. I was hoping to park away from the diner, so no one would see me on the scooter. But I took a wrong turn and pulled right in front, stuck at a red light. I stole a glance at the restaurant, and there was Jim on the other side of the large window, sitting at a big table with everyone there, waving at me and pointing me out. Busted. I parked right there and walked in, carrying my helmet and bag, which I got out of the rear storage compartment. I felt all eyes on me. Some of the guys I knew, like Jim and Bill, but others I had never met in person. I looked at their expressions. *Who the fuck is this guy*, they said. Perhaps I should have driven the car, I thought, first impressions and all.

In the strained silence at the table, I can sense that each person is wondering whether they should have come. So am I. I scan the table, two four-top tables pushed together in the rear of the diner. In one corner are two retired detectives, Pete and Bob, who had worked with Jon Burge. They have no connection to the Ealy case. It was the biggest gamble for them to come. They had gotten wind of a new round of federal indictments against more Chicago detectives, even those who had only worked with Burge on a few cases or for a few months. The rumor was that the new federal indictment would be a conspiracy case. The Feds would claim that the abuse and torture of suspects was widespread and the detectives had worked together to cover it up, making it then an ongoing conspiracy. Like a RICO charge, this meant that there was no statute of limitations. The detectives could get charged for cases more than twenty years old. A legal theory once designed for the Mob was now being employed against Chicago cops. The lawyers for the accused cops warned their clients not to talk to anyone, including the media and, incredibly, fellow cops, as this could be construed as part of the conspiracy. The cops heeded their attorneys, another benefit for those claiming abuse against the police, for now the cops were effectively silenced and could not point out the lies in these accusations. I knew that dozens of other cops were in touch with the two at this meeting, wondering if what was happening here could help them.

The two lawyers, both of whom have worked many wrongful conviction cases, remain quiet, only listening. These guys know me the least. It is unusual for them to come to the city on a weekend morning unless they are working on a big case. Jim Delorto and Bill Crawford are on the other side of the table. Jim is a retired federal supervising agent who had broken some of the biggest cases of his era. He had been an old-school cop, Italian from the neighborhood. He drives an older Lincoln Town Car, dresses impeccably, and gets right to the point, the way a good investigator always does. He knows the cases better than anyone, as he had investigated many of them. He commands the attention and respect of everyone at the table. Now he is a private investigator, getting many of his cases from cities whose cops have been accused of wrongdoing. Bill Crawford is a retired Pulitzer Prize–winning *Chicago Tribune* reporter.

Investigating the Ealy case had led me to him. He is a tireless investigator. I realize that I should have sat next to Jim and Bill at the other end
of the table. I feel all alone on my side of the table, out in some foreign
place. I barely know these detectives. Why should they talk to me? I am
only a patrolman.

What was it that brought us together? I knew, but I couldn't say. It
would be too strange to speak out loud. But the truth is that we were
seven men in search of a metaphor. Life without one had become
unbearable, untenable, and dire. There was no control over our lives, let
alone our imaginations. The Ealy case, the Wilson murders, they held a
mystery, a doubt, but nothing that could rise to the level of a metaphor
that we needed. The appeals court ruled that the detectives acted unlawfully when they asked Ealy to come to the station, so they tossed his conviction. Andrew Wilson showed up at central detention with bruises all
over his body. These cases, particularly the Wilson case, had been
deemed examples of police misconduct, corruption, or abuse. So be it.
There was nothing that could be done to undo these claims. Whatever I,
or anyone in law enforcement, wanted to say about them came off only
as pissed-off cops who wouldn't let the issue go. What we wanted was
something that could be used to paint our own vision, much as many of
the activists had painted visions of the city from the Wilson case, then
other cases. We needed a case that revealed itself in public records,
through trial transcripts, witness statements, and good, solid police
work. We needed it backed up by jury verdicts and expert opinion. We
needed one that proved itself through common sense. If there was any
veracity to my doubts about the Wilson and Ealy cases, then surely such
a case must exist. Surely there would be others. But we were looking for
a specific kind of metaphor, and I couldn't remember the word for it. It
was a long metaphor, one that had a narrative to it. Then it came to me:
allegory.

Several months earlier, Bill showed me the Anthony Porter case, a man
convicted of killing a couple in a park in 1982, the night before Ealy
killed the four Parkers. Porter was a gangbanger with a violent history.
He was tried and convicted. No less than six witnesses either put him at
the scene of the murders or actually saw him fire the gun. His lengthy rap
sheet compelled a judge to give Porter the death penalty, and he came
within fifty hours of being lethally injected. That's when some wrongful

conviction advocates at Northwestern University became involved, headed by a professor named David Protess, who ran the Innocence Project. At first, Protess and his students worked to get a stay of execution for Porter, based on the contention that Porter's IQ was too low for him to be executed. But after they conducted an investigation, they announced that Porter was innocent. They also argued that another man, Alstory Simon, was guilty of the murders. They had obtained a bizarre confession from Simon sixteen years after the murders. The Anthony Porter case was one of the biggest in the state's history—a man just fifty hours from being executed exonerated by then-Governor George Ryan. So powerful was the case that it compelled former Governor Ryan to place a moratorium on the death penalty.

The Porter case held so many of the same themes as the Ealy case: the year 1982, a predator freed from prison based on claims of police misconduct, accusations of police torture without any physical evidence or supporting witnesses. Bill and Jim explained this case to me over the course of several months, and Bill had written a lengthy account of it in an article. There was also the strange role of the journalists, who seemed, as they did in the Ealy case, too willing to buy the claims of police misconduct and abuse. The Porter case was more fantastic than Ealy's or the Wilsons'. Ealy had gotten out on an appeals decision, but Porter had come within two days of being executed and eventually got a pardon from the governor.

But after I met Bill and Jim and they showed me the Porter case, the familiar doubt set in. What did I really know about either one of them? What did I really know about the Porter case? How could I be certain they weren't kooks and they weren't setting me up? The only choice was to return to the crime scene itself, so I called Bill one day and asked if he had ever been able to contact the detectives who worked the Porter case. He told me no. That was a start. I got the names of the detectives from the case reports, then called the police pension board, telling the lady who I was and that I was working on an old case. Would she be willing to look up the detectives' names and tell me if they were still receiving pension checks? Yes, they were, she said after a putting me on hold for a while. Would she be willing to call one of them and give them my phone number? Yes, she would. A little while later my phone rang, and I was talking to the lead detective on the case, Charles Salvatore. I asked him about the Porter case, and he flew off the handle.

"That Porter was guilty. He killed that couple in the park. There is no doubt he killed them. It's right there in the investigation," Salvatore said.

Over the next few months, the detective eventually broke the case down step by step, and everything he stated matched exactly what Jim and Bill had told me. I knew then they were on to something, that their arguments had merit. This case, then, would be our allegory. With it, we might have some sway over the imaginative life of the city. We might create a vision in stark contrast to the one that had set so many killers free, like Ealy. There were still many questions. What form would it take? How would we sell it? How would we get people to listen to us? But the mere fact that we were getting together and talking was reassuring, was hopeful.

"Well," I say, as we sit at the table, breaking the silence, "maybe we should all describe how it was that we got involved in these cases." Then I recount how the Ealy case had called out to me, led me to the Wilson murders of Fahey and O'Brien. Bringing up the Wilson murders gets the detectives going, for they had been working at the time and remember the case well. The detectives then ask me about the Ealy case, and I go over it step by step. As we talk, the tension at the table subsides. Names are dropped, dates clarified. People pick up the menus, pass them around. The waitress approaches. I am hungry, so I order the BLT club with split pea soup. Others order. Everyone is suddenly reaching for the bread basket and butter. Soups come. The detectives recount how they had been accused of torturing suspects, the dark veil it imposed upon their lives, their ruined careers, the loss of social standing, living into retirement with the threat of a criminal case, and then prison hanging over their heads.

Bob describes his experience with a prominent reporter in the city. His sister had developed paranoid schizophrenia in her early adult years and had difficulty processing reality. It was, the detective say, evident to anyone who spoke to her even briefly. It was a tragic fate for her that left the whole family devastated. The sister had watched news stories connecting Bob to Jon Burge. Somehow this reporter got ahold of the sister, and the sister told her that Burge used to visit their home. She told the reporter that Burge and her brother Bob boasted how they tortured confessions out of suspects in one of these visits. But these claims were manifestations of her delusional state. Burge, Bob says, had never set foot in his house, didn't even know where Bob lived. The detective and Burge did not have a friendship outside of the job. Bob talks about seeing his mentally ill sister broadcast on the news, her delusional rants accepted as legitimate statements, the anger and sorrow that welled up in the family, how badly they want revenge against the reporter. As he speaks his face turns red, the rage brimming up. Afterward we are silent, shaking our heads in disgust.

The lawyers talk about finding inmates in the prison system who would testify that they had conspired with other inmates to make false accusations against Burge and his men. They could not get these men admitted as witnesses in cases, and they could not get any coverage from the media. These were inmates with direct testimony on crucial cases. These witnesses had names, dates, and times.

I relax a bit as conversation heats up, but I look around the table one more time. It is a Hamlet world we live in, one that begs contemplation or action, on the one hand, to play out endlessly in our minds the absurdities and injustices we perceive in the murder cases from 1982 and, on the other, to take some action against them. So many bars I had sat in meeting detectives for the first time, who told me the story of their cases. This meeting is, I hope, an initial step further, however wavering, however ridiculous. I can't be sure of the outcome. Who will listen to us about the Porter case? How will we frame the story in such a way to make it believable? No one knows yet, but it is reassuring to settle on the Porter case, to have this allegory.

"What I think we need to do now is set out the case Bill and Jim have been talking about the last few months, the double homicide in Washington Park in August 1982. You've all read about it. Bill and Jim know it better than anyone. Unless there are any objections, I think we should all get on the same page with this case and go from there. So, Jim, why don't you take it from here," I say.

Jim looks at me.

"I will, Marty, but before we get going, I just want to tell you how adorable you looked riding in on that scooter," he says.

Everyone at the table bursts out laughing.

10. ANXIETY

My partner and I approach Thirty-First Street in our unmarked car, Lake Michigan to our left. When I don't pull into the exit lane to head back to headquarters where we work, he makes an anxious gesture. We have no business heading south of Thirty-First Street. Some cars have tracking devices in them now, so anyone might see we are traveling somewhere we shouldn't be.

"We'll just say that we missed the ramp and had to go a little farther south," I say.

He nods, relaxing at a solid alibi, but he's nervous. He flicks a cigarette ash out the window, still smoking two or three times a day. My partner is a far better cop than I will ever be. He worked the West Side for more than a decade, including the area where James Ealy lived. He led the city in recovered guns, has been shot at five times. He can look at maps and name which gangs own which corners, name the leaders of that gang, and describe various arrests he's made there. But for all his hard work, for all the predators he's put in prison, he has little to show for it. He has never been promoted. He went through a nightmarish fraudulent lawsuit where his home and his livelihood were on the table. Some gangbangers claimed a civil rights violation, saying that they were arrested for no reason. They got an attorney and took it all the way to trial. He won the lawsuit, didn't have to cough up any money. Only his reputation was besmirched by the attorneys representing the defendants. Afterward, he was worn out and fed up. He had enough and wasn't going through it again. There are a lot of cops like him. It had gotten so bad at depositions with wrongful conviction lawyers that the first questions they would ask were about the officer's house, how much it was worth. This was their way of scaring the officer into settling the case, making the officer afraid they would lose everything they had. To a cop who was married with children, it was often an effective strategy. My partner had enough. He became a gang analyst at headquarters. No more arrests, no more street stops. He brought me down a few years later, when chronic back pain became too much for me to ride around in squad cars.

I glance over at him. In the years since I returned to the city, a great anxiety has unfolded. It had always lingered on the periphery, occasionally entering the lives of its residents, including the cops. It arose partly from the crime scenes themselves—like the apartment with the four Parker family members strangled to death—partly from the marriage between the criminal and the legitimate in the city. But most of all, this anxiety flourished from an unbridled creative freedom, one that gave free rein to interpret city crime. Such imaginative indulgences were almost inevitable, because people could, in this freedom, re-create the city and themselves in the most fantastic manner. Look at how Burge and his detectives went from being the best cops in the city to little more than the worst form of criminals, the transformation of Andrew Wilson and James Ealy from cold-blooded murderers to victims, once-obscure professors and their suburban students into heroic investigators.

The problem was that this creative license left the city undescribed, perversely so. The fantastic knew no bounds, no rules. Only the anxiety remained to illuminate, to unify. It was compelling merely in the manner it held the city's inhabitants. My attraction to it was, in its essence, neither moral nor legal—it was imaginative, for it offered the sole possibility of finding the authentic in the sociopathic city. But now it forced decisions on me. I was coming to believe many of the wrongful conviction cases were fraudulent. I thought the city may have let loose bona fide killers. I was talking to retired cops, attorneys, private investigators who shared my convictions. Once we had settled on one case in particular—the Anthony Porter case, where we had gathered compelling evidence that a true killer had been set free—we spoke daily on the phone and met regularly at West Side diners. We talked about media connections, making a movie, a documentary. Suspecting that Porter was guilty made his case technically an unsolved murder, and I was a cop. I had to do something about it.

Didn't I?

My partner shifts in his seat. He doesn't like this entire foray into the South Side. I can't blame him. Anything we were doing could be made into something that would destroy us. This creative license could easily turn on us. My partner was a great cop once. I wonder how many lives he had saved with all those recovered guns, how many homicides had been prevented. I think about what a bitch it must have been to go through the lawsuit and the trial, to wonder how things would turn out. This anxiety had been imposed upon the police for a long time. Now I was following it into uncharted territory, into the foreboding I perceived haunting many wrongful conviction cases. This was why we were cruising down Forty-Seventh Street, looking for a woman, a reported prostitute and drug addict, who was once the girlfriend of Anthony Porter, a man who had gotten away with a double homicide, much the same way James Ealy had gotten away with the Parker murders. Once again, these murders were in 1982. In fact, these murders took place the night before Ealy killed the Parkers.

"Why don't you turn that fucking radio down?" I say to my partner as we pull up to a red light. He turns up the volume with each new song, then plays drums on the dashboard or air guitar along with it, annoying the shit out of me.

"Why don't you blow me?" he says.

"Because I choke on small bones," I say.

"But you don't choke on big ones, do you?" he says, laughing.

I smile and drive silently. He got me.

A murderous abandon was the initial and oftentimes most intense anxiety that haunted the crime scenes of 1982. Anthony Porter's crime scene was no different. Porter, a gang enforcer and a notorious stick-up man on the South Side, was already facing a long jail sentence for another crime when he entered Washington Park on August 15, 1982. This was likely the reason for his abandon: he knew he was going back to prison. Two weeks before Porter entered the park, he had gotten in an altercation with a man over a barking dog. On August 1, Earl Lewis, thirty-two, was waiting outside a building with his sister and his dog near Fifty-Sixth and Michigan. Lewis, his boyfriend, his sister, and Lewis's dog had just emerged from Washington Park. Lewis's boyfriend had gone into the building. Porter walked down the street toward them and suddenly kicked Lewis's dog. Porter then walked into a nearby building. A few minutes later, Porter came out of the building. Lewis confronted Porter about kicking his dog. Porter told Lewis he would kick Lewis's ass. Lewis walked up to Porter, challenging him. Porter glared back and walked away. A few minutes later, Lewis was talking to his sister, who suddenly shouted out that Porter had a pistol. Lewis spun around. Porter put the pistol right to his head. The fact that Porter put the pistol right up to Lewis's head is an important detail. It was a revolver. Lewis turned his head, then heard the gunshot. Lewis was grazed across his forehead, but he didn't know that. He thought he had been shot in the head.

"The first thing I did, I held my ears, grabbed my ears and went over to a car and leaned on it thinking I was dead," Lewis testified.

Lewis remained on the car, slowing realizing he was alive. He looked up and saw a woman standing in the doorway of a building. He told her he was shot and asked her to call the police. The woman responded that there wasn't anything wrong with Lewis. The woman, Lewis said, turned out to be Porter's mother.

A warrant was put out for Porter's arrest. But that wasn't the only reason cops were looking for him. A team of officers assigned to investigate robberies in the district had also fingered Porter for nine separate armed robberies. They were looking for him so they could put him in a lineup and ask victims to identify him. Another reason police were looking for Porter was that two cops had spotted Porter in the neighborhood after the warrant was issued for his shooting of Earl Lewis. When these cops approached Porter, Porter raised a pistol and fired at them. They gave pursuit, but Porter got away. Porter was known among the police in that district also as a gang enforcer for the Black Gangster Disciples, one of the most violent gangs in the city. Cops tend to know who the gang enforcers are, not only for their own safety but because they are the first people the cops look at in gang shootings.

Porter grew up in the area of Washington Park. The park was within blocks of the projects along State Street, the worst of which was the Robert Taylor Homes. Some would argue these projects were as bad, or worse, than the Rockwell Gardens where Ealy grew up, but these projects on State Street were larger. They stretched out for miles, the "largest continuous stretch of public housing in the nation," according to the *Chicago Tribune*. Being right off the expressway and next to the CTA trains, they were ideal for drug dealing and notorious for the vast profits they made for gangs. These drug sales were one reason for the intense level of violence, as the various gangs constantly fought over access to dope markets. According to the same *Tribune* article, "95.5 per-cent of the Robert Taylor households were headed by women. Forty-one percent of adult residents had incomes of less than $5,000 a year; 84 per-cent had incomes of less than $10,000. Only 4 percent were employed." This is exactly the kind of world where Porter grew up. He only had a mother, who lived on welfare. He had eight brothers and one sister. Most of the brothers had long criminal records. One brother, Larry, had been shot and killed by the police.

Porter's strength as a gang member was violence, so much so that even the worst gangbangers were leery of him. Several residents in the projects told me that when Porter came around, he was almost certainly armed or had a gun stashed nearby. On August 15, 1982, when he entered Washington Park, Porter certainly knew there was a warrant out for him for the shooting of Earl Lewis. In fact, that day Porter's photo and physical description were on the daily police bulletin, meaning that of all the thugs and gang members in the city, Porter was at the top of the list.

This state of mind Porter was in, this criminal abandon, had grown familiar to me. I recognized it from the Ealy case, the night he strangled the Parkers. It was the same as when Andrew Wilson gunned down offi-cers Fahey and O'Brien at Eighty-First and Morgan, no different when Edgar Hope shot the rookie officer on a bus. Porter moved deeper into this abandon that night he entered the park, carrying his pistol, proba-bly the same pistol he used to shoot Earl Lewis and to shoot at two cops. In the park, Porter walked up to a twenty-nine-year-old man named Henry Williams standing next to a pool. Williams had entered the pool about an hour earlier with his friend William Taylor, age forty, to cool off on a hot August night. Both men hopped the fence to get in. They had also been drinking that day, buying several beers and a bottle of vodka. There was reason to celebrate. Earlier in the day was the Bud Billiken Parade, a celebration in the black community signifying the end of sum-mer and the beginning of the new school year. The parade ended in Washington Park. A section of the park was a large pool complex, com-prised of three different pools, with changing rooms and a set of bleach-ers next to it. The pools were enclosed by a fence that was easy to climb for neighborhood people seeking a late-night swim.

Porter walked up to Williams as Williams was putting his pants back on next to the pool, placed his pistol against Williams's head, and asked Williams if he had any money. At first Williams said he didn't, but

Porter asked him again and Williams admitted he did. Porter reached into his pocket, took two dollars, then told Williams it was his lucky day, and it was. Porter let him live. Porter pulled his gun back and headed up into the bleachers.

William's friend Taylor got out of the pool after Williams was robbed. Taylor did not know that Williams had just been threatened with a gun by Porter. Taylor began to dry himself off. As he did so, he looked into the north section of the bleachers, where he saw Anthony Porter standing over a man named Jerry Hillard. Taylor saw Porter shoot Hillard in the head. Forensic evidence would later show that Porter shot Hillard from a distance of only a few inches, meaning Porter held the gun right up against Hillard's head, just as he had held the gun right against Williams's head a few minutes before and just as he had when he shot Earl Lewis two weeks earlier. Porter, still holding the gun in his hand after he shot Hillard, ran down the bleachers, right in front of Taylor. Porter ran so close to Taylor that Taylor could see Porter was holding a revolver, the same type of handgun with which he shot Lewis. Taylor did not flee the scene. He went up the bleachers toward the wounded Hillard.

Other witnesses would tell police they saw Porter also shoot the second victim, Marilyn Green. She had been standing next to Hilliard. Green and Hilliard were a couple, engaged to be married the next year. Most of the evidence indicated that Porter likely shot her first, twice in the neck and once in the hand. One of the bullets that entered her neck went downward through her lungs and other vital areas before it exited her back, causing massive bleeding. She had no chance of surviving. Her descent into unconsciousness was slower. She did not remain in the bleachers after she was shot. Instead, she got up, took a few steps, collapsed, somehow raised herself up, and walked down the bleachers.

Two officers responded to the scene. When they arrived, they ran into Marilyn Green staggering from the bleachers. As they approached her, she held one hand to her neck and pointed with her other hand to the south. The two officers saw a man fleeing in that direction. They stopped him. It was Anthony Porter. They frisked him, but, finding no weapon, they let him go.

Right around this same time, Second District Officer B. Johnson was sitting in his car on a traffic stop with his partner, Officer J. Thompson, just outside the park. While his partner was writing out a traffic citation, Johnson saw Marilyn Green staggering toward him. She was covered in blood, and he saw that she had a hole in her neck.

"I asked her what had happened, and she tried to say something to me, but I couldn't understand her," Johnson testified.

Only people who have actually been near a shooting in a public place can know the chaos that follows, how difficult it is to discern the offenders from the bystanders fleeing in terror. Add to this the fact that none of the cops knew what they were running into when they responded to the park. It could be a gang fight with numerous gangbangers armed and shooting it up. There could be a wild shootout with the police. These are among the most intense moments of being a cop. As Officers Johnson and Thompson were helping put Marilyn Green in a squad car so she could be rushed to the hospital, they got assigned on the radio the job of a man shot inside the park. They replied to the dispatcher on the radio that they were dealing with another shooting victim, a female, in the same area. All the cops knew by this radio exchange that they were dealing with a multiple shooting in a crowded park, the day of a huge festival in one of the worst, most gang-infested areas of the city. After Marilyn Green was taken away, Officers Johnson and Thompson then headed into the park. Once inside, they stopped a man fleeing the area. They questioned the man, Mark Senior, and filled out a contact card before letting him go, satisfied he wasn't an offender. Senior would later become a witness.

Henry Williams, the victim who had just been robbed by Porter, fled out of the pool area, but as he jumped the fence, he was grabbed by two detectives, Perry and Dwyer, also responding to the shooting. They placed him in custody. It wasn't in the testimony, but I suspected the detectives didn't know if Williams was an offender or not, so, to be sure, they placed him under arrest. He was running out of the pool, which was closed. They could justify the arrest with a charge of trespassing. This way, they could hold him until they figured out what role he had played. It was a smart move. Williams told them that a man was wounded at the top of the bleachers. The three of them, two detectives and Williams, went up to the bleachers where Jerry Hillard was lying, still alive. When they arrived there, William Taylor, the friend who had come to the park with Williams, was also there. Detective Dwyer stated that Hillard was gurgling.

"When I got to Jerry Hillard, Taylor approached and he was telling Jerry Hillard not to go to sleep, otherwise he'd die," Detective Dwyer testified.

Dwyer called for a wagon, seeing that there was no time to waste getting Hillard to the hospital, but as he called, the wagon pulled up. He and his partner, along with Taylor and Williams, picked up Hillard and carried him down the bleachers. But something crucial in the case occurred as they were carrying Hillard. Dwyer heard Taylor and Williams whisper the name Porter to each other. Dwyer recognized Porter's name instantly, for Dwyer was an experienced robbery detective and every robbery detective was familiar with the name Anthony Porter. The fact that Taylor and Williams were whispering Porter's name amongst themselves was the first sign of what an open-and-shut case it was. No one was even interviewed, not even asked a question, and witnesses were naming Porter.

Hillard was taken to the hospital, two shots to his head. He would be rushed to surgery but wouldn't make it. But while Dywer, his partner, and Taylor and Williams were still at the crime scene, Dwyer confronted the two men and asked if Porter had anything to do with it. Right away, Williams admitted he was robbed by Porter shortly before the shootings. He told Dwyer that Porter put a gun to his head and took money from him. He also said that Porter went up into the bleachers after the robbery.

Back at the Area headquarters at Fifty-First and Wentworth, Williams repeated his story about being robbed by Porter. He admitted he did not actually see Porter shoot Hillard or Green, only that after the robbery he saw Porter go into the bleachers where the shooting subsequently occurred. Taylor initially said he did not see who committed the shooting. But at headquarters, Williams told Dwyer that his friend Taylor did see Porter shoot Hillard, that Taylor was just too terrified of Porter and his gang members to admit it. The case was eventually passed on to Detectives Salvatore and Gray. They got Williams to repeat his story of being robbed. They confronted Taylor. Around this time the detectives found a daily police bulletin and saw Anthony Porter's name on it. They saw he was wanted for a shooting two weeks earlier, the one where Porter shot the man after kicking the man's dog. They also saw Porter's rap sheet: two armed robberies convictions. They got back to Taylor and tried to get him to admit he saw Porter.

Looking over the various accounts of the Porter murder scene, it's hard to see how the police could have done a better job in this chaotic, brutal crime scene. Just six months earlier, five cops had been gunned down, four of them fatally. The two officers who encountered Marilyn Green outside the park rendered her aid, got her into a car and to the hospital as fast as possible. When that was done, they didn't sit back and start writing a report. They ran into the park and found a man who would later become a witness. The two detectives who arrived on scene placed Williams in custody, a man who would become a central witness in the conviction. They secured the crime scene, encountered William Taylor, who would also become a central witness. They carried the bloodied, gurgling Hillard down from the bleachers into a wagon and got him to the hospital. They could have just stayed there and waited for an ambulance. They didn't have to carry him down the bleachers. Then they protected the crime scene. After the crime lab came, they went to the hospitals to check on the condition of the victims, and then detectives returned to scour the area again for any evidence that might have been missed. They got Taylor and Williams as key witnesses. Two other officers who responded to the scene had seen Porter running. They stopped him. In doing so they become central witnesses in the case, undermining Porter's ridiculous alibi that he wasn't even in the park that night. Taylor and Williams were taken back to the Area station, where Detectives Salvatore and Gray eventually got statements from them. By the next day, a warrant was issued for the arrest of Porter. The police responded to a vicious homicide in one of the worst areas of the city, rendered aid, protected crime scenes, gathered statements and evidence that quickly led to the offender and an arrest warrant within a day: top-flight police work from patrolmen all the way up to the detectives.

The group of officers specializing in armed robbery cases, called the robbery team, approached the state's attorney in the case, saying they had Porter as a suspect in at least nine armed robberies. When he was in custody, they wanted to call the victims in these cases and see if they could identify Porter in a lineup, but the state's attorney nixed the idea, saying they would only go with the murders. One wonders what would have happened if the state proceeded on these robberies and got even a few convictions out of them. The reason is that after Porter got out of prison, many people decried the sixteen years he had spent in prison. But if he had gotten convicted on any of these robberies, along with shooting Earl Lewis in the head, he should been in a lot longer, like, say, at least twenty more years.

Back in the car with my partner, I go over in my mind the Porter crime scene. I often think about Marilyn Green's death walk in the park that night. I couldn't help but wonder if Porter was smiling menacingly when he shot her. I could see Porter was floating in that sociopath's euphoria, like Ealy and the Wilson brothers, like Edgar Hope. All these murders were in 1982. These were all men who simply enjoyed killing. Marilyn Green already had two children; one was four months old. Certainly there were images of loved ones, seminal moments of childhood passing through her mind. I wonder how much she labored to breathe, to remain upright. I wonder if she could taste and smell the metal of the bullet and the gunpowder. Certainly she could taste her own blood. I wonder what it must have been like for her to approach the cops, trying to tell them she had been shot by Porter. She was unable to speak, so she pointed in the direction he was running. Is there anything so humiliating, so terrifying as dying by murder at the hands of a sociopath? There is no fate about such a death, just a sudden, horrifying onset of evil, coming out of nowhere. One cannot look retrospectively from the moment of the murder and see any logic that brought one there.

"This is the woman we are looking for," I say as I place the mug shot on the dashboard between my partner and me. "She was once the girlfriend of Anthony Porter."

My partner studies the image and the physical descriptions. He can memorize a face in a moment and spot it easily in a crowd. This is another of my shortcomings as a cop. I can never trace faces on photographs to people on the street. I'm relieved he's reviewing it carefully. He looks at me.

"Why would she talk to us?" my partner asks.

"It's a long story," I say.

He won't be put off.

"Yeah, so?" he asks.

"I want to know if she's still around here. I want her to tell me that Porter admitted to her that he committed the murders," I say.

"Well, why the fuck would she do that?"

"Several reasons," I say. I pause, making sure I have his attention, because I need to run all this by him. He has a good legal mind.

"Well, I'm listening," he says.

"After Porter got out, he beat the shit of her. It was the second time he went off. He beat up another woman he had a kid with, then when the kid tried to step in, Porter started stomping on her. I think the girlfriend might want to tell the truth about him because he abused her so much."

My partner's silence lets me know he thinks my theory is sound. He turns it over in his mind, then starts shaking his head.

"So what the fuck are you going to do if she says he did it?"

"I guess we'll have to write out a supplemental report," I say, knowing that putting any of this adventure in writing will freak him out. "We'll both sign it."

"Like fucking hell we will, you fruitcake. We're not even supposed to be in this neighborhood, and you want to create paper documenting it? I'm not putting my name on anything. We're not going to even fucking talk to her. We'll find out where she lives if we can, then you pursue it off duty. That's a bad fucking move," he says, cutting the air with his hand, "a bad fucking move."

I start laughing. He sees I'm kidding about writing reports.

"Take it easy. We'll just take a look around," I say.

From my top pocket I pull out a folded sheet of paper with a few possible addresses of Porter's girlfriend, as well as her car plate with the make and model. The addresses were given to me by Jim, the private investigator at our last meeting. I couldn't help but drive by the addresses after he gave them to me. I was, after all, a cop, and I was starting to see the Porter case as a still-unsolved murder. Didn't I have every right to be here?

Didn't I?

It was a relatively simple case to convict Porter of the double homicide. The witnesses came forward and pointed him out. The state had as many as six civilian witnesses, but they only called two to testify, one being Henry Williams, the man who was robbed at gunpoint shortly before Porter gunned down Marilyn Green and Jerry Hillard. They also called William Taylor, an eyewitness. The cop who stopped Porter running in the park undermined Porter's claim that Porter was somewhere else partying with a fellow gang member at the time of the homicides. Porter's alibi witnesses fell apart in cross-examination, and Porter himself never took the stand. That was a crucial fact. If Porter truly believed he was wrongly convicted, why did he never take the stand? The real issue was whether Porter would be executed. Here Porter's long and exceedingly violent criminal life was exposed, including the shooting of Earl Lewis in the head over a barking dog.

There was testimony by a robbery victim in 1979 in the hearing to determine whether Porter would be executed. This robbery, ironically, took place in the exact same area of the bleachers where Porter shot the couple. In June 1979, Porter, along with several other men, struck up a conversation with a man named Douglas McGhee, a welder enjoying his vacation from work. McGhee said he came to the bleachers to enjoy the summer weather and check out the women in bikinis in the pool. Porter and McGhee began talking about a car for sale, McGhee saying he might be interested. McGhee left the park, went home and got the eight hundred dollars, and brought it back to the bleachers. Porter sent one of his shorties to go buy some beer. When McGhee realized they had no car for sale, he got up to leave, at which time Porter kicked him in the face, damaging McGhee's eye. Porter pushed McGhee down to the ground. Everyone began jumping on him, kicking him. McGhee said Porter was "the one doing all the talking during all the instigating. He was the big mouth. He was the ringleader. He was top show of everything, anything to be said it came out of his mouth." Porter then reached into McGhee's pocket and took his eight hundred dollars, all the money McGhee had saved up for his vacation.

"I went straight on to the doctor. My eye was swollen up, whole face was swollen up. The doctor wanted to really keep me in the hospital, but I was so upset, you know, so traumatized behind losing my money I couldn't stay in the hospital, told him I will go home and let my wife take care of it," McGhee testified. After four weeks, his vision slowly returned in the damaged eye, but not fully. Porter was sentenced to three years for the robbery, served one and a half.

Porter's character and criminal history made a sufficient impression upon the judge at sentencing.

"Anthony Porter, like a perverse shark in a frenzy of robbery, destruction, and death, you took two lives without reason, remorse, or shame, only to satisfy your appetite for violence. Accordingly, I have considered all factors in aggravation and mitigation, and I herby find no mitigating factor sufficient to preclude the imposition of the death sentence."

My partner points out a woman walking onto Forty-Seventh from Martin Luther King Drive. I slow down and we eye her. She looks over at us angrily. It's not her. I see what I think is a good spot at Michigan and Forty-Seventh, pull the car over there, and place it in park. People are walking by in both directions. It seems like a good place to wait, but it's noisy and there are people everywhere. We can also be seen by any of police vehicles driving down this main street, especially bosses, who might ask, "What are you doing here?"

"Let's move to the side street," I say.

"Yeah," my partner says.

After the Porter conviction, the anxiety expanded. First it went to the detectives who worked the case. This was nothing new. Detectives throughout the South Side were notified that many long-dead murder cases were suddenly reborn ten to twenty years after the fact. Some new witness seemed to always step forward, one who claimed there was a different offender or that they were coerced by the police. So it happened to the detectives on the Porter case. They awoke one day to hear Professor David Protess and his students at Northwestern University's Innocence Project announce that Porter was in fact innocent, that another man named Alstory Simon had committed the murders. This man, Alstory Simon, was a friend of Green and Hillard and was last seen walking into Washington Park with them many hours before their murders. The detectives learned Protess, his students, and his colleagues had obtained a confession from Simon. In short order, Simon's confession was accepted and Porter was pardoned by the governor. Protess carried a great deal of weight in the city. He had successfully argued that four other men convicted of rape and murder were wrongfully convicted. These defendants sued and won $36 million shortly before Protess took up the Porter case. In freeing these four men, Protess became an international celebrity. Students competed hard to get into his class. Nevertheless, the detectives were stupefied. Who was this guy Alstory Simon? Not one witness had ever mentioned him. Soon they learned they were being accused of framing Porter, of knowingly ignoring evidence that someone else committed the murders. Ultimately, there were accusations of torturing Porter as well.

But a measure of anxiety also began for the Northwestern activists. Right around the time Porter was released from prison in 1999 and Alstory Simon took his place for the murders, the state's attorney convened a grand jury hearing about the Porter case. Grand jury hearings are held in secret, so that what happens there is not immediately known to the public. But what happened in this hearing was that the Innocence Project was put under a legal microscope. The students, Protess, his private investigator Paul Ciolino, all of them were forced to testify how they were able to discover evidence in the Porter case that detectives, the prosecutors, the courts had failed to obtain. These transcripts lingered on the periphery for years, more and more people slowly discovering them, seeing them for what they were: a terrifying glimpse into the wrongful conviction movement. In the grand jury hearing, every single claim they made was torn apart by the prosecutor. In reading this testimony, one can perceive Protess and his students wishing the hearing had never taken place, hoping their statements would never get out.

But even with the testimony of the grand jury buried, anxiety moved into the Northwestern camp. Less than two months after the exonerated Porter ran into the arms of David Protess outside the Menard prison, a scene that would be broadcast around the world, Porter got into an argument with a woman who was the mother of three of his children. Porter began beating her. One of Porter's children, a daughter who had stood by him as he fought his conviction, attempted to step in and break up the fight, but Porter turned his wrath on her, and, according to an Order of Protection filed against Porter, hit the woman "around her body with his fists, pulled her down the porch stairs, threatened to kill her, stomped on her left leg and hit her on the back with a beer bottle."

"I want people to know what kind of man my father is," the daughter said in the newspapers. "It hurt me because he's my father. I have no love for him anymore. I can't forgive him. I'm going to stay out of his life."

In the face of such violence, Professor David Protess from the Innocence Project was quick to dismiss the batteries in a sophomoric psycho-babble.

"It's important to remember this is a very difficult adjustment," Protess explained after the first domestic battery. "You can't be incarcerated for that long and be expected to begin normal life."

Protess seemed to have forgotten about the time Porter shot Earl Lewis in the head, the time he beat a man senseless during a robbery. What about his other convictions, his title as a gang enforcer, his reputation as an armed robber? Perhaps Protess or his students had no idea what gang enforcer meant, though every cop who worked in Porter's district did. It meant that if the gang needed someone severely beaten or murdered, they turned to guys like Porter. Porter had been violent all his life, long before the conviction for the murders. His incarceration had nothing to do with it. These domestic batteries are likely indicative of how he had treated women his whole life. The fact that the reporters would accept such clearly ridiculous excuses by Protess is a sign in the case of Protess's strange power over the local media.

Then in 2006 Porter moved to southern Illinois with his girlfriend, with whom he had five children. Another verbal altercation escalated, and Porter began hitting the woman with a beer bottle. The bottle broke and Porter cut her with it, slicing her face so badly she required forty stitches. Later she refused to go forward with charges.

But these were smaller events, generating only a mild anxiety among Protess and his students. Unless he murdered again, they were largely manageable. What loomed larger was Porter's civil lawsuit against the city, the one claiming he deserved $25 million because he had been framed by the detectives. By 1999 it was axiomatic in the city that someone who was "wrongly convicted" was the victim of some police or prosecutorial malfeasance. Wrongful convictions had become big business, a kind of cottage industry. There were several law firms in the city and many law professors working at law schools who were taking up cases. There was the Center on Wrongful Convictions at Northwestern Law School, headed by an old colleague of Protess, Rob Warden. There was the People's Law Office, who had led the crusade against Jon Burge. There was another law firm, Loevy & Loevy, specializing in wrongful convictions. These lawyers, teachers, and students worked together on many cases and supported one another's claims. They adopted similar strategies, many of them apparent in the Porter case. One common strategy was their ability to discover some new witness or offender two decades after a murder, much like Protess and his students "discovered" that Alstory Simon was the offender sixteen years after the murders. They were wildly successful, winning as much as $70 million in lawsuits against the city.

These groups initiated a virtual tidal wave of claims against prosecutors and police. In the beginning of 1999, the year Porter was released, the *Chicago Tribune* ran a series of articles assailing the criminal justice system, claiming cops and prosecutors routinely convicted the wrong man. They held the Porter case out as a kind of paradigm of how bad things had become.

> In a chilling illustration of the death penalty's frailties, the very courts that have granted a new trial or sentencing hearing to nearly half of Illinois' Death Row population rejected the appeals of Anthony Porter, an innocent man who came within two days of execution.

Wrongly convicted in 1983 of shooting to death a couple as they sat in bleachers at a park on Chicago's South Side, Porter was saved not by the justice system, but by journalism students. Working with a private investigator, they proved Porter's innocence earlier this year by obtaining a videotaped confession from the real killer, who recently pleaded guilty.

This was the magnitude of journalistic opinion mounting as the civil trial unfolded. Governor George Ryan, who would soon be in jail on corruption charges of his own, had pardoned Porter. Recent huge settlements in other cases all but guaranteed Porter would be a wealthy man. In the face of all this, many people expected the city was going to settle with Porter's attorneys. No doubt Porter's attorneys did as well. Certainly Protess and the other wrongful conviction activists thought so.

But Detectives Salvatore and Gray refused to capitulate. Furious that the case had unraveled and that Porter was walking the streets, they demanded a trial, certain that not only were they completely innocent of any framing, but that Porter was guilty of the murders, regardless of his exoneration. The detectives had lived with the ignominy of alleged malfeasance, a frame-up, and torture in the case, allegations repeated over and over in the press that eulogized David Protess and his students. The press repeated the baseless claims that the detectives intentionally framed Porter for murders he didn't commit, as well as claims they had bungled the investigation from the beginning. These were seasoned detectives, detectives who had investigated hundreds of crimes, just like the detectives in the Ealy case. The notion that a group of North Shore coeds, journalism students, could interview a few witnesses and suddenly announce they had solved the case was laughable to cops.

What drew the ire of the detectives even more was the fact that Porter began claiming torture as his civil trial approached. Some sixteen years after his arrest and Porter starts claiming the detectives had tortured him, just as Ealy suddenly claimed torture after his arrest and confession. Porter claims he was hit in the back with a phone book, that he was smothered with a typewriter cover. This form of torture was the best choice, because it left no marks, which conveniently explains why Porter had none on him in photos taken after his arrest. As in the Ealy case, there was no evidence of abuse, no claim by Porter of torture at the time of his arrest. Porter made no statements to the state's attorney, nor made any claims after his criminal trial. Even in his appeal to the Supreme Court, Porter never said anything about torture. These accusations drew little scrutiny from the media, who never investigated the suspicious birth of such claims so many years after the fact, especially in light of the fact that Porter never confessed. Porter claimed in an absurd tale that the detectives tortured him but he never caved in. They never noticed that these torture accusations had all the earmarks of a legal Hail Mary pass because they suddenly took shape as the attorney for the detectives announced he would not settle the case. Facing a trial, Porter needed some legal ammunition because his case was so weak, so he went to torture claims. It was an indication that torture was by now an inmate cliché, a standard defense tactic, no matter how ridiculous. Porter was housed in the county jail at the same time as the Wilson brothers, Edgar Hope, and James Ealy, all men who claimed abuse. Later Porter was sent to death row, joining a collection of other condemned murderers who had been arrested in Area 2 by Jon Burge and his men, many of whom also claimed torture.

Certainly in the Porter murders, the detectives didn't need a confession. They had an airtight case from the beginning, unbiased witnesses coming forth right at the scene of the crime in a public park. Why would they want to pin the arrest on Porter and leave the real offender on the street? What would be their motivation? The only answer was that by 2005, the year Porter's lawsuit went to trial, the wrongful conviction zealots had successfully painted Chicago cops as the worst thugs in the city, men who had no motivation for justice at all, who would arrest anyone for a crime, they were so crooked. This was one reason why Porter could get away with claiming torture right before the trial and no one batted an eye. No one was skeptical at the timing of the accusations, at the absurdity of them. Rather than taking a second look at the case, the media stuck with a narrative of Protess and the Northwestern students as crusading heroes and Chicago police as racist thugs. The media replayed over and over the image of Porter emerging from prison into the embracing arms of David Protess. To many cops, especially those who had worked the Porter case and those who had dealt with Porter on a regular basis, it was a fantastic transformation of Porter, from homicidal maniac into folk hero.

For cops, this embrace was a strange image, a perverse alliance. It was one thing to free a guy you believed was innocent, quite another to develop this kind of solidarity, friendship with a guy who would walk up to someone and shoot them in the head as casually as going shopping or getting on a bus. To free a guy like Porter, if you think he is wrongful convicted, you do it because you do your duty, but you don't make a friend out of such a guy, don't cast him as a hero. A natural piety would temper your feelings of justice with a dark anxiety over the threat Porter posed to innocent people. But this was not the case with Protess and his students, or with any other wrongful conviction activists in the city. Not only did they embrace Porter after he was released from prison, but they brought him to Northwestern University and paid him money to give talks to journalism students.

This making a victim out of Porter was particularly enraging to the detectives, because they had spent several days looking for Porter after the warrant was signed for his arrest. One story was handed down to them that gave them pause. The detectives went to check out Porter's mother's apartment after the murders and began searching, telling Porter's mother that he needed to turn himself in. One of the detectives went into a room where there was a Murphy bed, searching as he spoke to the mother. He approached the bed, but was called away by his partner before opening it. The story handed down to the detectives was that that Porter was hiding in the bed with a loaded shotgun. Porter allegedly said he was going to execute the cops if they found him.

Nevertheless, the civil case went forward. It was a familiar nightmare for Chicago cops. The detectives went from solving a simple murder case into becoming defendants themselves, just like the detectives in the Ealy case went from solving the murders into taking the blame for Ealy's liberation. The detectives lived in the anxiety full-time now. Many ominous outcomes loomed for them. What would be the ramifications of Porter's accusations? What would happen if a jury embraced the torture allegations? Would they be forced to pay a settlement from their own pockets? Would they have to pay money to a man they knew was a killer? Would these allegations against the detective in the civil lawsuit then turn criminal? Would the detectives be indicted? Would they face prison? What about their reputations? Porter had already been released, claiming a police frame-up. Already their reputations were besmirched. How bad would it get? Would they end up like the Burge detectives who were tried in civil court? The Burge detectives won these cases, only to have attorneys double down on their public relations campaign against them, calling them every manner of criminal. The Porter detectives had to review each step of their investigation through the eyes of a malevolent lawyer as they imagined the upcoming trial. They had to imagine how anything they did could be turned into appearing devious or illegal.

Porter was released in 1999. The trial took place in 2005. That was some six years the detectives had to live in the anxiety of this civil case hanging over their heads, six years watching Protess and the students wallow in the limelight as they blamed the detectives for a great injustice, just as the detectives were blamed in the Ealy case. This was among the worst period for cops, the limbo between the accusations and the trial. There were depositions, evidence gathering, constant articles in the newspapers condemning their investigation and echoing the claims by Porter's lawyers and the wrongful conviction advocates that the detectives framed Porter. Many detectives facing lawsuits like this tell their attorney they are willing to settle. They just want to get it over with and get on with their lives. The risks are too great and the stress of the ongoing legal proceedings, ones that could take years, can ruin one's life. Both detectives in the case, Salvatore and Gray, were already retired at the time of the civil trial.

Yet they wouldn't give in. They rejected any settlement in the case. They angrily demanded that it go to trial. Their attorney, Walter Jones, initially wanted to argue that the detectives acted in goodwill and according to procedure, but had somehow gotten the case wrong, convicted the wrong man. Then Jones began to dig into the evidence, saw how passionate the detectives were. He reviewed the evidence, re-interviewed witnesses, even found some new ones. Jones also had access to the grand jury transcripts investigating the Northwestern claims. These helped him see even more clearly how ridiculous were the claims by the Northwestern sleuths. Other detectives and cops involved in the case volunteered their help, many of them retired, traveling from all over the country. Jones began to see clearly Porter was the killer. He changed his strategy accordingly. This was the reason he stunned Porter's lawyers by refusing to settle the case. Now the anxiety expanded into the world of Protess and his students, as well as the university. The cracks were starting to take shape in their case in the public, in a legal proceeding. Already their case had been obliterated in a grand jury hearing. During the trial, Jones broke the case down step by step, and, in a brilliant summation speech, he showed the absurdity of the claims against the detectives because the incontrovertible evidence indicated Porter was the murderer.

The jury saw it clearly and ruled in favor of the detectives. Suddenly, the most high-profile wrongful conviction case in the state's history had just fallen apart, a man just two days from being executed—and the jury awarded him nothing for his fifteen years in prison, not a nickel for his claims that the detectives had conspired to frame him. A grand question now lay in front of everyone at the end of the trial: How could a man be declared wrongfully convicted, then lose the trial where that claim was tested? The journalists at the trial were stupefied. A shell-shocked reporter walked up to Walter Jones and asked how it could be that Porter received no compensation for his years in custody, for his wrongful conviction. Jones lifted his hand and pointed to Anthony Porter, saying, "The killer has been sitting in that room right there all day."

Now the anxiety exploded among the journalists. Many had been echoing the claims of Protess and the students since they made their first claims that Porter was innocent. What was it that a jury saw that they didn't? Well, for one, the jury reviewed all the evidence. They did not merely accept the claims of Protess, Ciolino, and the students without checking it over, asking simple questions. A question floated around the room but was never asked: If there was nothing wrong with the investigation into the murders, what was Anthony Porter doing free? He had been convicted in a criminal trial. Six witnesses had placed him at the crime scene. One of the witnesses had been robbed at gunpoint just before the couple was murdered. A cop had stopped Porter running in the park right after the call of the shooting came out on the police radios. Porter was wanted on another shooting two weeks earlier, a shooting that showed clearly he was willing to murder over nothing. An eerie silence followed the jury's verdict. Not one journalist in the city reviewed the case, not one of them explored why the jury ruled against Porter, why Walter Jones flatly stated Porter was the killer. Not one confronted Porter's lawyers about the torture claims, never explored where they came from. Not one approached the detectives whose names had been dragged through the mud for six years and asked their side of the story.

My partner is playing air drums again, slapping the dashboard with one hand, his knee with the other. The knee is his cymbal.

"Hey, Ringo Starr," I say, "would you mind putting a lid on it?"

He ignores me, plays louder. One of the most annoying aspects of his drum playing is that he keeps perfect time. He catches every drum roll, every lick. His perfect imitations make it even more difficult to ignore him. I put the car in gear.

"Let's look around the alleys for her car," I say. He just nods and keeps playing. I start humming another song in a completely different style of music to throw a wrench in his escapades. If that doesn't work, I'll ask him questions about the old days working the West Side.

We pull onto the west alley of Prairie from Forty-Eighth, letting the car move only by its idle. We look left and right in the backyards of the buildings where cars are parked, many of them junkers. About halfway up the block, there is a three-flat with a large backyard. About six cars are parked there. One is green. I see its plate. It belongs to this woman.

"That's it. That's the Chevy," I say.

"I see it," my partner says. "Just keep going. Don't look at it."

From a window on the first floor, we can see people watching us. There are three males on the front stoop. One of them walks around and eyes us. Clearly they are lookouts. It's a dope house, for sure.

"Let's go park up the street where we can keep an eye on the house," I say.

"No, let's get the fuck out of here," my partner says.

"Just a few minutes. Come on. I want to see if she comes out. Maybe she will be with Porter, and we'll know they are still together," I say.

As I say this, I let my foot off the brake and coast out of the alley, turn right twice, and park on the street. They know we are watching, but they don't know why.

"We're not even supposed to be here," my partner says.

"I know. Just a little while," I say.

I put the car in park, turn the radio down a little. We move our seats back, crack the windows a bit, and wait. My partner lights another cigarette, two in an hour now. He's nervous. My mind slows down a bit. I've always like the mentality that arises from sitting on a building or a car, waiting. It's almost dreamlike. Porter was once two days away from dying by lethal injection. He was right up close to his death. He had already picked out his coffin and made his arrangements. Then he walked out of the prison free, pardoned for the crime. He could never be prosecuted for it again. What a feeling that must have been for a killer. Years later Porter would actually get paid to speak at Northwestern University, arriving with an entourage of fellow gang members. I wonder if any of the students had the nerve to raise their hand.

"What about that guy you shot in the head over the barking dog?" or "Why did you slice up your girlfriend's face?" "What does it mean to be a gang enforcer?"

I'm shaking my heading thinking about it. It seemed to me that such a kid would be spurned in the class. At this point, such questions were heresy in the city.

My partner sees me shake my head, lost in this rumination.

"What?" he says.

"Nothing. I'll tell you later," I say.

"You're a fucking fruitcake," he says.

"Fuck you," I say.

We sit for a while, nothing happening.

"Fuck this shit," I say to my partner. "Let's try something else."

"Like what?" my partner asks.

"Let's go up to the building and ask if she lives there," I say.

"Oh, sure we will. And when a fight breaks out and we call for help or lock one of them up, we'll just say we happened to be driving three miles outside of our beat, and we just felt like knocking on this one door for no reason," he says.

He has a point.

"Well, how about this? How about we tell them we are from special victims and we are looking for the mother of a juvenile in custody and we change the name a little bit? Her name is Tamara Kelly. We'll say we're looking for Theresa Kelly?"

"No fucking way. We're not even supposed to be out here," my partner says. But I can tell he is thinking about it. He was great at creating such frauds when he worked the street.

"If there is the slightest tension, we'll get out. We're gone," I say. "I'll do all the talking. There won't be a complaint because they'll believe the story. C'mon. I need ya."

"Oh, fuck it. All right," he says.

We get out of the car and walk slowly and casually toward the house, not even looking up. We don't want to look like cops serving a warrant or as if we are looking to lock someone up. Before we even get to the gate, two male gangbangers come onto the porch, along with a woman.

"How you all doing today?" I say.

The two thugs say nothing. The woman just looks at me.

"Wondering if you could help us out. We have a juvenile in custody back at the station, and we're trying to get hold of his mother so we can release him. No big deal, just a retail theft. He's not very cooperative and he keeps giving up different names. The last one we got is Theresa Kelly. Are you Theresa Kelly, ma'am?"

"No, I ain't."

"Well, do you know if Theresa Kelly lives here?"

"Where do you work out of?" she says.

I am getting a little nervous. Maybe she is not buying it. If she makes a complaint, we could get really jammed up.

"Juvenile section, special victims," I bullshit.

She doesn't press it. The two thugs remain silent. My partner and I remain at the gate. If we try to approach the building, there will be trouble. They got their dope in there, for sure. We keep our body language relaxed.

"So anyway, we got to get this kid back home. He's been there all day, so we're looking for this Theresa Kelly," I say.

"You mean Tamara?" she says, pointing up to the third floor.

Bingo. She lives upstairs.

"Tamara did you say? That might be her. Is she home?" I say.

Two shorties come out onto the porch, staring at us, eating Popsicles.

"I don't know," the woman says.

I don't know what to do. It's too risky to walk past the gangbangers. They might have dope or something else in there. We don't have a warrant and our reason for being there is bullshit. They clearly want us gone right away. Walking up the stairs would be too risky. No one even knows where we are. It dawns on me that I don't even remember my call sign on the radio, and the radio isn't even on the right channel for the district we are in. *You stupid motherfucker. You fucking dumbass.* I finger my radio, look at it. My partner catches my eye, sees what I am thinking.

"I got the right channel," he mumbles to me. Then he looks up at one of the kids.

"Why don't you help us out, little man, and see if she is home upstairs and then we'll be gone," he says, a great move.

"Do it," the older gangbanger says, and the kid runs up the stairs. From an open window, we can hear him tapping on the door and the long silence afterward. He tries a few more times. Nothing, but we know now where she lives. The kid runs back downstairs.

"All right, then. You wouldn't happen to have her phone number, would you?" I ask.

The woman shakes her head. She wouldn't give it to me anyway. It is a stupid question. We turn and walk back to the car, relaxing a little.

"You the man, you know that?" I say to my partner.

"We're not doing this shit anymore," my partner says, but I can tell he enjoyed it.

I put the car in gear and pull out, go about two blocks up, and park again. We have both been silent, but now we want to talk about it. I pull out a notebook to jot down some information. My partner reaches over to turn the radio up again when he sees someone walking on the other side of the street, right toward us. His gaze fixes on the man. I look up as well. He has long hair, is small, but wiry. Has that frenetic gait. He's headed right for us. Could it be Porter, we are wondering. My partner puts his hand on his gun, slides it out slowly. I put my hand on mine. I roll the window up a bit. He walks toward the front of our car. He's just crossing the street. He isn't approaching us. He looks over at us, nods.

We nod back.

11. HOLLYWOOD

I am in my underwear on a winter morning, my guitar strapped on my shoulder as I sit next to my desk, surrounded by boxes and stacks of transcripts and documents. I am a little woozy from pain pills I took first thing in the morning. One cat, Frances, is looking at me from a shelf above; another, Elizabeth, is on the couch behind me. I think they hate living with me when they see me pick up my guitar, but they endure it, particularly when I sing loudly, with everything I have. Such is the case this morning. Pain pills after a pot of coffee will do that. I am working on the Beatles song "All My Loving," trying to get the 12/8 rhythm of John Lennon's guitar in it. But I can't. I look at one of the cats when I sing, as if I mean the words for her. She looks away, anxious for me to finish. When my phone suddenly rings, I curse, because it means putting down the guitar, grabbing my cane, and raising myself up to get to it before it goes to voice mail. Time and time again, I tell myself to keep the cell phone close to me, but I always forget. I put the guitar in the stand, grab the edge of my desk, and pull myself forward, moaning from back spasms. Then I step forward gingerly. The first step is always the most painful until the back muscles relax a bit. The cane goes out first, followed by my left leg. Who the fuck is calling me this early in the morning? As I get to the ledge by the front door, my third cat, Dill Pickle, runs out of the way from under a chair, startling me. I jump backward, which causes me to grab my back in pain.

"Get the fuck out of the way, Dill Pickle, or I'll turn you into guitar strings," I say when she darts under my legs.

Dill is a big calico cat I rescued from the common area of my condo building after another tenant tossed her out. I came to my back door during a cold rain shower a few years earlier, and there she was on the steps across the way, sopping wet and meowing loudly. All the weight of the world seemed to be on her shoulders. She had been hanging out for weeks. Many people took pity on her and fed her, but no one could take her in. Who could just throw out a cat like that, I asked myself. I already had two cats. She stared at me and I said, "Okay, c'mon in," as I held open the door. If she picked up on what I meant and she wanted to come in, fine, I thought. I wouldn't push it. She didn't need any further encouragement. She ran down the stairs across the concrete common area and into my kitchen, dripping, the other two cats running for cover. I put out some wet cat food and clean water, and set out a little pillow in the corner where she was hanging out. She was skinny and sickly. The hair on her head was matted down in a strange way. It gave her the air of a poet, so I called her Dylan after Dylan Thomas. (I didn't know what sex she was.) But after I took her to the vet and she got healthier, she got fat and lazy and revealed herself lacking in any poetical sense at all. She meowed a lot the first few months, so much so that I thought of changing her name to Sylvia Plath, but I was already used to Dylan. She also meowed at the window, wanting to go outside, so much so I finally opened the window to let her out. (I lived on the ground floor.)

"Go on out if you're so unhappy here, you ungrateful, selfish beast," I told her.

She leaped onto the grass and basked in the sun. Whenever a neighbor walked by, she sat down on the sidewalk blocking their way and rolled on her side. Few people could resist stopping and petting her. Then when they stood up and walked away, she darted in front of them and rolled over again.

"You shameless whore," I said to her when she came back in, wagging her tail.

The other cats watched, fascinated, then, after seeing Dill go outside for a few months, they ran out, but they always stayed near the window and checked in every half hour or so. Soon all three were hiding in the bushes, attacking each other and running in a wide circle in the common area. They looked up from the grass and watched all the birds above. They held their whiskers to the wind and smelled all the scents, often in a kind of trance. They would hide in the bushes and watch things go on from that perspective. All the cats liked going outside so much, it became a morning routine. They would sit on my bed staring at me, waiting for me to wake. When I stirred, they darted off the bed and ran to the windowsill, staring at me, then the window, as if it wasn't clear to me after a few years what they wanted. It was difficult to sleep in when three cats were watching you intensely.

"Get the fuck out of here, you worthless creatures," I would yell at them, and they would jump off the bed and run into the living room. Then slowly they would creep back in, jump on the bed, and stare at me again. What a life they led. Wake in the morning, go outside, hide, play, chase birds, smell things, sleep in the sun. Then, when afternoon came around and I got ready for work, head inside and crash out in front of the window.

Dylan's name was a mistake, I decided. She got fatter and lazier. She never wrote any poetry at all. Sometimes I said, "I sang in my chains like the sea," to get her going, but it never clicked. She threw up on my Walt Whitman paperback one morning, to which I took great offense. I started calling her Dill, a shorter, less noble nickname for Dylan. One day, while eating an incredible corned beef sandwich on rye bread from a kosher market, I looked at her looking at me. I held up the dill pickle that came with the sandwich. It was fantastic, one of the best pickles I had ever had.

"You're as dumb as a dill pickle," I said, showing her the pickle to strengthen my simile, then taking a bite out of it.

She looked at me, looked at the pickle, wagged her tail, and then meowed.

Dill Pickle. It stuck.

Dill Pickle circles in and out of my legs as I put the phone to my ear and sit down on my couch. She rubs her cheek against my leg. I believe she remembers that I rescued her and feels no end of gratitude for it. That is why she always clings to me. It's an endearing trait in her. She always has to be near me. I reach down to pet her. She rolls over on her side, purring, a really sweet little creature. She owns me.

"Hello," I say into the phone.

"This is unbelievable. I can't fucking believe it. It's a fucking outrage. We've got to put a stop to this."

It's Peter, a filmmaker from the West Coast. Peter is older, had grown up in Chicago, but settled in Los Angeles.

"Hello, Pete."

"I don't fucking see how this happened. That poor fucking Alstory Simon."

"Yeah."

Peter had purchased the rights to the first book I had published, a collection of stories, mostly about my real-life experiences hauling dead bodies to the morgue. Over the course of about a year, we had hashed out many storylines aimed at turning the book into some kind of cable drama, the kind that ran for an hour every week. We had a character loosely based upon me, someone who had wandered into the police job after years in the service industry. Our problem was that we had many scenes, but no narrative drive. As we were talking about making a show based upon this book, I was working on the book about Ealy and exploring other wrongful conviction cases. I told Peter about the Anthony Porter case and the community of people I was working with on it, the journalists, lawyers, retired detectives, et cetera. At first, I couldn't get Peter interested. Finally, I half jokingly told Peter I wouldn't talk to him until he reviewed the documents related to the Porter case. My feeling was that having a character exploring these cases would be a great narrative for our series. The main character could become obsessed with them as a police officer, just as I had. The character could be driven to uncovering them. Peter finally promised he would explore the Porter case. This was his first phone call since he read about it.

What was so compelling about the Porter case was that the malfeasance that took place was not some obscure conspiracy theory. It did not require a great deal of interpretation. It was right there in the public record, in the documents and court transcripts, particularly the grand jury transcripts from 1999. Now Peter saw it clearly. I sit on the couch, letting Peter vent for a while. This venting is common after people familiarized themselves with the case. As Peter rants, Dill Pickle climbs on my lap, rubbing against my arm. Soon I will be covered in her fur, the price you have to pay for her love. As Peter and I talk that morning, we move away from the notion of writing a cable drama. Here, Chicago's native resistance to fiction resurfaces. Peter realizes, as almost everyone who takes a second look at the Porter and Ealy cases does, that you cannot make up characters and deal with these murders in any disguised or diluted way. You can't clutter them with creative devices or transform the themes into symbols, and, most of all, you can't fictionalize them. The reality of the stories themselves is too fantastic. After all, what use is fiction in a city that exists solely upon its own conspiracies, its own crimes? And so almost without thinking about it, Peter and I—and everyone involved in our enterprise—organically move into the form of a documentary. We will just tell the story of the Porter case.

Peter's interest is the first instance of the stories moving outside the committee we have formed, a crucial, exhilarating step. We have had no such luck with the local media. There was hardly a contrary voice in the city as Protess and his Northwestern students trumpeted the claim of innocence by Porter, a claim that included the theory that the detectives had framed Porter. Just a few weeks earlier, Bill and I had traveled into the far northern suburbs to meet with another Chicago journalist, this one a columnist for the *Tribune*. We had sent him our documents and information, asking him if he would be interested in writing about it. As we talked to him, we could perceive the light going on, just as it had for Peter. By the end of the meeting, he guaranteed he would write a column about the Porter case, Protess, and Northwestern's Innocence Project. Then two days later came his e-mail saying he could not do it. The editors at the *Tribune* would not print it. They would not give him a reason, just told him to forget it.

Another editor at a major magazine said there was a convincing case in our documents, but he couldn't do the story. He said he doubted anyone in the city would write about it. There was too much political liability for anyone to publish it. After all, the editor said, the newspapers had given wide voice to the arguments of Protess. How would they look if the entire case was a sham? But what about the fact that an innocent man may be wasting away in prison, we argued. What about the furor over a wrongful conviction? What about the fate of the detectives in the case? We just got shrugged shoulders in response. Bill and I wondered, where was all the passion about wrongful conviction now?

Not only did we have little luck in getting attention to the story in the city, but some of us were becoming pariahs, none more so than Bill, even though Bill had worked for the *Tribune* for twenty-seven years and won the Pulitzer Prize. His passion for the Porter story met with no takers, no one in the city save a few media reps who would tell him off the record they believed him, but they couldn't do anything with his story. In growing frustration and anger, he sweated over Alstory Simon lingering in a prison downstate for a murder Simon did not commit. Bill sent copies of his conclusions all over the city, to every media outlet. Nothing. It was a bitter pill for him to swallow: Here in the city that virtually invented the wrongful conviction movement, Bill couldn't get anyone to budge on a case that held the greatest evidence of a wrongful conviction. In his frustration, he had become disgusted with many of the people involved and lashed out at them. He cursed some of them out, sent nasty e-mails. Finally one media outlet, the *Chicago Reader*, which had been a vocal supporter of David Protess and Northwestern, finally called Bill about an article. Our hopes were ignited, then dashed. The story that followed had little to do with the Porter case, but focused on the fact that Bill had cursed out some of these officials. Many of us on the committee had to rub our eyes when we read it. The fact that Bill lost his temper with a few officials and journalists in his attempts to free an innocent man was seen as newsworthy? My mind went back to the hallway of the Burge hearing in the Dirksen Federal Building, the activists cursing the police, calling the cops motherfuckers, racists, scum. No one batted an eye.

The refusal of the local media to take a deeper look at David Protess and the Innocence Project was even stranger given the discovery by Northwestern University in 2011 that Protess had altered evidence submitted to the state's attorney and subsequently was fired by the university. Once again, Protess was claiming a wrongful conviction in another case. The prosecutor subpoenaed e-mails by Protess and his students in this case. At first, the university fought the prosecutor, arguing that the e-mails and documents generated by Protess and his students were legally protected, since the students and Protess were journalists. The prosecutor countered that they were not journalists, that the Northwestern investigators were in fact working for the defense. After a long court battle, watched closely by the city media, the judge ruled in favor of the prosecutor, and the e-mails and other documents were submitted. In the process of giving up these e-mails, Northwestern became aware that Protess had altered one of them. This is a serious crime, altering evidence specifically requested by a prosecutor.

For some reason, Protess was never charged with obstruction of justice, but this discovery, along with other accusations of malfeasance on his part, ultimately led to an internal investigation by the school, whose spokesman eventually admitted that Protess had regularly lied to the school about his investigations. In response, they fired Protess from his tenured position. Strangely, the ever-contentious Protess took the firing without contesting it legally. He admitted altering the evidence, but claimed it was for altruistic purposes. This was a strange, suspicious twist of fate for a man once regarded internationally as a crusader for justice and for the oppressed. It was not surprising to the detectives in Chicago, nor was it surprising to those of us who had explored the Anthony Porter case. But what did it mean that a professor who had helped free a dozen inmates, many of them murderers, was now revealed as a liar and someone who would alter evidence in a wrongful conviction case to further his designs? One wonders what a field day Protess and his students would have with any detective who was found altering evidence in criminal cases, one who would be discovered routinely lying in capital murder cases. Every single case that detective was involved in would be reviewed by wrongful conviction lawyers, just as they had pored over every single murder conviction by Jon Burge. They would re-interview crucial witnesses, review all the evidence. But none of this happened after Protess was fired, and Bill could get no one to listen to his claims about the Porter scandal, no one to write a story. None of us in the city could.

To us, particularly the retired detectives who had worked during the ascendance of the wrongful conviction movement, there was a cruel, conspiring silence among the media. There was also a fear on my part that Bill's plight might be prophetic. I began to wonder if my own pub-lisher would back out of the contract I had about the Ealy story, the col-lection of strange essays and stories showing how all these murders were connected in fantastic ways. Perhaps they would back out, and I, too, would join Bill and the detectives in the city's unpublished, imaginative wasteland.

I look at my reflection in the TV as I recline on my couch, Peter still talk-ing away on the phone. Dill Pickle is sleeping on my hip, purring away. I still have all these back problems and they're getting worse. I don't know how Peter will work out. I suddenly notice there is a break in his rant. I listen. Peter is listing things we need, money, and need to do— editing, traveling back and forth from Los Angeles. It sounds like a mountain of work, rising at all hours of the day to drive places and set up the shoots, carrying equipment, driving all over hell. My back is barely functioning now. I tell Peter I have to go and will call him later. I roll over on my other side. The pain pills are making me drowsy. Dill Pickle jumps off of me. Then, when I settle back down, she walks up my leg to my hip and sits down again. I stroke her neck a little. Where will we get the money? Can we get people to talk on camera? I feel myself falling asleep on my couch, Dill Pickle still on me.

"You crazy motherfucker," I whisper. Her tail swishes up and down a few times. We both nod off, Dill purring away on my hip.

12. OPIUM DREAMS

It's quiet in my hospital room, just the hum of machines monitoring my blood pressure and the elastic bands on my legs squeezing to prevent blood clots. Occasionally there are sounds in the hallway of a worker pushing a machine past the door or the conversation of nurses. It's morning now, very early; I can tell from the light in the window behind the drawn shades. I keep the blinds down. It's unpleasant to be drugged up and have the light beat down on my bed, causing me to sweat. It's almost as bad as the late nights when I can't sleep, just watching time go by on the clock. There are still four days before they will take me in for surgery and fuse the vertebrae in my back. I grab the bars on the side of the bed to pull myself up and to the right, an easing of the pain that will lend itself to another narcotic slumber.

When I awake, I glance at the clock, fifteen minutes before I get another shot. My life is now measured in increments of two hours. On the second hour, they give me a shot. At around fifteen minutes before this second hour, the pain would begin in my leg and back. Without the painkillers, I might be yelling again, rolling in my bed. In just a day or so of being on the narcotics, I have come to depend on them, to look forward to the euphoria in the minutes after they go through the IV into my arm. Then I would dread the remaining time, the stoned-out malaise afterward, a malaise that increases each time I take another shot. This is how junkies feel, I realize. I reach for the call button.

"It think it's about that time," I say when the nurse comes in.

"It sure is," she says, after looking at the computer screen with my information on it.

She leaves and comes back a few minutes later with the syringe. Only with these drugs am I able to hang on, but they take away all coherence, leave me in a dream world save the brief interlude when they begin to

112

wear off and the pain starts to come back. It had taken more than two days to find the right combination, two days I only remember as a nightmare, waking up with my leg twitching violently and me yelling. The nurses were in contact with a pain specialist, and they inched the opiates and anti-inflammatories up to the edge of safety. Still, I awoke yelling. My blood pressure was sky-high. I feared a heart attack. At one point, they came in and told me there was an anomaly in my EKG, and I started to think this might be it. I recounted the rivers of whiskey and beer, the steaks, the butter.

The second night was the turning point. I awoke in my hospital room and didn't know where I was, my leg twitching again from the pain down my back. I didn't know how I got in this room and couldn't account for the last four days. The room was foreign, sterile. I didn't know my name. There were tubes and machines, darkness outside the room and quiet. In my delusion, I thought I was in an embalming room. Something must have happened and they thought I was dead, I theorized. I couldn't move, couldn't flee. I had seen TV shows where people believed someone was dead but they weren't. They woke up late at night locked in a refrigerator with dozens of other bodies, unable to get out, no one able to hear them. This imagery came back to me. It's strange in a state of delirium what knowledge comes back to you and what doesn't. The back pain was so bad I was close to passing out again. If I were in the embalming room, that meant there were dead bodies all around me. Even if somehow I could crawl onto the floor, I would see them laid out on gurneys. Perhaps I would bump into one in the darkness and they would fall upon me, gangbangers bloody from gunshot wounds, traffic crash victims. Then for a moment I wondered if I hadn't already died and these were my first moments on the other side. That's how fucked up I was.

Somehow my knowledge of the morgue remained in my imagination, even though my identity didn't. I had brought many bodies there when I worked the wagon. I somehow remembered that people who die from what is called natural causes usually don't come to the morgue, never endure an autopsy. They are picked up by funeral home drivers and taken discreetly away, usually at the guidance of a loving family. Bodies that arrive in the morgue have some tragedy about them, the people have suffered some dire ending, like murder victims. I thought that if I somehow managed to get down from the bed and out into the hallway, I would see dozens of them. I imagined them lining the darkened corridor, some with bloody sheets on them, gaping wounds. Even if I could get down from the bed, I decided it might be better to just remain in the room until some staff arrived the following morning. But I couldn't. I couldn't last in this level of pain for that long. I would have a heart attack, surely, or stroke out. If I somehow only made it halfway down the hallway, I might be stuck there with the bodies. What if I crawled into the autopsy room itself and couldn't get out? There might be bodies in there still cut open, blood and organs on the floor. What if I had to spend the entire night there?

There were no sounds anywhere. I figured everyone had gone home for the night and left me. What if it was a holiday? What if I had to remain in this condition for two or three days? All I could do was yell, so I did. Maybe there was still a janitor, a night watchman. I moaned louder and louder, the pain so overwhelming. Suddenly a petite woman walked into the room wearing scrubs and a name tag. She was nervous, holding one hand in the other and turning them.

"What's wrong?" she asked.

"Where am I?"

"You need to sit back, breathe through your nose," she said.

"Where am I?" I said.

"Please, sit back."

"Goddamnit. Where am I?"

"You're in the hospital."

"What hospital?"

"Lutheran General?"

"Where? Where is it?"

"Park Ridge, Illinois. Sit back," she said.

She came closer to me.

"Why am I here? What happened?" I said.

My mind raced with possibilities. Car accidents, wounded, heart attack. Had I just emerged from a coma?

"You have a back problem. You are scheduled for back surgery,"

"What about this pain? Why am I in such pain?"

"It's your back. That's why you are here. We've been trying to control it. We're working with a pain doctor," she said.

"Why can't you give me something for it? Why can't you give me a shot?" I asked.

"Because we've already given you so much and it's not working. The fact that you have dementia is not good. I'm afraid your body just can't take anymore. We can't give you any more until I talk to the doctor. I'm waiting for the phone call from the doctor now," she said.

"I'm not sure I can take this pain," I said, writhing on the bed, but relieved I wasn't in a morgue. I was grateful to be talking to another human being.

"Breathe in your nose and out your mouth, steady," she said.

"Oh, for Christ's sake," I said, panicking.

I could tell she was alarmed about my condition, afraid something worse was going to happen. It increased my anxiety. Was a heart attack looming? She left to call the doctor again, and I writhed on the bed, telling myself to concentrate on something else. In a few minutes she arrived with three syringes.

"The doctor wants me to try these. They are very powerful and you will fall asleep again," she said.

I watched the first drug go in, followed the stream with my eyes, the warmth in my arm.

"This is a painkiller," she said. I fell backward, felt my eyes roll back into my head, and I slept.

The following days I remained in and out of coherence. But when I could think somewhat straight, this night haunted me. Why had I concluded in the drugged-up state of mind that I was in a morgue and not simply a hospital? Why would my imagination go there? I had wandered in this collection of murders, starting with Ealy's in 1982. These murders had become a kind of measure of my life in the city, taking place the same year I first returned to the city and unfolding all my time here. They were taking a toll on me. All murder victims go to the morgue for an autopsy, all the victims of James Ealy, Anthony Porter, Andrew and Jackie Wilson, Edgar Hope. The bodies are cut open to determine the specifics of the homicide. What a thing for the family of the victims to go through. What a place to end up. The bodies are noted, photographed, and diagrammed for the trials. After these autopsies, things get all fucked up.

Ealy had one trial, then had the trial tossed on appeal. It was remanded for another trial, but the prosecutor could not use any evidence obtained by the detectives, so the case just faded away and Ealy got out. Andrew and Jackie Wilson had two criminal trials and two civil trials. The families of Fahey and O'Brien had to sit through them all, had to hear the medical examiner discuss the autopsy over and over again.

Andrew Wilson was sentenced to death but was given life because of his torture allegations, and he became a hero in the correctional system, a kind of godfather. Edgar Hope had two criminal trials and once petitioned for clemency from the governor, who himself would end up in jail. Many people believed the governor championed the wrongful conviction movement only to distract the public from the scandals that would end his political career and put him in prison. It was hard to imagine: Hope shot three cops, two fatally, and he actually entertained the possibility of getting out. Anthony Porter was convicted, sentenced to death, then was sprung sixteen years later, pardoned so that he could never be convicted of that crime again. After that night in the hospital, I began to have this feeling that the souls of murder victims waited somewhere; they were never set free. How much worse it would be for them when their killers were freed from prison.

But then maybe I saw myself waking up in a morgue for other reasons. For a moment in the dream, I wondered if I had already died. Perhaps it was the fact that I found myself in solidarity with cops who were accused of the worst crimes—torturers, racists, thugs, men who were portrayed as if they enjoyed brutality. Perhaps there was a warning to my dream, telling me my imagination was all wrong. Maybe it was telling me that in getting these murders wrong, terror loomed, terror even in the next world. I tossed and turned in my hospital bed all that week after the narcotic dream, a separate anxiety emerging apart from my anxiety about the surgery on my back.

There is still another week in the hospital, four days on these painkillers, then three days to recover from the back surgery. I fear more dreams, awaking again in the morgue. I have to confront it, get a handle on it, but I know after I get out of the hospital and the pain subsides, I will take up the murders again. I will take a stand on them. Perhaps I am stuck with them the rest of my life. I turn to my right side again and fall into another narcotic asleep, the TV blaring some midmorning show.

When I awake, my doctor is in the chair next to me, watching television. His feet are up, as if he were sitting at home. He is wrapped up in the television program. I like his style, one reason I have stayed with him through the surgeries. I like the unpretentious manner with which he spoke to the nurses and staff, and I like his directness. I stir and he looks over.

"This is too painful," I complain.

"I know," he says.

"Are you sure this surgery is going to work?" I ask for the fiftieth time.

"No doubt about it. You'll be as good as new," he says.

"I'll play basketball again?" I ask.

"No doubt," he says, his gaze returning to the TV.

He hates all my questions. Sometimes I would bring a whole list of questions with me into his office and hand them to him. He would read a few, then tear it up.

"Just stick with me," he'd say.

But now I think about me ever getting back on the basketball court, the idea of artificially straightening out a spine.

"You're out of your mind," I say.

"You'll see. I've done thousands of these. Get some rest," he says, standing up, and walks out the door. The nurse comes in with another shot. It has been two hours already. I am so strung out; I am swimming in the drugs, as bad as any junkie in the city. I feel the warmth again, fall back to sleep.

When I wake up, the afternoon sun is fading. Glare from the window has subsided. There is a shift change in the hallway. The chatter among the workers is pleasant. Soon the evening nurse will be on duty, a welcome relief because the day nurse never changes my bedpan or sheets, never offers for me to get a bath. The evening nurse will help me out. She will move me around the bed and get the old sheets off and the new ones on, give me a bucket with soap and water and a washcloth, my toothbrush and toothpaste. All the while she keeps up a friendly conversation, tells me about her family. After she leaves, I change my underwear and T-shirt. She doesn't make me wear the gown. Friends will be visiting soon, bringing a hot dog from across the street, with tomatoes, pickles, relish, peppers, and mustard, along with some fries. What would I have done without my friends, I ask over and over. I won't finish the hot dog, but it will be a great smell and wonderful to look at. I raise the bed a little, push two pillows under my head. It's also a long interval since the last pain shot, over an hour. I am now as lucid as I am going to get.

When I first arrived in the city in February 1982—the same month Andrew and Jackie Wilson shot Officers Fahey and O'Brien, the same month Edgar Hope shot a rookie cop on a bus and James Ealy raped a woman in the Rockwell Gardens—I would have believed the claims of the wrongful conviction activists about the police. But now I don't. I have changed, but I don't know if for the better or worse. It's so difficult to be certain about anything in Chicago. I pull my legs close to my chest again in my hospital room. The pain is starting. I will need another shot soon, and will lose whatever lucidity I have mustered. I want my imagination back, to be able to stand by it, to have it free me, not hold me in captivity. Just then, I can smell the fries and hear the footsteps outside my room. Two friends come in swiftly, carrying a white bag. They set it on the moving table next to the bed. I tear it open: two hot dogs and two large fries. It is just so beautiful. The hot dogs are so colorful, so pungent and symmetrical. There isn't much time before the next shot. My friends sit down in some chairs next to me. One pours some water. The other changes the channel. I take one bite of the hot dog and swirl some fries in the ketchup, but I can't muster the energy for a second bite. My leg begins to shake again and the nurse comes in with the syringe.

Ten days later I am finally home in my condo, recovering from surgery, which was deemed successful. There is little pain in my back save the scar from surgery, but I am weak, getting around with a walker that has wheels on it. I had stayed at some friends' house after the surgery, watching movies all day with their kids, sleeping on the sofa in the basement. Then I finally came home, staring with a mixture of dread and excitement at my desk with the boxes of court transcripts and newspaper clippings about the murders of 1982 next to it.

Late that night I arise from bed, using the walker to go the bathroom. When I return to bed and lie down, my skin becomes clammy, my heart races. It seems as if all the walls in my bedroom are closing in on me. I feel as if I were dying, at the same time I am filled with a sense that there is no meaning in life, as if the only thing that life boils down to is some kind of dread or terror. The sense of terror is familiar, like the night I awoke in the hospital thinking I was in a morgue. I feel as if I am still under the spell of this horror and I will never escape it. My bedroom is too small. I rally, use the walker, and make it into my living room, opening all the shades on the windows first, then sit in my chair. I turn on the TV to hear a human voice. The sweating won't stop and I'm breathing heavily, afraid I will pass out. I try to reassure myself that everything is okay, but I don't believe my own reasoning. To be conscious seems to be living in a state of terror. I come close to calling an ambulance, then I recall that there is some medicine I have for anxiety when flying. I get up and find the pills in my kitchen, take two, then sit in my living room again. I begin to wonder if this kind of consciousness is permanent, the culmination of my twenty-five years in the city. More than ever, it feels as if it will be with me the rest of my life.

In the mornings these nighttime panic attacks hang over me as I begin taking up the transcripts and reports of the various murders. I have gathered them from lawyers, from the archives, and from tracking down detectives and cops who worked the cases. I attempt, as much as possible, to look at them from the perspective of the police. But I am only reading about these murders, studying them secondhand. What the detectives in these cases must have actually lived with, the years of staying up late reviewing what had happened, seeing their names smeared in the papers, for capturing killers like Ealy, Porter, and the Wilsons, only to be called racist thugs. So many killers set free. Detectives attended the autopsies as part of their investigations, in addition to reviewing the murder scenes, poring over the photos, dealing with the relatives. I can see the imagery of those autopsies lingering in every aspect of their investigations. That night and the next four, I have more panic attacks, crawling out of bed and sitting in my living room, where I open all the windows, turning on the TV just to hear a living, real voice.

It is in this state of mind I return to the winter of 1999, when Anthony Porter was released from prison. It was two months before Ealy would get out after serving his sentence for trying to murder the prostitute, Ealy and Porter both returned to the streets. By 1999 there were dozens of inmates claiming torture, asserting that even as the allegations against Burge and his men took shape and investigations were initiated, Burge and his men were still so jaded and crooked they continued torturing suspects. Most incredible in these allegations, the detectives were allegedly still using the same methods: typewriter bags over inmates' heads, phone books. The city had written tens of millions of dollars in settlement checks to these inmates. Scores were eventually set free. Detectives all over the city waited through the months, then years of allegations and lawsuits. Their retirement years were spent in a deep anxiety. Would they, in their seventies, be sent to prison? The cops had their own lawyers, many of whom advised the detectives not to discuss their cases, particularly amongst themselves. So there came a point in the city when the detectives who investigated murders were in a verbal straitjacket, unable to defend themselves, taking the Fifth. Their silence allowed the wrongful conviction advocates greater freedom to condemn them, to make their pleading of the Fifth seem incriminating. What a time in the city, the killers and their advocates free to say anything, to make any accusation, the police who tried to get them in prison silenced.

Panic attacks make sense. They are an appropriate state of mind in the crooked city, where the anxiety never resolves. In their epiphany, the world suddenly seems much different than one had imagined it, darker, terrifying and totally hopeless, as if the mind guiding the world were evil. Certainly it is in Chicago, where we all live in a sociopath's fantasy. Worse, in a panic attack, one suddenly sees oneself in a new relation to this evil, connected to it in previously unforeseen ways. I imagine the hundreds of police officers succumbing to these attacks in the years they were accused of torture and other abuses, the nights they lay awake after articles in the paper called them all manner of monsters, like the detectives in the Porter case and the Ealy case, like Burge and his men. I imagine them seeing their investigation obliterated and guys like Ealy and Porter out on the street again. I also see these panic attacks moving into the lives of the wrongful conviction advocates, whose investigations are beginning to fall apart. Protess was let go from Northwestern. He changed evidence solicited by prosecutors. So many witnesses and inmates were saying Protess and his investigators offered them money and reduced jail sentences for their statements.

In this mind-set, I return to the issue of confessions. Much of the wrongful conviction movement is based upon condemning the methods by which the police obtained a confession. But the Porter case acted as a kind of window because this was the first time these activists obtained their own confession, an illuminating glimpse into their methods, their integrity. To get this confession in the Porter case from Alstory Simon, Protess enlisted the help of a private investigator in the city named Paul Ciolino, a flatfoot who showed up as a pivotal character in several wrongful conviction cases, obtaining crucial statements from witnesses and inmates. Ciolino was flashy and cocky in the media. He bragged about his ability to get people to talk. He also had generated suspicion over his methods, claims that he went overboard and broke the law in getting people to do his bidding. There were, for example, claims he had manipulated statements by promising wealth through movie and book deals. But the mere fact of Ciolino working with Protess seemed strange. What was a flashy, street-talking private investigator who boasted of his ability to get people to talk doing working with a professor and his students at one of the country's most elite journalism schools? Why did the school need a private investigator? As journalists, or journalism students, weren't they the investigators?

Alstory Simon had only lived at the projects near the murders for a short time, though he had lived in projects throughout his life with his mother. He had met his father only a few times. There were several arrests on his records, a few for dope, domestic battery, a gun arrest, and some armed robberies, for which he had done time. Simon claimed he carried guns in the projects for protection and that he stayed away from the gang life, mostly because he had friends who belonged to different gangs. He was in his forties at the time of the Porter murders and had never been pinched for any violence involving guns. He had never been accused of shooting anyone. Simon and Inez had known each other since they were kids and had been lovers. One time, Inez called and asked Simon to come to her South Side home, where Inez lived with an uncle who was abusing her, beating her regularly, and holding daily meetings with local gangbangers. These gangbangers would hang out and get high. The uncle was also running a prostitution ring out of the house. I have to wonder if the uncle was forcing Inez into prostitution as well, given the fact that she turned tricks later in life to fund her drug addiction.

Alstory visited Inez at this home and saw what was going on. He pulled a gun on the uncle and told him to get out. He got the gangbangers out as well and ended up staying at this house for several months with Inez before they moved. At the time of the murders, Simon lived with Inez Jackson and her children in the projects, nicknamed "The Hole." They had only been married about two months. Inez's children claimed repeatedly that Alstory was an excellent father to them. He brought money and groceries home, gave advice to the kids, and encouraged them to get jobs and stay out of the gangs. Inez's children loved Alstory. What broke up their marriage, Simon told me, was his inability to deal with Inez's drug and alcohol addiction and his discovery that she was turning tricks in their apartment while he was out working. Inez's life was filled with abuse, drugs, and alcohol. Simon may have been the only decent men she had ever been with. Simon never liked the projects where Inez lived because of the gangs there. He wanted to get Inez and the family out, but Inez wanted to stay. Inez was friends with the victim Marilyn Green. That was Simon's connection to the couple.

Alstory Simon confessed to the murders in 1999, sixteen years after the fact. It seems incredible for a man with Simon's street smarts to confess after one visit from Paul Ciolino, early on a February morning. It was an amazing feat of persuasion: to convince someone who had kept this secret so long to suddenly spill the entire story to a stranger, a stranger who appeared without warning at his front door, particularly when there was already another man in prison for the killings. After Ciolino got this confession and Porter was freed, Simon went to prison. A few years later, Simon claimed his confession was coerced, that he had been threatened by Ciolino the morning Ciolino came to his house.

This is what Simon said happened:

In the winter of 1999, David Protess and his students arrived at Simon's apartment in Milwaukee. Simon had moved to Milwaukee shortly after the murders. He had a steady job and was living with a girlfriend. The students arrived at his apartment already convinced Simon was the offender and that Porter was innocent. They had discovered what they claimed were anomalies in the case. They pointed out, for example, that witnesses stated Porter had fired from his left hand but was right-handed. The mother of Marilyn Green also mentioned that the last time she saw her daughter, she was with Simon and his wife, Inez, and she had told detectives this fact. The students also went back to the pool and "re-created" the murder, concluding that some of the witnesses could not have seen what they said they did. At Simon's apartment, they brought up the double homicide to Simon. Simon told the students he and his then-wife, Inez Jackson, had walked with Jerry Hillard and Marilyn Green up to the entrance of the park that night but had seen unsavory characters (guys like Porter, perhaps?), so they decided to leave, stopping for ice cream before they went home. The park was crowded that evening because of the Bud Billiken Parade.

When the students visiting Simon at his Milwaukee home then told Simon they believed he was guilty of the murders, he became enraged and kicked them out. Then a few days later, Simon answered his door again, early on the morning of February 3, 1999. Simon was strung out from a coke binge with his girlfriend the night before. His girlfriend had already left for work. Standing in his doorway was Paul Ciolino. The private investigator arrived without Protess or any students, accompanied only by an assistant. It was 6:30 in the morning, sixteen years after the murder. Simon didn't have his shirt on. Simon claimed Ciolino and his partner barged into the apartment. He also said Ciolino was armed and was brandishing his weapon, claiming he was a "police investigator." Ciolino and his partner made an incredible announcement to Simon: Ciolino said he had statements from witnesses declaring that Simon was guilty of the 1982 murders for which Porter had been convicted. Ciolino pulled out two documents, showing affidavits from Simon's ex-wife, Inez Jackson, and her nephew, Walter Jackson, who was in prison for his own murder conviction. Both Inez and Walter Jackson claimed in these affidavits that Simon was the killer. Inez claimed she was with Simon the night of the murders and had witnessed Simon kill the couple over a drug debt. Walter Jackson claimed Simon had admitted to the murders during conversations together.

Simon entered a fantastical world. Four detectives had pored through the case, prosecutors had found nothing naming Simon as the offender, and a jury had reviewed the evidence and declared Porter guilty. The Illinois Supreme Court had reviewed the case. As many as six witnesses had fingered Porter as the offender or put him at the scene. No one, not one witness in the park, ever mentioned Alstory Simon's name. Nor did any witness ever step forward to detectives and place Simon at the scene of the crime, let alone in the park where the couple had been murdered. That Ciolino should have such evidence sixteen years after the murders must have been mind-boggling to Simon, especially the claims of his ex-wife, Inez Jackson. Simon said he told Ciolino and his partner to get out, but Ciolino refused. The armed Ciolino, Simon claimed, warned Simon he had better cooperate. Accidents happen in people's apartments all the time, Simon claimed Ciolino said. Ciolino dropped another bomb. He told Simon the police were on their way to his apartment at that very moment to arrest him. That wasn't all. Ciolino told Simon he was wanted in connection with another murder in the Milwaukee area, three murders now hanging over his head. Ciolino warned Simon about the death penalty. Just a little while earlier, Simon was walking around in his apartment with his shirt off, recovering from a night of partying. Now he was being told that he could be executed for a double homicide and another murder.

Ciolino pulled out a videotape, which he placed in Simon's VCR. On this tape was an African American man, unknown to Simon, who claimed he was in the park the night of the murders and had witnessed

Simon shoot the couple. Simon's world was now imploding. Now another witness, on tape, was claiming Simon had killed the couple. As Ciolino and Simon continued to talk, a news story came on the television in Simon's apartment. On the show Simon saw his ex-wife, Inez, declaring to the reporter that she was with Simon the night of the murders and that Simon had murdered Marilyn Green and Jerry Hillard over a drug debt. Her statement was being broadcast all over the country. Accusations were pouring in on him. His ex-wife was fingering him as the killer on the news. Walter Jackson had also fingered Simon as the murderer. Then there was the man on the tape claiming Simon was the shooter. Simon nevertheless tried to shake it off. He told Ciolino that he was crazy, that he had never killed anyone, but by now he was panic-stricken. The death penalty hung over his head.

Simon claimed that Ciolino said he had a plan. He told Simon that if Simon would confess to the murders (Ciolino just happened to have a video camera with him), Ciolino could promise that Simon would not get the death penalty. In fact, said Ciolino, the private investigator could guarantee with his connections to Northwestern's Innocence Project that Simon would only do a few years in prison and that afterward they would all become rich from the movie and book deals they would sign. All Simon had to do was confess to the crimes in court and apologize to the victims. Simon would simply claim the killings were in self-defense. Overwhelmed, Simon rallied. One more time Simon denied committing the crimes. He said he wanted to talk to a lawyer. No problem, Ciolino told him. Then Ciolino assured Simon that he could get him an excellent lawyer, someone who was a friend of Ciolino. The private investigator called Chicago lawyer Jack Rimland, who shared office space with Ciolino. Rimland, said Simon, had jumped in his car and was making his way up to Milwaukee. Overwhelmed by Ciolino's claims and coercion, Simon said he gave in. Ciolino and Simon went about making the taped confession, Ciolino writing what Simon would say beforehand. Ciolino worked it out so that Simon would claim self-defense in the shootings, would argue that the male victim, Hillard, had charged at Simon and Simon shot. They would say it was over a drug debt. Simon would claim he accidentally shot the female victim Marilyn Green (three times?).

Simon would also confess that he was with his ex-wife, Inez Jackson, in order to corroborate her claims that she witnessed the shooting. The story concocted by Ciolino had to some degree match the real actions of Alstory and his then-wife, Inez, on the night of the murders. In truth, that night the couple had gone out for ice cream. So they both stuck with that story. Inez had claimed in her affidavit that after Simon shot the couple to death in the bleachers, without her having any idea that he was going to kill them, the two then went out for some ice cream. Two people with no previous murders on their record gunned down a couple in a crowded park, a couple they had been friends with, and then walked to a nearby ice cream parlor.

I sit back in my chair at home, sip some coffee. My back is starting to hurt more where the staples are holding my skin together. I pull myself up on the walker, shuffle into the kitchen where the tray holding all my pills sits. I look for the pain pills, norco-something. They are white and oval, hard to confuse them with the pills for inflammation, antibiotics, stool softeners. For a moment I think about not taking the pill. It'll be tough coming off them; I've been on some kind of painkillers for months now, including the shots they gave me in the hospital every two hours. But the pain is still there. Not today, I figure, and I pop the pill, shuffle back to my desk. I sit back and turn over Simon's account of his confession. I think about the visit itself, why Ciolino even went to the apartment to begin with. It's a strange connection between Ciolino and Protess. Why would a private investigator go and get the statement, and not Protess and his students? The entire enterprise to free Porter was part of a journalism class at Northwestern. Why wouldn't the students and teachers at least go along with Ciolino? After all, they had been there just a few days earlier.

Ciolino boasted in the press and on his company website that he "bull-rushed" people in his investigations, including the confession he obtained from Simon. Ciolino said that Simon "never had a chance." What made the relationship between Ciolino and the Innocence Project even stranger was Ciolino's background. One would think that Protess, a professor at Northwestern, would conduct investigations of the highest caliber, without any stain, especially when his investigations often claimed unsavory tactics by the police and dubious events in the backgrounds of cops. All anyone had to say, for example, after the wrongful conviction movement took shape was that a cop had worked in Area 2 under Jon Burge and his cases were automatically suspect.

Why, then, would Protess allow a private investigator who boasted of "bull-rushing" targets to be a part of his investigations? Ciolino was once accused of knocking and pounding on the door of a person who was involved in a dispute with his client. An affidavit alleged that Ciolino threatened to "put a bullet" in the man's head. This is the same accusation Simon was making, that Ciolino barged into his apartment and threatened violence against Simon if he didn't cooperate. Ciolino was also once placed on probation by the state for "acting as a private detective without a license." I try to imagine the incident as Simon claimed it happened. Did Ciolino really walk into Simon's apartment with his gun drawn? Why wasn't Protess with Ciolino? It was almost as if Protess was shielding himself, the school, and his students, as if Ciolino was the guy who did the dirty work.

So, too, with the claim that Ciolino asserted he was a "police investigator." Impersonating a police officer is a felony. Any evidence rooted in such an alleged ruse should not be allowed into a courtroom. The case should immediately stop and be investigated. Ciolino's claim of being a cop explains to some degree why Simon allowed Ciolino to enter and remain in the apartment to begin with. Otherwise, there is a good chance Simon would simply have told Ciolino to go away. Simon lived in some rough neighborhoods, where you just don't let anyone into your dwelling. People raised in the projects know about probable cause and legal searches. They have a common understanding of the rights police have to enter someone's home.

"During this whole time, Ciolino kept telling me that they had all the evidence they needed to convict me, that I was going to go down for these murders and end up on death row, and there was nothing I could do about it," Simon said in a statement.

Why didn't Ciolino and Protess simply bring their collection of affidavits and paperwork to authorities and seek a warrant for Simon's arrest? Why didn't they contact the prosecutor in Chicago and let him deal with it? Simon said that at one point he went to call 911, but Ciolino's partner blocked him from using the phone. Any confession arising from such coercion would be grounds to reject the confession. Cops who did this would face sanctions, lawsuits, and perhaps criminal charges. Barging into someone's dwelling, armed, with the intent of getting them to make a statement, those would be the elements of coercion. They would be, if proven, crimes. Ciolino's claim of bull-rushing a statement began to take vivid shape. I wondered why he brought a camera to record the statement. How could he be so certain he was going to get a confession that he brought the equipment? Who would be willing to give a recorded confession to a double murder sixteen years after the crime to a complete stranger when someone else was already convicted of it? Who would give this confession early in the morning to this stranger unless there was some powerful incentive?

The nature of Ciolino's bull-rushing became even more vivid in the videotape Ciolino brought to the apartment, the one that portrayed a man claiming he had witnessed Simon commit the murders. Eventually, the gun-toting private investigator stated he made the tape as a ruse. He had hired an actor to claim he was a witness to the murders in 1982. Ciolino admitted that he knew the actor had witnessed nothing about any crime. It was just a tactic to put more pressure on Simon, he said. This tape played a powerful role in terrifying Simon into confessing, Ciolino hanging the possibility of a death sentence over Simon. This fake tape was a key reason why Simon gave the confession.

Then there was the allegation by Simon that Ciolino discussed what kind of sentence he could get for Simon. Simon claimed that Ciolino promised he could keep Simon off death row if Simon confessed, could get him only a few years in prison. If a cop began bartering sentences, which he has no control over, as a way to garner a confession from a suspect, the case would be tossed out of court. He would face sanctions and lawsuits, perhaps even be fired or face criminal charges.

Then there are the accusations by Simon that Ciolino promised Simon wealth from movie and book deals. It wasn't the first time a witness or an inmate would claim Ciolino or Protess or other wrongful conviction advocates had encouraged them to change a statement with the promise of wealth and celebrity. These accusations arose from independent sources in many cases, years apart, including several key figures in the Porter case. One wonders what would happen to the police in a case when key players, unrelated to one another, started announcing that they had been offered money, in the form of book and movie deals, by detectives for their statements. The wrongful conviction advocates would assail such a case, would demand that the officers be investigated, fired, then charged. They would demand that the cases be dismissed. Then they would begin reviewing every single case the officers were involved in, seeking evidence of similar malfeasance.

Yet going back all the way to the beginning of Protess's career of freeing inmates, there were allegations that he offered money through movie and book deals in exchange for changed testimony. A witness in one of Protess's most high-profile exonerations claimed Protess tried repeatedly to get the man to change his statement. In addition to profit, the witness said Protess even offered sex with one of his students. The man told prosecutors that Protess became irate when he didn't cooperate with Protess's plans. The man, who had no apparent motives to make such claims against Protess, never backed down from these claims.

All these accusations by Simon paint a disturbing picture of his so-called confession, of why a man would come forward almost two decades after the fact and confess to a double homicide in a manner of hours to a stranger who arrived at his apartment. Here is a longer statement by Simon submitted by his lawyers in an attempt to have his case reviewed:

> After showing me the videotape and the affidavits, Ciolino said I want you to see something, and they tuned the TV to a station that was doing a story about the murders. The TV story presented the same professor who had previously come to my house with the girls, saying Anthony Porter was innocent, and the story also included a videotape of Inez saying that she saw me shoot the victims. Ciolino also showed me a signed statement where Inez said she saw me shoot Jerry Hillard and Marilyn Green.
>
> After seeing this story on TV, I was no longer just angry. I was scared to death. For the first time I believed that I was actually going to be charged with committing the murders. One of the men then turned the TV off and Ciolino said that he was going to level with me. He said that the men were not "police" investigators, but actually, were "private" investigators who worked for the professor who they had just shown me on television. He said they had all the evidence they needed to put me on death row, and that the Chicago police were on their way to arrest me right then. He said that once the police get to my house there would be nothing more he could do for me, and this was my one and only chance to help myself by giving a statement saying that I shot the two victims in self-defense.
>
> Ciolino said that he and the professor wanted to free Anthony Porter, that when he got out, millions of dollars were going to be made on movies and book deals, that I would be entitled to a lot of the money, and that they were not concerned with hurting me. He convinced me that he was actually trying to help me by giving me a way out before the police got to my house to arrest me. He said that if I gave a statement saying I did the crimes in self-defense, that he would get me a free lawyer, that the professor could make it so that I only had to serve a short time in prison, and that when I got out, I'd be taken care of financially, and would not have to work again. I told Ciolino that this was all crazy, that I did not kill anyone,

and that I could not believe they were doing this. At one point, Ciolino put his hand on his gun and said that we could do this the easy way, or we could do it the hard way, but either way, I was going to give a statement. I even attempted to get to the phone to call the Milwaukee police, at which time the other investigator, who was also armed, stood in front of the phone and blocked me from getting to it. Ciolino told me that people have accidents in their homes all the time, and that we could even have an accident right now.

By this time, I was convinced that if I did not say I shot the two victims in self-defense, that they had enough evidence to convict me of murder and that I would end up on death row. Ciolino asked me if I could read, and when I said that I could, he told me to read what was in the papers he had. He wrote on a pad of paper and said that we would practice my statement until I memorized it well enough to say on videotape. I then read the affidavits Ciolino gave me, and he told me to just say that I only shot Jerry because I thought he was going for a weapon, and that Marilyn getting shot was just an accident because she just got in the way. Ciolino emphasized to me that it was important for me to say when I shot them that I was in fear for my life and that shooting Marilyn was just an accident. He said that he would make sure that it was a self-defense case.

After we practiced the statement several times, Ciolino had me say the statement on the videotape. I had the papers he showed me next to me when I was giving the statement so I could remind myself of things if I forgot what he wanted me to say. At some point, Ciolino made a phone call and told me that attorney Jack Rimland would be representing me. He assured me that, just as he was doing with Anthony Porter, Professor Protess would be able to pull the strings necessary to have me released from prison after a short time.

Yet of all these accusations made by Simon, it is the ones that Ciolino openly admitted to that are the most disturbing. This was the moment Simon stated he wanted to see a lawyer and Ciolino told Simon he would get one. In my apartment, I lean forward, place the documents that describe this part of Simon's confession in front of me. I've read them a thousand times. It was an elemental, mendacious violation of due process. Not only did Ciolino offer a lawyer, free of charge, so long as Simon confessed, but, Simon alleged, Ciolino called his lawyer/friend Jack Rimland that very day and told him to drive up to Milwaukee. Here was an attorney who was supposed to represent Simon, working with the very guy who wanted to get Simon put in prison for a double homicide. Any lawyer who was representing his client fairly would shout into the phone, "Get Ciolino the fuck out of that apartment right now. Call the police if you have to. He has no fucking right to be there, and don't say a word about any murders. Keep your mouth shut." It's called the Fifth Amendment, the right not to incriminate oneself. But Rimland did the opposite. Rimland encouraged Simon to confess to the crimes. It was an egregious abuse of civil liberties. Rather than represent his client, rather than utilize the mountain of evidence that Porter was the killer and not Simon, particularly all the eyewitnesses, Rimland worked with Ciolino to get Simon behind bars and to set Porter free.

Simon claimed Rimland traveled to Milwaukee that very day and furthered Ciolino's confession plans, again working pro bono. When, I wonder, did a Chicago lawyer ever drive to Milwaukee and represent a client for free? How was it that Rimland just happened to be available that day to drive up to Milwaukee in the morning? Was this whole thing planned out between the two men beforehand? Ciolino just happened to have camera equipment with him, just happened to have affidavits, a fake witness statement recorded on a VCR tape. Ciolino just happened to go to Simon's apartment when the news broadcast Inez Jackson's statement accusing Simon of being the murderer. Now Ciolino just happens to have a lawyer available for Simon.

On this morning, Simon claimed the plan was hatched among the three men to have Simon plead guilty to the murders. Simon would claim self-defense, and both Ciolino and Rimland promised him he would only get a few years in prison. They told Simon with the money they would make off the movie and book deals, Simon would never have to work again. One wonders what the wrongful conviction advocates would do if they uncovered allegations that a cop promised to provide a lawyer to a suspect in a murder case, told the suspect they could guarantee a short sentence, told the suspect that he would become wealthy if he went along with the plan. But for the lawyer to join in on the plan and encourage his new "client" that he would guarantee a short sentence if he confessed? It's difficult to wrap one's mind around it.

Sure enough, the following day, Simon's new lawyer stated to the media that his client could get the death penalty if convicted. The death penalty? One day after Rimland becomes Simon's attorney and Rimland is talking about the death penalty? Is this what Rimland, Protess, and Ciolino would call legal representation? There were at least six eyewitnesses who put

Porter at the scene of the murders. Each one of those witnesses undermined the argument that Simon was the offender. In the twenty-four hours since Rimland became Simon's attorney, how could Rimland have looked at the evidence? How could he have interviewed any of the witnesses, who would have told them they saw Porter at the murder scene? The attorney could not have examined the evidence that showed Porter was indeed in the park the night of the shootings, even though Porter's entire defense was that he was somewhere else. Rimland ignored the testimony of the witnesses at the grand jury, who continued to finger Porter as the killer. He ignored the blatant rejection of the arguments by Protess and his students by the grand jury that Porter was innocent. He didn't challenge the so-called confession his client gave to Ciolino, a confession that would certainly be shot down in court. He didn't point out the dirty tactics alleged by Simon against Ciolino, the claim that Ciolino barged into the apartment, that Ciolino was armed, that Ciolino was told to get out repeatedly, that Ciolino claimed he was a police investigator, that Ciolino could guarantee Simon a short sentence, that his client was under the influence of drugs when he made the statement. Instead, Rimland got in front of the media and acknowledged that his client was facing the death penalty. He advised his client that pleading guilty and thirty-seven years in prison for the murders was a good deal, a deal that gave Porter his freedom and made Protess and his students heroes once again. It is the duty of a lawyer to represent his client to the best of his ability, to take whatever evidence exists and fight for the innocence of his client. But Rimland did none of this. Simon described how Rimland conspired with the very people who were trying to frame his client for the murders.

I have to stand up for a few minutes and stretch my back. I can only read sections of Simon's confession before stopping. In the decade I have been a cop, after all the accounts of coercion and torture alleged against the cops, I have never seen a guy like Alstory Simon so completely set up. It makes my blood rise, but I have to push on, knowing it gets much worse. A few months before Simon was to be sentenced for the murders, Rimland headed a meeting of an organization called Illinois Attorneys for Criminal Justice. There he gave an award to Protess, Ciolino, and several students for their work on the Porter case. "David Protess and his students utilized their talents as investigative journalists and successfully uncovered crucial evidence resulting in the freeing of Anthony Porter," Rimland announced at the meeting, the same lawyer passing out an award to the very people who were trying to pin a double murder on his client, praising them for their work against his client.

I sit back, look out my window. Simon said he went along with the plan. He confessed to Ciolino. Simon turned himself in at a Chicago Police District, Rimland there representing him. Assured by Rimland and Ciolino that he would receive a short sentence, Simon said he kept his mouth shut about the plan. The six months between the time Simon turned himself in and then confessed were a nightmare. Over and over Simon changed his mind. He thought about pleading not guilty, but every time he did so, Rimland reminded him that if Simon didn't take the deal, he could get indicted for another murder in Milwaukee and then Simon could get the death penalty. Simon said Rimland never told him about the grand jury and how the testimony in that case destroyed the claims by the Northwestern investigators, solid evidence that could have exonerated Simon. Simon said he got into several shouting matches with Rimland about the deal. At one point, Simon decided he should hire another attorney. But in the end, Simon stuck with the plan, terrified he would get charged with another murder in Milwaukee he knew nothing about and get the death sentence. He confessed to the murders in open court, his lawyer taking a deal for thirty-seven years in exchange for the confession. Simon's lawyer, Rimland, did not call any of the original witnesses to testify that it was Porter who killed the victims, not Simon. He did not call any of the detectives who were still certain Porter was the offender. Rimland did not bring up the grand jury hearing that ridiculed the case by Protess and his students. A few months after Simon was sentenced, Rimland sent Simon a letter in prison saying he no longer represented him. And that was supposedly the end of that.

Outside it's getting cloudy. There will be some rain soon. The winter has been too warm. That means walking on some slippery surfaces if I go out for something to eat. Certainly I will have a panic attack tonight. I know it. I will awake long before dawn and begin sweating, my heart racing. I will find myself thinking about death and will end up in this same living room, turning on the TV to hear a living voice. There's this image in the back of my mind that I will never be free from the feeling of waking up in a room I believe is the morgue, trapped with all these dead bodies. It's perhaps wiser to set aside the story of Simon's confession, to set aside the image of the real murderer, Anthony Porter, now roaming the streets, and Simon stuck in a prison cell, but I leave it alone.

Several years after Simon confessed and was sentenced, the central witnesses who signed affidavits against him—his ex-wife, Inez Jackson, and her nephew, Walter Jackson—admitted the affidavits were all lies. They came forward and signed statements with Simon's new lawyers, admitting the whole thing was a part of a jailhouse scheme. Both Inez and Walter said they were told by Protess that he would deliver on certain promises, but Protess never did. Inez said Protess promised her money from movie and book deals. She said Protess promised he would get Walter Jackson out of prison early and he would also get Inez's son out of prison. Walter Jackson also said Protess failed to get him out of prison. Inez, wracked with illnesses from a life of doing drugs and acquiring AIDS, also stepped forward. New attorneys for Simon traveled to Inez's apartment in Milwaukee and taped her confession right before her own death that she had lied about Simon being the killer. Inez said she couldn't live with the fact of dying without telling the truth about the case. Three people in the case now officially stated that Protess and Ciolino offered wealth through movie and book deals if they would change their testimony, Inez Jackson, Walter Jackson, and Alstory Simon. The case against Simon had completely blown up, but he was still in prison.

I try to sit upright in my chair, but I can't get much energy going. I am tired from concentrating, too drugged up. I think about what happened to the detectives in the Porter case, all the accusations made against them, the accusations of torture, of a frame-up. I think about Simon's confession. It was one kind of crime for the police to smack a guy around in custody because they believed he murdered their coworkers. It was quite another to set up an innocent man and put him in prison for your own wealth and celebrity, and, in doing so, releasing a guy like Porter onto the street.

I'm tired from reading the documents again. I want to sleep, but I can't face the panic attacks to come.

13. IN CUSTODY

Prison looms. At any moment I feel as if I will be taken into some kind of custody. The feeling that I am criminal, illegitimate, has been with me a long time, but now it moves to the forefront, and I'm glad for it. Perhaps there will be some kind of indictment, then a trial. Perhaps I will be on TV, handcuffed, scurried into a bond hearing, which will be denied. I can see myself locked up in a cell for most of the day, my meals arriving by a tray, three times daily. There will be a toilet, a bed, a sink, and a desk. For some reason, in this incarceration I imagine the authorities will allow me a file cabinet, office supplies, and a phone. Outside the prison I will get reports about other wrongful conviction cases.

My crime is, for the most part, my imagination, what it has become. I let it roam throughout the murder cases of 1982, especially the Ealy case. I have this feeling that I live in a story half-told. I recall telling the story of the Ealy murders to coworkers in the parking lot of my district, then moving into the Wilson murders and then Porter. These cops were held spellbound by the account of how Ealy got off, how Porter got himself released from death row and was out walking the streets. Those of us who meet regularly at the diner, we started to have this feeling that these stories would catch on, would stir imaginations as ours have been. We're planning a documentary with Peter, but this is on hold until my back recovers, until I get straight again. But even with these plans, I feel some looming penitentiary.

I reach over for my cane, push down on it with one hand to raise myself up. There are some things I need to do before I'm locked up. It means breaking some more rules. *In for a dime, in for a dollar*, I think. The city policy is that no officer on leave for medical problems, for what is called an Injury on Duty, can travel beyond the city limits. There are too many cops, they said, who use medical leave to take unofficial vacations. Inspectors could be sent to your house to check on you. Sometimes they even filmed you. *Well, so what*, I think. I have to make this trip. I need to get closer to the works of James Ealy. There's a little town called Trevor, Wisconsin, right across the state line from Illinois, about an hour's drive. I have to go there. Unless I get in a car accident or some trouble kicks off when I get there, the city will never know. It will be my first venture out in months, since my back went south and I had the fusion surgery.

From 1999 until 2006, I do not know what James Ealy had been up to. There are no arrests on his rap sheet. I have no idea how he ended up in the northern suburbs of Chicago, in a place called Lake Villa. He lived in an apartment. I need to go to Trevor, Wisconsin, because a woman had lived there up until the she was murdered by James Ealy in 2006. Her name was Mary Hutchinson. She was strangled to death by Ealy at her place of work, a Burger King restaurant. She was thirty-five years old, married, with a daughter. I had worked in the service industry long enough to know what a brutal job it is to run a fast-food joint. Mary put in long hours, often seven days a week. Though she had been with the company for several years, she had only worked at the current restaurant, the one where she was killed, for a short time. She had moved to this restaurant because she had been robbed at another outlet, pistol whipped in the course of the robbery. I know how tough the job must have been, busy all the time, workers not showing up or quitting without notice. There is accounting, ordering, hiring, firing, inventorying, problem solving, incredible rushes of patrons arriving without notice, machines breaking down, smart-ass punk kids stoned out of their minds causing disturbances, treating you like a servant. And then you get pistol whipped during a robbery.

Yet despite the dangers and hard labor of her job, Mary was very well liked by her employees and by the people in the community. Many kids who had worked for her attended her funeral or called to give their condolences. There was an elderly woman who Mary hired, in her eighties. She wiped down tables, collected trays. Mary gave her a ride home every few weeks and stayed to help the woman clean her apartment, this after working sometimes seven days a week herself. The newspaper accounts described how pleasant Mary was, how she introduced family members to everyone at the restaurant. Mary's father also came by one day to collect some ice for a picnic. James Ealy, who worked at the restaurant, carried out the ice to the car for him, the father having no idea that this man helping him would soon murder his daughter. The fact that the company hired Ealy without checking his background became an issue in a civil case, when Mary's husband sued the company, alleging that they did not conduct a sufficient background check. All the time Ealy worked there, Mary had no idea what Ealy had done in his life, that he had raped a woman on a stairwell, then, six months later, strangled a family of four to death, one of them a three-year-old boy he raped before killing. She didn't know he was tried and convicted and that Ealy would claim he was tortured by detectives, an almost standard defense in Ealy's time. She didn't know he was thrown back into society on a legal technicality, the detectives taking the blame. Nor did she know that Ealy then tried to kill a prostitute after he got out and then served another five years. She never knew all the time Ealy was working at the restaurant what kind of predator he was.

From the newspaper articles I had collected, I learned Mary Hutchinson had some relatives in Trevor. Now, after the years of researching and writing about the murder, I want to make contact with them, to see the family of a victim. But I don't have any addresses, nothing to go on. On my computer, I find a person with the same last name in the town, and write it down. That's all I have, except that some of the articles in the paper said Mary had lived in a trailer park.

As I get ready to make the trip to Wisconsin, my mind goes over the killing. Mary heard the phone ring early one morning at the restaurant when she was alone. She had arrived in the morning to do inventory. She no longer was willing to stay late at night, after being robbed at another restaurant. This call was brief. Then there was another call that lasted thirty seconds.

Ealy was driving by the restaurant that morning on his way home from work. He had worked at the Burger King with Mary, long enough that Mary considered him a friend, but Ealy had quit and found a job at another restaurant, working the midnight shift. I see him turning a corner on his way home and spotting Mary Hutchinson's car in the parking lot. That's when it dawned on him to call the restaurant to make sure Mary was there. No doubt the familiar rush of adrenaline hit Ealy, along with another witless plan. All of his crimes were so clumsy, so poorly executed. I believe it was because the lust of the crime overpowered his planning. Some would argue Ealy wasn't highly intelligent, but they said the same about Porter. Yet Porter fooled the entire city about the murders he had committed and had gotten himself exonerated. Ealy had escaped a quadruple murder conviction. These two killers weren't idiots. They were intensely calculating. No, in my mind, it was Ealy's sexual lust for murder that always clouded his judgment, along with the fact that he was broke, deeply in debt, and needed money. But, really, did he think he would get away with the robbery of his former boss? Didn't he know he would have to kill her? I believe that when the desire to kill rose up in him, there was no stopping it. He knew Mary was alone in the restaurant, knew also there was money. But I don't think it was the money that guided him. No, Ealy was not a simple thief or burglar. He was a complex monster. The other murders and rapes were proof of that. "I don't know why there is so much evil in me," the police said Ealy confessed to them. So as he approached the Burger King, he called Mary, checking to make sure she was alone, and he must have been satisfied by what he heard.

Like the Parker strangulations, no one will likely know exactly how Ealy killed Mary, how he got in the back door. Did she let him in, or was the door open? Did he still have a key from when he worked there? Mary was wearing a bow tie, part of her uniform, no doubt. She seemed like the kind of person who was always prepared for work, always wore fresh uniforms, probably always had one hanging clean in her bathroom or closet. No one will ever know what words were exchanged, if Ealy went right to work. I can imagine him talking to Mary, perhaps letting her know what was about to happen. Stab marks in Mary's back indicated to investigators that Ealy had to force her to open the safe. Perhaps she wouldn't do it at first and tried to talk him out of it. Maybe she begged. Maybe she knew that once she opened the safe he would kill her because she could identify him. Ealy stabbed her repeatedly with the screwdriver to get her to open the safe. How painful that must have been, how horrible the sounds must have been. Mary had been working alongside Ealy for months, had even told him she considered him her protector. After the safe was open, Ealy took the bow tie off her and wrapped it around her neck, pulling it tighter, just as he had used artifacts in the Parker apartment to strangle the Parkers, belts from coats, panty hose. Oh, how long had it been? The woman on the stairwell, the four Parkers, the prostitute who got away, and now Mary. I imagine Ealy's face was up against hers, that menacing glare in his eyes. Perhaps he whispered curses or even gibberish as the life receded in her, a woman who was merely working a tough job to support her family. Probably all of Ealy's victims died too quickly in his mind. I imagine he wished they could gasp and struggle longer, to prolong the killing. Ealy went into the safe and grabbed the money, some $1,700, and took off. To think they once had him locked up on the rape when he was seventeen and they let him out. Then they thought they had him on the quadruple murder and they let him out of that one too. Then he got out after the assault on the prostitute. Each crime the police did their job, did their utmost to put Ealy away.

The police went back to work again. The police task force formed to solve the murder set up roadblocks several days later, searching for possible witnesses. They drained a pond next to the restaurant looking for evidence. They interviewed seventy current and former workers. That's how they got Ealy. They interviewed him, asked him his phone number, wrote it down. Then when the phone call records that morning came back, they matched Ealy's. They got a warrant and found the exact number of bills and coins hidden in his bedroom. Ealy thought that when he called Mary and blocked the caller ID on his cell phone he wouldn't be caught, but that was easy enough for the detectives to get around. Ealy confessed, then later denied it. His lawyer argued that the police unlawfully arrested Ealy when they went to his home and confronted him, obtained evidence there. He was still awaiting trial for the murder as I prepare to go up to Trevor, six years after the murder.

I limp out of my building with my cane and head to my car. Inside it, while the engine idles, I plug the address into my GPS, a tool I covet, for it tells specifically how to get somewhere. This is especially valuable when I leave the city. There seems to be no coherent layout in the suburbs; the roads wind in different directions. You often move from one town to another without even knowing. Since I have gotten out of the hospital, the feeling of being lost unnerves me, initiates the first shades of anxiety that might lead to a panic attack. The GPS will guide me through all the interstates and exits, particularly those around O'Hare Airport, where planes are flying right over you as they land and take off. Because I live on the edge of Lake Michigan, it takes a few minutes for the GPS satellites to catch. I sit with one leg out of my door, waiting. Three months ago I couldn't sit in a car, so I'm making progress. Suddenly the woman's voice on the GPS speaks.

"Recalculating," she says confidently, assertively.

"Go one hundred and fifty feet. Then turn right."

I admire her confidence, but there's a coldness about her, as if she's waiting to pounce on any fuck-up. And she does. When I take the wrong turn or the wrong ramp, she waits a few seconds as if she's calming her temper.

"Recalculating," she says, with an undertone of disgust. "Can't you get anything right?" is what she wants to say.

Sometimes I want to remind the GPS lady that I have roamed the city streets for years, that I know them as well as she does. I want to remind her I only need her for the suburbs, but she isn't the kind of woman you can say that to. She's right, though. I do need guidance. One thing the murders of 1982 reveal is that one never really knows where he or she stands in the city, one never knows anything for certain. Look at Burge, look at all the detectives in the cases. Look at Protess and his students. But that isn't entirely true. There is one thing that's certain every year that I have lived in the city: James Ealy will kill again. Murder is the one certain act of his life. The trial judge, the prosecutors, and the detectives all knew. The judge railed about the fact that Ealy would strike again after the appeals court tossed Ealy's conviction.

"Turn right," the navigator woman says, a half block away from my house.

"I'm turning right. I know how to get to the expressway from here," I argue.

"Proceed point five miles. Then turn left," she answers.

"You think I don't know that? You think I don't know to turn left less than a half mile from my house? Man, you really burn me. You know that? You really piss me off sometimes," I say.

I turn left where she said.

I'm a good half hour past the airport. This is the longest I've sat in a car since before the surgery. I can feel my back stiffening up. Ever since my panic attacks started, I've had problems in enclosed spaces. The windows on my car are broken and can't be opened. I feel myself getting a little anxious. *Perhaps I should turn around and head home*, I think. What if I have an attack on the road, away from the city? What if someone trying to help me calls the authorities? What if the police department finds out I'm heading to Wisconsin? In the beginning of a panic attack, one's mind always begins racing. I shake my head. *To hell with it*, I think, *I'll just keep going.* But now I want badly to get past the suburbs and the billboards, out into the country, where it's quiet.

After Ealy was arrested for strangling Mary, police ran his rap sheet and saw the quadruple homicides. A brief media storm followed the announcement, residents of the community wondering how a man could get away with murdering four people. The prosecutor in the county where Ealy strangled Mary condemned the ruling. It was one of the first indications that the decision by the appeals court was as much geographical as it was legal. Such interpretations of the law were common in Chicago, but foreign and repugnant outside the city. It was this firestorm from the media that first called my attention to the case. I read the accounts of the Parker murders and could not see the police misconduct, could not see what the police had done wrong in their investigation. That's what had drawn me into the murders. I found the appeals court decision that had let Ealy go, printed it, and read it over and over. I could not see what the detectives did wrong, nor could I clearly understand what the appeals court lawyers were arguing. Then I ran into the newspaper stories about the Ealy case. Ealy's murder of Mary Hutchinson faded in the press after a short time. Then, it was largely forgotten. All that remained was the criminal trial.

The GPS lady guides me into Trevor. She takes me through a bunch of side streets until suddenly a large lake is before me. It has been a warm winter so there's only a little ice in the middle. She tells me to take a few more turns and then says we have arrived at our destination, a nice medium-size home on the shore of the lake. I pull into the driveway, place my cane on the ground, and push myself up, my back so stiff I have to wait a minute. I begin walking toward the back door of the house, which is open. Only the screen door is closed. There's music coming from inside and a big sign that says Beware of Dog. This could be Mary's family. Will they be angry at me, tell me to get out? Will they call the police? Will the dog attack me? I knock. The dog barks. He sounds big and I can hear him running toward the screen door that separates us. I place my foot on it so he can't push through and attack. *Christ*, I think, *am I going to be attacked by a dog in Wisconsin?* But he's a big golden retriever. He runs only to the door and begins wagging his tail and sniffing at me. I knock again.

A kid, about high school age, comes to the door. He tells me he remembers the murder but he's not related to Mary Hutchinson. As he speaks, my spirits sink. The entire trip seems like a bust. I feel like a fool, wandering around this little town I know nothing about. I thank the kid and head back to my car. The lady on the GPS is silent now because we have reached our destination. I'm on my own again. I miss her. It's quiet in my car. The door is open and I can hear the wind. A part of me wants to leave and continue driving west, as far away from the city as possible, to get away forever. All of my siblings have headed west and remain there. Only I came back. They were wise; I was the fool. But it wouldn't be practical for me to just leave. I need a job, a career, and I have one. Where would I go, anyway, especially with a bad back? From the driveway I can see the road that winds to the front of the house and along the lake. It's quiet and I figure I may as well head down there. Perhaps there will be a public bathroom, because I have to use one before heading back to the city. My back is starting to hurt again. Perhaps I will need a pain pill soon. I idle along the lake. There are homes all around it, but no one's out. Then around a corner there's a public boat launch with a Porta-John.

I park next to it and clamber out of the car again, really having to go now, latching the door after I stand inside. The wind blows through the small opening at the top of the john, so strongly it whistles. I'm forty-eight years old, standing in a Porta-John along a lake I don't even know the name of, searching for family of a murder victim I also don't know. I can hear small waves rolling up on the shore. The sound of pissing is loud because the stream has to fall a long way into a hollow place. I make some circular motions with my piss, trying to find the spot that makes the loudest noise, as if that increase in volume would give my existence more significance. It's a long, fulfilling piss. When I finish, I button up and turn around. I try to pull the latch open, but it won't move. I try jiggling it, then hammering it with my palm. Nothing. Right away the anxiety from the panic attacks starts. It comes rushing on like a wave. I try pushing the door with my body, but that only causes the Porta-John to sway and I know if I hit it any harder it may tip over, all the feces and urine and God knows what else at the bottom washing over me, including my own piss. (How's that for irony?) And I would still be trapped, stuck inside a feces- and urine-filled prison. What's more, I could easily fall with the door against the ground, imprisoning myself for good in the john. *Is this it*, I ask myself, *a Porta-John next to a lake?* My heart racing, I pick up my cane and try to use the rubber end of it to smash the latch open, but there isn't enough room in the small space to raise it high enough. My hand hits the top of the Porta-John, causing a slight cut. Perhaps I would get an infection as well. I pause, trying to get my mind together, but the panicky scenarios came rushing forward. It might be days before anyone walks by and would hear my cries for help. If it gets cold tonight, I could freeze to death.

I see myself frozen and stiff, being discovered by some resident walking their dog. The local police would set up a crime scene, see that the latch was stuck, explain to the papers my absurd death. What was a Chicago cop doing in a Porta-John more than an hour from his home, the journalists would ask. Later they would print the fact that I wasn't even supposed to leave the city. How relieved the wrongful conviction advocates at Northwestern would be, for word of our documentary and my book had already spread there. They knew we were investigating Northwestern and Protess. How relieved they would be that I froze to death in a Porta-John. So would the journalists like *Chicago Tribune* columnist Eric Zorn, with whom I have been arguing about the cases, our antipathy escalating. Just then I pull the door in toward me rather than away and turn the latch easily with the other hand. The door swings open. I fall out of it, panting, sweating. The wind hitting me is a relief. I walk to the edge of the shore to embrace with my eyes the wide, placid landscape of the lake and stand there for a long time. I look around. No one saw me in my panicked condition. Calmed down, I remind myself that Ealy's trial is scheduled to begin soon. I will attend as much as I can, particularly the opening arguments. It will be the first time I will actually see him.

All these years in the city together and we will finally meet.

I reconsider the decision to head home. What kind of investigator am I, leaving the town after one failed attempt at connecting with Hutchinson's family? Why not stick around a bit? I walk back to my car and retrace the roads back to the center of the town, just a few blocks long. On my way back, I see the sign for the trailer park, so I pull in. Slowly I coast down the rows of trailers, all well maintained. These are clearly all working people, like Mary, toiling away at tough jobs but only able to afford a mobile home. Almost every trailer has a name on it somewhere, but I can't find any that say Hutchinson. Certainly some neighbors are watching me, leery of a car that seems to be casing the area. Probably they all look out for one another. Soon the cops will come to check me out. It will be too strange, almost impossible to explain my presence on the property, getting out of my car slowly with a cane, showing them I'm a cop from Chicago and then going over the account of why I'm there. It would be ridiculous. It seems as if it would take me hours to explain to anyone how I arrived in the trailer park. So I pull out, get back on the main road into town.

There on the corner is a pizza place just opening for the day. The sign says they sell slices. I look inside and see a lone woman working. Perhaps this is an opportunity, I figure, so I pull into the parking lot and slowly get out of my car. Clearly I'm the first customer of the day. All the pizzas are still whole. After I order one of the slices, I wait, hoping the woman will strike up a conversation.

"So how are you today?" she asks.

Bingo.

"Well, I guess I'm doing okay. I am a little disappointed, though."

No one would buy this line in Chicago, I think.

"Oh yeah, why is that?"

"Well, I'm a writer from Chicago and I came up here to interview someone, but I can't find them. I thought since it was a pretty small town, I would be able to track them down without an address, but I'm leaving town empty-handed," I tell her.

"Well, who are you looking for?"

Christ, I think. *Could this get any easier?*

"Do you remember that poor woman named Mary Hutchinson who was murdered at the Burger King?"

"Yeah, I do. I used to see her around town a lot. Her husband was around after she died. But I heard he moved to Tennessee with their child. Haven't seen him for a while. They used to live up at the trailer park."

"That's what I heard, but I couldn't find a trailer with their name on it. I'm writing a book about the guy who killer her," I say.

"Yes, I heard he was from Chicago and killed several people there but got away with it."

"Yes, it's true. Four people."

"That's hard to believe."

"Yes, it is."

"How did he end up here?" she asks.

"I really don't know. I'm hoping to find out," I say.

My spirits sink at the thought that the husband and daughter are gone. I will never get a chance to see them.

"You know, the husband, I forget his name, he used to hang out at the bar over there."

She points to the only bar I can see about a block down.

"I'll bet you they could tell you more," she says as she hands me the slice.

It's still early in the day, just about lunchtime if you eat a little early. There are only a few people in the bar, an old man who looks like he spends much of the day there and a group of women in the back. The women act like coworkers who just got off some shift or who are getting together on a day off. They're putting some shots down along with beers. Looks like a long day of drinking ahead of them. I sit at the end of the bar, near the door, hanging my cane on the stool next to me. The old man starts talking to me in a drunken ramble. I can't make out what he's saying. The bartender is older and I figure he's probably the owner as well. I shouldn't be drinking with all the medication I'm on, so I will have to order a drink and milk it. I'm getting tired and will have to head home soon anyway. When the bartender sets down my beer, I place a twenty-dollar bill on the bar and say, "Why don't you let me buy a round for the bar, especially those ladies over there?" The owner nods, happy for the sudden influx of business and quickly goes to get the drinks. The drunken old man looks at me gratefully when he gets another beer. He stands up to walk toward me, but I turn away to the bartender, and he sits down. I don't want to get tied down talking to some local drunk. The women eye me from across the room, hold up their glasses, and say thanks.

The bartender comes back my way after he's served the drinks.

"So where are you from?" he asks.

"Chicago. I'm a strange mix. I'm a writer working on a story about a murder that occurred up this way back in 2006. Perhaps you remember it. Her name was Mary Hutchinson."

"Sure I do. Her husband used to come in here all the time."

"You say used to?"

"Yeah, he moved to Tennessee a while back with the daughter. You said you were a strange mix. What do you mean?"

"Well, I mean in addition to being a writer, I'm also a cop."

I can see him get a little nervous, the thought going through his mind I work for the Liquor Control Commission or something.

"Don't worry. I'm a Chicago cop. I'm just looking into the Hutchinson murder case. It interests me."

He relaxes.

"Yeah, crazy how that guy got away with murdering all those people in Chicago," he says.

"Yeah. It is. I was hoping to talk to the family up here because I saw they lived in the trailer park, but I guess they are gone," I say.

"They are, but her father still lives there," he tells me.

"No shit?"

"Yeah, my bookkeeper knows him real well. You want to talk to her?"

"Yeah, I'd love to," I say. "Let me get one more round for everyone."

"Oh, you don't have to."

"No, no. I'm happy to," I say.

The owner calls out his bookkeeper, who says she will take me to Mary's father, so I walk with her out to my car and drive back to the trailer park. It has gotten colder, but is still sunny. We pull up in front of a trailer. It seems so strange to be standing at the front door of a trailer in a town I had never heard of before. An older man answers, opening the screen door and standing on the porch without a coat on. We shake hands and I quickly explain who I am, that I'm writing a book about Ealy and I'm also a cop. He listens to me patiently, then from a few statements makes it clear he knows Ealy's history, knows about the appeals court, the judges who put Ealy back on the street. He bears in his countenance that hollow fatigue that could be confused for something else, like an illness, but I recognize it instantly. His daughter was murdered in 2006 and it's now 2012 and the trial hasn't even started yet. The defense attorney in his daughter's case is making similar arguments about the police lacking probable cause as the lawyers did in the Parker murders. Why not? It worked before. These motions are no doubt one reason the case is dragging on.

The father tells me he has never missed a hearing. He tells me he and Mary had been very close. He's from the East but had migrated to the Midwest in search of steady work. He had lived in Chicago, then moved out to a rural area where there was factory work. That's what he had done all his life. When he was laid off a job once, Mary got him work at the Burger King for several weeks. He tells me he had visited her at work many times, had even met James Ealy. Mary was very easygoing with the other workers, very friendly. The father mentions several times that they frequently took road trips on his Harley-Davidson together. He also tells me that his relationship with Mary's husband deteriorated after Mary's death. The husband had taken his granddaughter to Tennessee and he rarely hears from either of them anymore. I exchange phone numbers with the father and drive the woman who helped me back to the bar, finish my drink, and head home.

Traffic picks up as I get closer to the city. I will soon need another pain pill. I shouldn't have had the booze, but it seemed necessary, part of the cost of doing business. It led me to Mary's father. In the morning I will get up early and go to the YMCA for the first time in months, walk the treadmill until I am exhausted. I have to strengthen my back so I can return to work. There's a dull feeling where they fused the spine. When I am better, we will begin shooting the documentary. I will also work on my book about Ealy every morning.

Planes from the airport are flying right above me, large trucks on either side of my car. A familiar anxiety comes upon me. The motions Ealy's attorney was asking for in the case make me nervous. Could Ealy beat this case as well? Is he that lucky that he can get away with another killing, one with a mountain of evidence, just like the Parkers'? One of the articles in the paper reported that Ealy made incriminating statements about Mary's murder, said he told the cops to tell Mary's family he was sorry. Will these statements get thrown out? Will Ealy's attorneys throw sufficient doubt upon them? No, it is absolutely impossible, I repeat to myself over and over. The town where Mary was murdered is far enough away from the city.

Isn't it?

14. TAKE ONE

Traffic on Lake Shore Drive isn't moving. The two left lanes are under construction and it's morning rush hour. I consider getting off at Fullerton, but I know from experience the side streets will be just as bad. I had neglected to have the air conditioning in my car fixed before the summer rolled around. Now it only blows hot air. On top of that, none of my windows open, so my car is a kind of moving furnace. I would normally open the door and brace it with my left knee anytime I attain a speed over twenty-five miles per hour. That would bring in a cool breeze, especially on Lake Shore Drive, where the temperature is always a little cooler, but at a standstill, it's pointless.

I'm heading to the Near North Side to pick up Peter, the filmmaker. We're going to a movie set on the West Side to prepare shooting our first interviews for the documentary. Peter called me a few days earlier to let me know he needed a ride. That meant each day he was in town I had to drive from the Far North Side where I live down Lake Shore at rush hour, pick him up, and head to the West Side, also at rush hour. It's a lot to ask, I think, but we need the interviews. I warned him about the air conditioning on the phone, but it hadn't seemed to register with him. He's an older guy, and the temperature is supposed to approach one hundred degrees by noon. Already I'm dripping sweat. I take a sip of hot coffee, dehydrating myself even more. As I wait in traffic, I keep trying to call Peter, but he never answers. Just then my phone rings. Peter, finally, I figure.

"Marty, who the fuck is going down to pick up Ricky at the bus station?"

It isn't Peter. It's Rick, the lawyer. Rick has been at the center of many wrongful conviction cases and represents cops accused of torture.

"What?" I say.

"I said who's going to pick up Ricky at the bus station?" Rick says.

"Are you kidding me?"

"No, I'm not kidding. He's on his way right now from Milwaukee. You said you wanted to interview him and I got him. Get someone down there to pick him up," Rick says, then hangs up.

Rick had come across Ricky Shaw in the prison system while defending Burge. Shaw was a former El Rukn gang member, a high-ranking general in the gang. He had just finished up serving twenty-five years of a fifty-year sentence. Shaw held vast knowledge of gangs, prison life, and many offenders who had made claims of torture against detectives in the Chicago Police Department. Rick tried to bring Shaw into Burge's trial as a witness, to show that many of the claims against Burge were made up in prison, but the trial judge limited the scope of Shaw's testimony, so much so that Shaw couldn't tell all that he knew. It was a ruling that infuriated many cops and lawyers, testimony that would go the heart of the case against Burge. What made the limiting of Shaw's testimony so frustrating was the fact that many wrongful conviction cases, like Porter's, were built upon claims of convicted killers. Why were their statements accepted in courts, but not Ricky Shaw's, many of us wondered. In addition to Shaw's knowledge about what was going on in prison, Shaw had also grown up in the same neighborhood as Anthony Porter and knew Porter in prison. Now Shaw, just a few days out of prison, is on his way to the city on a bus. He would, Rick said, be arriving in an hour.

Shooting an interview with Shaw has been a goal this week. Peter assured me that he had spoken to Shaw and Rick, and that we would interview Shaw a few days later. But apparently he had it all wrong. I still can't get ahold of him. It's burning up in my car, but I have to think fast. What if I go and pick up Shaw? I try to imagine a Chicago cop picking up an El Rukn general a few days after the gangbanger got out of jail. What will Shaw do if he knows I'm a cop? Will he go berserk? I haven't brought my gun, but even if I had, how would I explain it if something went off? How would I tell the responding cops how and why Shaw and I got into it? It would take hours. I would have to talk about the book and the documentary. Then I begin to wonder about not getting to Shaw, of losing this opportunity. I can see Shaw arriving at the station, hanging out for a while, then walking away, our hope for an interview gone. Perhaps he would get on another bus back to Milwaukee, perhaps head over to some friend's house. He's on parole. He had to get permission to leave Milwaukee and come to Chicago. Perhaps he doesn't even have enough money to get back home. He would be stranded.

This image of a solitary Shaw at the bus station and me trapped in traffic unable to reach him is illuminating. How can it be, I wonder, that we are the only ones going after an interview with him? Even though the judge in the Burge trial ruled much of his testimony inadmissible, aren't journalists interested in what Shaw has to say? Here's a general in the El Rukn gang, now the Black P-Stones, also a potentially relevant witness in some of the biggest wrongful conviction cases in the city's history, yet no journalist or activist has made the effort to sit down with him. What information he could provide. Some might argue that you can't trust a guy with his criminal record, but Protess and the students at the Innocence Project interview career thugs all the time, and build cases upon their claims. They believed Porter. Why not interview Shaw?

The Black P-Stones, after all, are not just some local street gang. In the 1960s they had created a powerful criminal enterprise, known for their brutality. They ran a vast drug and prostitution empire. At one point their leader, Jeff Fort, had made contacts with Moammar Gadhafi, the leader of Libya, in an attempt to get money and support. For this support, Fort and his other gang leaders promised to commit acts of terrorism on American soil. Gang members purchased what they thought were sophisticated weapons for an attack on a Chicago Police station, but they were really talking to FBI agents, who had infiltrated the gang. Wouldn't it be worthwhile to hear what Shaw, a general in this gang, has to say? I wonder how much attention Shaw would get if he were making the opposite claims, if he were saying he has more information about police abuse and corruption. I wonder if the journalists and courts would be willing to listen to him then.

My phone rings again. It's Bill. Word is spreading about our emergency. He's heard Shaw is on the bus. Bill jumped in his car and is heading downtown from the western suburbs. Bill says he will pick up Shaw. I will head to Peter's condo and try to track him down. But now I worry about Bill, a man approaching seventy in a car alone with Shaw. This guy has been in the joint for more than two decades. Perhaps Bill is too easy a mark for him, an irresistible opportunity, so I call Bill back and tell him to remain in a public area at all times.

The traffic starts moving. I get off at Michigan Avenue and make an illegal right-hand turn toward Rush Street and Peter's condo building.

Even if I get ahold of Peter, how will we get a camera crew in time? I park in front of Peter's condo building and head up to his unit, wet with perspiration. It's a fancy Gold Coast condo. No one answers, so I go back to the doorman and ask him to call up there, flashing my badge. Still no answer. I approach the doorman again, saying I think my friend in the unit may be ill, as he was supposed to meet me some time ago and he hasn't been answering his phone. Is there any way they can do a check on his well-being? The doorman, growing weary of me, leads me to the administrative offices, where an older woman listens to my story. She won't budge until I flash my badge again. They take my ID and return to the room, leaving me in the lobby. While they're gone, I call Bill to see if he's okay. Yes, he says, he and Shaw are waiting at Manny's Deli, along with Jim, who, I know, has a pistol. My frustration with Peter is beginning to boil over. Where the fuck is he and why wouldn't he answer his phone? Will every interview be a clusterfuck like this?

The doorman is getting cabs for tenants, a buck for each one, which he quickly sticks in his pocket. Many of the cars parked illegally out front are his as well, probably ten bucks a piece, I figure. I had been a doorman for more than a decade. It's pleasant to watch him. He's good, never missing an opportunity for a tip. Perhaps I should have remained being a doorman, I think. I mean, look at me, waiting in a lobby for a filmmaker I can't get ahold of, trying to shoot an interview with an El Rukn general that probably won't pan out. Must I always move about the city in such desperation? As if in answer to my thoughts, two ladies who work for the condo building walk up to me, angry. One of them is the woman I spoke to about checking Peter's condo. They ask to see my police badge one more time, write down the number, and tell me the person who answered the door had no idea who I was. They then tell me I will have to leave the building. Back in my car I sit with the door open for some ventilation, completely out of ideas, and furious. Did I have the wrong room number, the wrong condo building? Why the hell would Peter not answer his phone? The doorman approaches, tells me I have to move. What will I tell Bill and Jim?

I put the car in gear and begin to drive, heading home because I can think of nowhere else to go. I will tell Bill to buy Shaw lunch then get him a ticket for the trip home. My phone rings. The caller ID says Peter.

"Where the fuck have you fucking been? Do you know what we have been dealing with?"

"Don't yell at me. It's not my fault," he shouts back in a whining, guilty voice, like a spoiled child.

"Not your fucking fault. Are you fucking kidding me? Who the fuck's fault is it?"

We both pause. As much as I want to lay into Peter, there's no time. We will have this argument later.

"Can you get a camera crew to the studio right now?" I ask.

"I'll call you back," Peter say.

Peter is somehow able to scare up a cameraman. He explains to me that the battery in his cell phone had run out. When the management banged on the condo door, he was sleeping, so Peter's friend answered. The friend didn't know me and therefore didn't recognize my name. Peter was asleep in the next room. Couldn't the two of them connect the dots, I think. I'm starting to have some real doubts about working with this guy. I swing back to Peter's condo to pick him up, little conversation going on between us at first. He freaks out when he feels the heat in the car. He was wearing a nice white dress shirt, which is sopping wet within a few blocks.

Ricky Shaw looks like an ex-con. Though in his forties, he has the build of a guy who works out regularly in the yard, not simply to stay in shape but as a requirement for survival. He also has that stare about him, one that always measures a situation to find some leverage in it. Shaw had been living for two decades in a world where you have to be willing to fight over something as insignificant as a bag of potato chips. We shake hands and go into the room where we will shoot the interview. The cameraman is there, as are Bill, Jim, and his partner, John Mizzola, and, of course, Peter and me. We make small talk while Don sets up. Shaw is talkative, a good sign. I'm afraid at any moment he will clam up, change his mind about the interview. I'm also worried he will start asking for money or gifts. That's the way ex-cons are. In every situation, they are looking for leverage. Giving Shaw any money would get us in a lot of trouble, particularly since we're asserting that Protess and Ciolino offered money and other incentives to inmates and witnesses in exchange for their testimony. But Shaw is broke, fresh out of prison, and he has been hustling all his life. Soon I figure it will dawn on him to play us for the interview. Just then, from the corner of the room, Peter mentions something about lunch and I steel him with an icy glance.

"Why don't I run out for sandwiches? That way we can keep working but still get something to eat," I say, hoping to keep everyone at the studio focused on the shoot.

"No, there's a great Italian place down the road. I've known it for years. Let's go there and when we get back, the cameraman will be set up and we can get going," Peter says. He clearly likes the notion that he's in charge.

I move over to Peter and whisper that we should shoot now, while Shaw is willing to talk, but he waves me off condescendingly. This delay could ruin us. After the screw-up in the morning, I'm really growing fed up with the guy. The six of us then pile into two cars, Shaw riding in the backseat with me, and we head to the restaurant. After we sit down at the table, Peter goes over the menu and grills the waitress. He wants ice tea with an orange, not lemon, and only a few ice cubes. *A few ice cubes*, I mutter to myself, *Jesus H. Christ*. Time, opportunity are slipping away. I watch Shaw surveying the restaurant. He's scanning the table with his eyes as Peter breaks into another story about his childhood on the South Side. I have heard these stories about four times by now. The guy thinks he's Mr. Chicago. We haven't even ordered yet. Shaw's mind is wandering. He isn't listening to a word Peter says, but Peter doesn't notice. Peter doesn't understand what it's like for a guy who has been in prison for most of his life to now sit in a nice restaurant. Most of the entrees he doesn't even recognize. He looks around at how well dressed everyone in the restaurant is, how easily they order anything on the menu. You can see him contemplating how he doesn't even have a dime to his name. He's thinking about Peter being from Hollywood, imagining the money out there. Then it comes, right around the same time our food is served.

"You know, I been wanting to do this interview and all, but I need me some new underwear and socks. I really do. I need a job and I need something to get around, to get me started," Shaw says.

The conversations stop. Everyone shifts uncomfortably at the table. I send another icy glance at Peter. Peter looks away. I want to leap across the table and grab him by the neck. Will we lose this interview because of his stupidity?

"Well, you're doing the right thing. That's the most important part," Jim says.

Jim's right. The only card we can play on Shaw is morality. When Shaw was busted for his armed robberies, a fellow gang member and accessory on the robberies had turned him in. Shaw had been raised in a good family home. All his siblings turned out to be good people. He slowly recognized in prison that there was no real solidarity in the gangs and that the gang life was all wrong. He had vowed to change his life, and he dropped out of the gang. Stepping forward to testify in the Burge trial was a bold, courageous move on his part. The entire prison population would be aware that he was speaking on behalf of Burge, threatening the opportunity for many of them to get out, to file lawsuits. That took guts. Even so, Shaw is a hardened ex-con. He had learned to live life by manipulating every situation to his advantage. I look at him again, wondering if he could make it on the outside. I couldn't be certain. I couldn't be certain he would even come through with this interview.

Jim steps in, a real veteran. The waiter had cleared our dishes. Jim reminds Shaw about how he had turned his life around in the joint, getting out of the gang and testifying at the Burge trial. He tells Shaw that this interview is part of the process, that it may help the police gain a foothold on the gangs that dominate the city. Shaw respects Jim and listens carefully, nodding his head. Jim also reminds Shaw that his efforts may help kids stay out of gangs, something Shaw mentioned frequently. I don't know what we'd do without Jim. I catch Peter's eye and make a forward motion with my hand, letting him know we have to get going, get the fuck out of there, but then he calls the waitress over and asks about the dessert menu.

"No, we're not having dessert. We're leaving now," I say to him as I stand up and stare hard into his eyes to let him know how intense my anger is.

After we get back to the studio and mike ourselves up, I feel more relaxed, more in my element. Shaw describes growing up in a decent home with loving parents, but he couldn't resist the call of the streets. He got involved in a neighborhood gang, but after getting arrested, a friend told him about the El Rukns, the former name of the Black P-Stones, one of the most powerful gangs in the city. Shaw's specialty was robbing people and businesses. He says that his friend would call him at home and ask if he wanted to go and make some money. "Pick me up," Shaw would say. They would get in the friend's car and drive out to the suburbs. Once there, Ricky would wait in the car while his friend went into a store. The friend would come back and tell Shaw what the place was like. Shaw would get out, hiding his gun, enter the place, and rob the store owner at gunpoint. They would do this to several stores in one day as they made their way back to the city. Shaw gave a cut of his proceeds to the gang. Because he was intelligent and tough, he moved up the gang hierarchy quickly. Soon he made the rank of general, one of the highest positions in the El Rukns.

Shaw tells me that he worked with many offenders who had been arrested in Area 2, a collection of five districts on the Far South Side of Chicago. Burge had worked this area much of his career and moved up to the post of commander. He had established a reputation as a no-nonsense investigator who had an unprecedented closure rate for his cases. He developed excellent confidential informers. Later, the activists who brought him down claimed this closure rate was another sign that he used brutality to get confessions from suspects. But I had spoken to many detectives and cops who spoke glowingly of Burge's investigative skills and his character. In the activists' quest to bring Burge and his men down, Area 2 had become a buzzword for police abuse, particularly after Andrew Wilson showed up at the downtown lockup with bruises all over his body.

When Shaw was in the county jail just after his arrest, he says inmates asked him where he had been arrested. When he told them it wasn't Area 2, they told him, "Too bad, you could have claimed torture." He says these lessons on claiming torture were also spread around the street from gang member to gang member so that everyone was aware of them. Lawyers, he says, came to the prisons, spreading the word to make contact with anyone arrested in Area 2. It didn't take much for the inmates to realize the opportunities. Another rumor Shaw says he heard throughout his years in various Illinois prisons was the fact that inmates believed they could make great wealth through movie and book deals based on their stories. Movie and book deals. There it is again.

After Shaw caught his fifty-year sentence for the armed robberies, his role as a general in prison gave him crucial contact with these inmates who were claiming torture. He became their confidant. He reviewed their cases with them. Three inmates in particular Shaw got to know well: Melvin Jones, Darrell Cannon, and Aaron Patterson, all three claiming that they were abused by Burge and his men. Shaw says the abuse claims by Patterson, Jones, and Cannon were lies. Nevertheless, all three of them beat their cases. Shaw describes how each one had been tutored to claim torture. As Shaw tells us these stories, we all steal glances at one another, particularly when Shaw mentions Aaron

Patterson, one of the most high-profile wrongful conviction cases. Patterson had scratched a message in the Area 2 holding room after he had been arrested for a double homicide, a message claiming he had been tortured. This was either an act of a desperate man who had been brutalized or a sign of how reflexive torture claims had become for killers. Patterson's etchings became crucial evidence in his claim that he was falsely convicted, part of his quest for exoneration and a huge payout from the city. It didn't last long because Patterson was charged on a slew of drug charges years later and received a long sentence. Then, in prison for these crimes, he tried to kill another inmate and was charged with attempted murder.

Shaw had also grown up in the same area as Porter and knew him when Shaw was a kid. He describes Porter's reputation for violence and how people stayed clear of him. He says how all the inmates in the prison believed Porter was the killer in the double homicide and were shocked when he got out. He says that seeing a death-row inmate get out energized every inmate and gave them hope of doing the same. None of the inmates, Shaw contends, believed Alstory Simon was the offender.

As Shaw speaks, I mark once again the arbitrariness that pervades the wrongful conviction movement. There is a balance in the law, a demand that the same criteria be applied equally to all events and people. Yet Shaw's disturbing claims reveal a vivid inequity. By what authority did Protess and other wrongful conviction experts put stock in the accusations of these murderers, and disregard others? Why would Protess and other wrongful conviction advocates believe a predator like Porter, yet wholly ignore the claims of someone like Shaw? Why, for example, was Porter taken up as a wrongful conviction case, yet no other law firm in the city specializing in wrongful conviction cases would take up Alstory Simon's claim? The supporters of wrongful conviction cases often claimed there was a thin blue line of secrecy in the police department, but was there no other group that would fight for the rights of Alstory Simon? There was more evidence that Simon was wrongfully convicted than there was for Porter, yet Simon wasted away in prison, while Porter roamed free.

We take a break and I walk out to the street. Porter's wrongful conviction narrative reveals the larger purpose of the city. It is the strange and fantastic allegiance between the criminal and the legitimate in Chicago, an allegiance aimed always at resolving the sociopath's enduring dilemma: the fact that the city could never reveal its true criminal nature, yet never completely deny its crimes. The purpose of such narratives had always been to romanticize crimes, deny them, recast these narratives as something else or simply obfuscate them. Look at Ealy. His lawyers immediately set about the hard work of employing these narratives on behalf of their client, miraculously transforming Ealy from murder offender to victim of police misconduct. So, too, did Protess and Ciolino in the Porter case, transforming Porter from death-row killer to victim of police abuse and misconduct. And so did they against Alstory Simon, transforming a working stiff with a coke problem into a killer, and coercing a confession from him. Now Shaw is claiming it's common practice. These narratives accomplish their goal by deflecting away from the crime scenes themselves and moving to places like the interview rooms at the police districts. No doubt Andrew Wilson got his ass kicked while in custody. Likely other police killers got smacked around. But systemic torture? Electrocution? What freedom these myths provide to their adherents, what power. Activists like Protess wage any claim whatsoever, no matter how baseless or destructive. Is there nothing now that can't be claimed or argued? Shaw paints a vivid world. No wonder he was ignored while killers like Wilson, Porter, Hope, and Ealy were given full voice. Small wonder the judge would not let him speak at the Burge trial. Small wonder the judge had no interest in what Shaw had to say. No one batted an eye when these claims of torture and misconduct came out of nowhere, with no evidence. But where, in truth, was the systemic abuse and fraud—in the police interview rooms or the law offices, university classrooms, and newsrooms?

It's becoming clearer to me why the journey to people like Shaw is so fraught with failure, miscommunication, and menacing threats, why I feel such hopelessness about it. Did I think it would be a simple task to confront these narratives that had taken hold of the city? After the shoot, we all go our separate ways. Jim gives Ricky Shaw a ride back to the bus stop. I suggest he give Peter a ride as well, as it's somewhat on his way. I won't have to listen to Peter gripe anymore. I get on the expressway, still roasting in my car. I fight the feeling that likely none of this will work out, that our work on this story is doomed and that something terrible will happen to all of us involved, particularly me, because I'm a cop. But what else can I do? I'm already too deep into the story. I am imprisoned by it.

What's most important, what I always have to do, is check my story over, review it. All of us at the shoot believe Shaw's story. But what good is that? Who the hell am I? I have no university backing me up. But I had a plan in mind, even before I interviewed Shaw. After the shoot, I get a copy of the interview. I carry it to four of the best cops I know in the city, to their homes, their side jobs, wherever, and I play all three hours of it. I pick these guys not only for their expertise in identifying a person who is lying or telling the truth, but also because they will tell me their reaction without bias. If Shaw were lying, they will tell me and I will have to deal with it. I will have to tell Peter, the detectives, and Bill and Jim. *Shaw's a liar*, I will have to inform them. My colleagues watch Shaw's mannerisms, the movement of his eyes, the construction of his statements and narratives. All four tell me they think he's telling the truth.

No doubt about it, they say.

15. CHUCK'S STORY

Charles Salvatore, whose friends often call him Chuck, became a Chicago Police Officer in 1968, the year of the riots at the Democratic National Convention. He worked until 1998, retiring as a sergeant. Ten of his years on the job he worked as a detective, just over seven years in Area 1 Homicide, the South Side, and a few years as a bomb and arson detective. His partner when he was a homicide dick was Dennis Gray. Salvatore and Gray were in the same academy class. They would run into each other after the academy while working various units on the job, and they often hung out together after work. When they both made it to detective, they partnered up. Both men realized they shared a common mind-set as cops apart from their friendship.

"Me and my partner Denny were on the same page. In our investigations, we threw the sand up in the air and wherever the wind blew it, we went. We didn't care who was involved or what it meant," Salvatore told me.

Another sign of Salvatore's commitment to crime scene investigation is the fact that he taught the subject for nineteen years at a community college.

One technique Salvatore pursued in his investigations was the relationships he built with prosecutors. After a case was completed, he would approach the state's attorney and asked how he could have testified or prepared the case better. Often tensions between detectives and the prosecutors are strained, but in working with the prosecutors this way, Salvatore honed his skills as an investigator. He developed a keen knowledge of the law, including the requirements for probable cause, and had a good reputation with prosecutors. It came as quite a shock to him, his coworkers, and many prosecutors when he was accused of framing Porter. A detective with such a meticulous eye to crime scene investigation is not likely to be one who, suddenly, out of nowhere, abandons the evidence in favor of pinning a murder on an innocent person.

I had tracked Salvatore down more than a year earlier. It had taken me a while to win over his trust. We finally met for breakfast on the West Side, spending several hours talking on a summer morning. Salvatore knew the Porter case so intimately, so specifically, it was clear he had painstakingly processed all the evidence, every statement. As we talked about the Porter case that morning and several others, one point arose among all others, one central point.

Salvatore and his partner worked the third watch on August 15, 1982, meaning they started work in the afternoon. The Porter murders were early in the morning of that day, just after midnight. When the detectives were briefed on the case, they were told there were two witnesses being questioned, Henry Williams and William Taylor. But Taylor, the one who actually saw the shooter, was hesitant to come forward because he was afraid of Porter. Williams and Taylor told detectives they were friends and had come to the park to go swimming. It was common for people to hop the fence and jump in the pool on hot evenings, so common the police rarely took action over it. This evening in particular the cops would not do much, because it was after the big South Side Bud Billiken Parade, and the cops couldn't get tied down with petty trespassing arrests. Williams stated he had just come out of the pool and was toweling himself off. Williams said a black male he identified as Anthony Porter approached him and put a gun to his head asking if he had any money.

Salvatore and Gray then interviewed Taylor, who confirmed Williams's story without naming Porter. Taylor was aware of Porter's gang, the Black Gangster Disciples. He had seen Porter committing brutal armed robberies on elderly people. Taylor was afraid not only for himself but for his elderly grandmother with whom he lived. Porter and his gang, Taylor said, knew where he lived. Here is Salvatore's testimony about Taylor's fear of making a statement against Porter:

Q: Mr. Williams had told you that at the time that he was, that you were in the room with him, that Mr. Taylor had told him that in fact he had seen the events?

Salvatore: That's correct.

Q: All right. And you told that to Mr. Taylor, yes?

Salvatore: That's correct.

Q: And after that, after you told that to Mr. Taylor, did you ask him, "Is it really true that you saw it," or words to that effect?

Salvatore: Words to that effect.

Q: And what did he say?

Salvatore: At first he didn't say nothing. At first he, he was a blank, and then he said, "I didn't see nothing. I didn't see nothing." And then I said, me or Dennis said, "You know, William, your buddy just said you seen it. Your buddy just said you saw the shooting. Now, you know, did you or did you not see the shooting?" And he wouldn't have eye contact with me. He kept on looking down and he kept on—his legs were jumping up and down, and he said, "I didn't see it. I don't know nothing. I didn't see." And again one of us, either me or Denny said, "You know, what's going on? You know. Talk to us." And again he kept—no contact. He kept on looking down, you know, and he says, "I really don't want to get involved." He says, "I got a ninety-five-year-old [grand]mother. I just don't want to get involved, you know" and that went on for a few minutes.

Taylor's reticence to finger Porter betrays an underside of gang life that few of the suburban Northwestern students or Protess knew about, the frequency and ease with which the gangs can destroy a murder case by bribing, intimidating, or killing witnesses and their families. This is one reason the resolution rate for murders is so difficult to maintain. Many of them are gang murders. The gangs control the neighborhoods and can easily get to any witness. Taylor's fear was real and justified. Porter's gang, the Black Gangster Disciples, could very well come after him. It would be nothing for them to murder Taylor or his grandmother. After all, Porter's willingness to commit violence for little or no reason was a valuable asset to a street gang. But Salvatore and his partner Gray were sharp. They gave Taylor a ride to his grandmother's residence so he could see that she was okay. It was a chance for Taylor to get to trust the detectives and relax around them. Then Salvatore and Gray went to Harold's Chicken and bought several dinners, brought them back to the station, where the four of them—Detectives Gray and Salvatore, witnesses

Williams and Taylor—broke bread together. At this point Williams nudged Taylor and told him to come clean. That's when Taylor told them, yeah, it was Porter.

In order to get approval for felony charges, detectives had to call the state's attorney, that is, the prosecutor. The prosecutor reviews the case and determines whether he will sign an arrest warrant. These moments are often a source of conflict between the prosecutors and detectives because the detectives often believe they have sufficient evidence to proceed, but the prosecutors want more. This was particularly true in the Porter case. The prosecutor who arrived at the Area station was David Kerstein, a cautious attorney with extremely high requirements for probable cause. His refusal to sign an arrest warrant for Porter frustrated the detectives. Their frustration was not without reason. They had two solid witnesses, one who actually saw Porter shoot Green and Hillard, and another who was robbed at gunpoint by Porter, then saw Porter go into the area of the bleachers where this witness subsequently heard shots. Porter had a warrant out for a shooting two weeks earlier. But there was more. In the course of looking for Porter for the shooting a week earlier, two cops had spotted Porter. When they approached him, Porter raised a pistol and fired at them, then fled. That meant in the course of just a few weeks, Porter had shot one man in the head, fired at two other cops, robbed a man at gunpoint, then killed a couple in the park. This was a far cry from the heroic, victimized Anthony Porter that Professor Protess and his students would sell to the public sixteen years later. It was clear Porter would kill anyone, anytime, including cops. In the minds of the detectives, there was an urgency to get him in custody before he shot anyone else. It would be a difficult thing for the detectives to live with if Porter killed more people, including fellow cops, while they already had two solid witnesses against him, just as it would have been difficult for the detectives in the Ealy case to live with Ealy killing more people if they had decided not to ask him to come to the station to answer some questions.

Nevertheless, Kerstein still had some reservations about the reliability of the witnesses, partly because they had been drinking that night, so he suggested to Salvatore and Gray that they all go back to Washington Park and go through the crime with Taylor and Williams. The detectives agreed. They warmed to the idea of seeing the scene themselves to help write their own reports more clearly. In the pool area of the park, Taylor and Williams walked the two detectives and the prosecutor through the entire homicide. Satisfied, they all headed back to the parking lot. But as they were leaving, Gray pointed out to Salvatore that there were several people in the area of the pool and they should canvass them, meaning they should see if they knew anything about the murder. This willingness to seek out new witnesses is illuminating. Why would two detectives trying to frame Porter go out of their way to find new witnesses? If they were framing Porter, they would have avoided talking to any more possible witnesses, witnesses who might undermine their false story. But Gray walked over to the group. Suddenly Salvatore heard his partner calling out to him. Salvatore went back to the group. Kerstein followed.

Listen to this, Gray told Salvatore.

A man named Kenneth Edwards told the detectives and Kerstein that he was in the pool area when he heard shots. He looked up and saw a man with a gun in his left hand, extended, firing and hitting a victim. There it was again: the left hand. Edwards said he knew Porter from the neighborhood, and he saw Porter shoot the couple. Edwards was with another man, Eugene Beckwith, when Gray approached. Beckwith told the detectives he was with Edwards the night before and he also saw the shooting, though he didn't see that the shooter was Porter. He did, however, observe Porter in the park a little while earlier when Beckwith hopped the fence to get in. Edwards and Beckwith told the detectives they were with two other men, Mark Senior and Michael Woodfork, both of whom had also witnessed at least some part of the shooting. Mark Senior also put Porter in the park. That brought a total of six witnesses, two of whom were eyewitnesses, as well as the police officer who stopped Porter running in the park. It was a solid case. All the statements provided by both groups of witnesses matched up, even on slight details: They saw Porter standing over the victims. They saw Marilyn Green get shot, Jerry Hillard go down. They saw Green stumble down the stairs and out of the park, holding her neck. There was one thing they also all agreed on. The Northwestern investigation claimed Alstory Simon was the offender and that he was with his wife, Inez Jackson, at the time of the shooting. All the witnesses agreed there was only one woman in the bleachers, the victim Marilyn Green. How, then, could Northwestern argue that Alstory Simon and Inez Jackson were at the scene of the crime when not one witness put them there? Inez Jackson was the only witness who actually placed Alstory Simon at the crime scene. She would later go on to recant this statement, saying it was contrived with Protess.

These witnesses are crucial not simply in their statements but in the manner in which Salvatore and Gray discovered them. This account of the investigation refutes entirely the claims brought against the detectives in the civil lawsuit—that the detectives conspired to arrest Porter and did so without probable cause. These witnesses and how they would be discovered also undermine almost the entirety of the claims by the Northwestern professor and students. When Edwards's narrative of the shooting was identical to Taylor's, down to the detail of claiming that Porter shot with his left hand, Edwards instantly confirmed to the detectives the fact that the original witnesses, Taylor and Williams, were telling the truth. Other facts were also confirmed. Porter's attorneys in the civil trial, for example, were claiming that detectives framed Porter and had no probable cause to arrest him. Yet how could they be framing Porter when the detectives found an eyewitness who repeated the same story as an eyewitness obtained many hours earlier? In some far-flung wrongful conviction fantasy world, it might be argued that the two eyewitnesses were obtained through some grand plotting by Detectives Gray and Salvatore, that the two detectives somehow designed it so that they would find identical eyewitnesses so many hours apart. But it was the prosecutor, David Kerstein, who wanted to return to the park, not the detectives. Kerstein witnessed the two detectives stumble upon Edwards, and he heard Edwards make his statement that Porter was the shooter. Kerstein himself heard Edwards repeat the same narrative of a shooting that Taylor provided earlier: Porter shot the couple with his left hand, then fled southbound through the park.

Clearly, there was no frame-up. Clearly, there was probable cause. Porter's attorneys in the civil trial stressed the fact that the two detectives put Taylor in their car and "took him for a ride" to see his grandmother before he admitted it was Porter. They suggested that this time away with only the detectives was when the detectives put the screws to Taylor for him to identify Porter. But these claims make no sense in light of matching witness statements. The detectives had a second eyewitness who said the same thing Taylor did, that Anthony Porter shot from his left hand. On top of that, all the circumstantial witnesses agreed as well, even to the detail of the offender standing over the seated victims. One of the circumstantial witnesses stated he was robbed by Porter shortly before the homicides, putting Porter at the scene with a gun, robbing people in the park. The matching witness statements refute the claims of malfeasance. The claim that the detectives took Taylor "for a ride" makes no sense. It was a solid investigation.

Here the transcripts of the secret grand jury hearing from 1999 become most illuminating, most disturbing. In this grand jury, which was convened to get to the bottom of the Innocence Project investigation, Protess, Ciolino, and the students were forced to undergo questioning by the prosecutor. It was the first time a wrongful conviction investigation was placed under such scrutiny, under oath, by a prosecutor. This prosecutor had reviewed all the documents, case reports, and transcripts of Porter's criminal trial. He had access to all the witnesses. In this grand jury hearing, it's clear that none of the Northwestern investigators picked up on the significance of the detectives discovering independent eyewitnesses so many hours apart. By their testimony, Protess and his students did not even seem aware of this fact. But the prosecutor in the grand jury saw it clearly. He pounced on this fact as he grilled Protess and the Northwestern students. Consider this exchange with one of the student investigators, Tom McCann:

Q: Do you remember what Kenneth Edwards told the police that night?

McCann: No.

Q: Are you aware that Kenneth Edwards told the police that night that Anthony Porter was the person who shot and killed Jerry Hillard and Marilyn Green?

McCann: No . . .

Q: Did you look at the police reports?

McCann: I did.

Q: Do you remember a police report that summarizes the testimony of William Taylor and Henry Williams?

McCann: I think I read that . . .

Q: So now you see that in addition to Williams and Taylor there was another person who told the police that Anthony Porter was the shooter that night?

McCann: Yes.

Q: As well as three other people who witnessed the incident?

McCann: Right . . .

Q: Did you do anything to investigate them?

McCann: No.

Here was an ominous admission by the Northwestern investigators. They never even troubled themselves to speak to the second group of witnesses. It's feasible by their testimony they didn't even know that one group of witnesses was discovered long after the first group. If they had, certainly they would have realized how illogical their claims were. Rather than talk to all the witnesses, Protess and his students only focused on the first group of witnesses, Taylor and Williams. These two were the only ones who testified at Porter's criminal trial. None of the witnesses from the second group were called to testify. Therefore, the statements of this second group played no role in the conviction of Porter, but their statements are crucial to understanding the truth of what happened that night and how sound the police investigation was. They are crucial to understanding whether Porter was the offender or not. How many murder cases have six independent witnesses putting the offender at the scene, then another police witness putting him there? How many have two completely independent eyewitnesses? Not many on the South Side of Chicago. But McCann was a student. Maybe one can excuse a young student for being too eager, too careless. Perhaps one could assume that as the professor in charge of the investigation, Protess, did more research. Maybe he guided the students with a steadier hand. He was, after all, a professor at one of the most prestigious journalism schools in the country. But under questioning, Protess admitted he did even less investigation, that he didn't even read the testimony of the second witness, Henry Williams, the man who was robbed right before Porter shot the couple.

Q: Did you at the same time read the testimony of Henry Williams?

Protess: No, I did not read the testimony of Henry Williams. I . . .

Q: I am sorry. Go ahead.

Protess: . . . I have not read the testimony of Henry Williams. My students showed me a summary memo of what he had to say.

Q: Aside from your testimony of your reading of the testimony of William Taylor, have you read any other testimony of any other transcripts of testimony that was taken at the trial?

Protess: No . . .

Q: Yeah. So you read opinions from court and the testimony of William Taylor?

Protess: That's right.

Q: Nothing else?

Protess: Well, in terms of documents . . .

Q: Yeah. I am not trying to trick you. You read all those affidavits over the course of time, but his background you didn't read any other testimony?

Protess: That's correct.

Q: —other than Taylor? You didn't read Williams's?

Protess: Correct.

Protess admitted that he read only the testimony of William Taylor, the eyewitness. At this point, it would be hard to call the actions of the Northwestern students and Protess an investigation. By their own statements, they hardly looked into the case at all. They ignored four crucial witnesses. They also ignored the manner in which this second group of witnesses was discovered. Instead, they focused solely on the testimony of the eyewitness in the criminal trail, Henry Taylor. The reason for this becomes painfully clear as the prosecutor continued questioning.

Q: You didn't read any of the police witnesses?

Protess: That's correct . . .

Q: Let me ask you a follow-up question, professor. You at some point read the police reports that were obtained . . . ?

Protess: Yes.

Q: You were aware that there were four other young men who were interviewed by the police, were you not, in connection with the shooting the same night that Taylor and Williams were interviewed?

Protess: Yes.

Q: Those people being Beckwith, Senior, Woodfork, and Edwards, correct?

Protess: I don't recall the names, but I do remember what you are saying . . .

Q: Mr. Edwards identified Anthony Porter as the shooter that night, did he not?

Protess: I would have to go back over the report.

Q: Please do so. I direct your attention to page 4 of the August 16, 1982, supplementary report under ZO RD 290330 authored by Salvatore and Gray?

Protess: Unfortunately I don't have my reading glasses, but I'd ask you to read it to me.

Q: I will be happy to read it. "Kenneth Edwards was interviewed and he related he and three of his friends, Woodfork, Beckwith, and Senior, went to the Washington Park swimming pool about midnight on the day in question, 16 August '82, Sunday. Kenneth related that he and friends entered the pool area on the north-side fence. He observed four people in the gallery area in the uppermost northwest section (victims and offender, unknown male black). They were sitting and talking to each other. Kenneth and his group proceeded further down the pool area and he and Eugene Beckwith began to swim. Approximately fifteen minutes later Kenneth had come out of the pool. He heard a shot and looked up and saw a muzzle flash from a handgun. He then observed the offender Tony Porter standing over one of the victims and fired two more shots at the victim at point blank range." Do you remember reading that?

Protess: No . . .

Q: And your students didn't investigate those four men, did they?

Protess: No.

Q: You didn't ask Paul Ciolino to find those four men?

Protess: No.

Q: You didn't go out yourself and look for those four men?

Protess: No.

Q: None of your group ever conducted any interview of those four men?

Protess: That's correct.

And so it went. The first time the Northwestern investigation was put under a legal microscope, it completely fell apart. It was hard to see any actions by the Northwestern investigators that indicated they wanted to get to the truth of the case. Rather, what emerged was their clear intent to undermine the case. If they had been interested in getting to the truth, clearly they would have read all the witness testimony and statements and then sought these witnesses out. Instead, they focused on one witness, William Taylor, the only eyewitness who testified in the criminal trial. If they had looked at all the witnesses, they would have seen clearly how Salvatore and Gray obtained the second group after they returned to the park the following day with the prosecutor. The prosecutor's shock over Protess's investigation is justified. He asked how it was that Protess was not aware of a crucial eyewitness in the case, one who validated Taylor's entire testimony. This was a double homicide case. The entire criminal justice system had been transformed by Porter's exoneration. This was the case that ended the death penalty in Illinois. Dozens of other inmates at the time were claiming they, too, were wrongfully convicted. The prosecutor pressed McCann:

Q: Did you go out and talk to them [the second group of witnesses]?

McCann: When I was doing this, it was only Anthony Porter. And we went with the two witnesses that appeared in Court (Williams and Taylor). And when we got William Taylor's affidavit, we didn't look back at the other ones.

Q: But, Tom, what did you tell us your purpose was, what were you doing this for?

McCann: To find the truth. But I am a college student. I mean this took a long time.

Q: Let's go with that. You are a college student, I understand that. Who told you to quit when you got to the Taylor affidavit?

McCann: No one. We only had a very short time so we decided to look at the alternate suspect.

Q: Did anyone tell you not to interview those four guys?

McCann: No.

Q: Did anyone tell you to go back and see whether or not they saw Porter in the stands that night?

McCann: No.

Q: Did you think for a minute that that might be important?

McCann: I did not.

One can see how the students' youthful enthusiasm carried them away. Their naïveté, their idealism, moved to the forefront in the grand jury questioning. One can see their enthusiasm clouding their better judgment. The prosecutor chided McCann about not checking with the other witnesses. Likely McCann and his fellow students were caught up in the idea they could right a great wrong. They could, as students, transform the justice system and get a person they believed was an innocent man out of prison. This enthusiasm prevented them from taking all evidence into consideration, from covering all the bases. Under oath, it is a glaring hole in their claims of Porter's innocence. Yet what also emerged in their account was the fact that Protess provided no leadership, no guidance. He only fueled their fire to undermine the case. The importance of a thorough investigation was crucial for many reasons, not the least of which is the dark shadow a false conclusion would impose upon the lives of the students. Freeing a killer like Porter and putting an innocent man like Alstory Simon in prison would haunt them the rest of their lives. A truly benevolent teacher would be keenly aware of this possibility. It would guide him to be cautious, thorough. What would happen if Porter killed again, just as Ealy did? Porter would stomp his own child in a vicious attack, then several years later he would slice the face of his girlfriend with a broken bottle. Protess could manage these incidents in the press. But what would happen to the lives of these students if Porter gunned down more people? What if he killed a child or raped someone? These students came to Northwestern to learn the art of investigative journalism, to investigate fairly. What appears from the grand jury hearing is something altogether different, something extraordinarily dark and sinister. The students had no idea what they were getting into.

One also wonders what the detectives would think of these statements by Protess and McCann in the grand jury after all they had been through, all the accusations they endured of framing Porter for the murders, the ruin of their reputations. One wonders what Alstory Simon must have thought when he read this testimony in his prison cell: the Northwestern investigation didn't talk to all the witnesses. One wonders what the cops responding to the crime scene would think of these admissions. Cops had to run into a crowded park knowing at least two people had been shot. Were they running into a gang war, a gunfight? The cops were all aware that five officers had been shot that winter in a one-month period, four of them fatally. Two cops had to put Marilyn Green, bleeding to death, in a squad car, then rushed back into the park to investigate. Two other detectives had to carry Jerry Hillard down the bleachers. He was on his last breaths, making a snoring sound, an indication for a victim shot in the head that he didn't have much more time. Witness Henry Taylor had put his life at risk, and those of his family, in testifying against Porter. Wasn't there a deep moral obligation for Protess to at least interview every witness?

The detectives' investigation also undermined another key claim by Protess in the wrongful conviction investigation. As with so many wrongful conviction cases, a witness suddenly comes out of nowhere many years after the crime to retract his statement. The police, the prosecutors, the initial defense attorneys somehow failed to uncover this witness or a new piece of evidence, yet suddenly the activists, some of whom are twenty-year-old college kids, are able to find it. This is exactly what happened in the Porter case. William Taylor was the only eyewitness used in the criminal trial against Porter. Protess, Ciolino, and the students took specific aim at his statements. The other witness, Henry Williams, also testified in the trial, but he never actually saw Porter shoot Green and Hillard. On top of that, Williams had died by the time the Northwestern investigators became involved. His testimony always remained on the record, unimpeachable.

In 1999, after a bizarre series of meeting with Northwestern investigators and their allies, Taylor suddenly signed an affidavit retracting his original statements. In this retraction, Taylor now said he never saw

Porter shoot Green and Hillard. But how does this so-called retraction hold up to the facts of the investigation? This claim doesn't hold up for the same reason the claims of conspiracy also fell apart: Salvatore, Gray, and Kerstein returned to the scene of the crime and found another witness, Kenneth Edwards, saying the exact same thing Taylor had said, even down to the detail of the fact that Porter fired from his left hand. How could Taylor be lying in his original statement, how could that statement be false, when it matched another witness in such detail? It's impossible. The question then becomes why? Why did Taylor retract his statement? This was a key question because the Northwestern investigation claimed that many people changed their stories after Protess, Ciolino, and his students got involved. Porter changed his story, so did Inez Jackson and her nephew, Walter Jackson, so did Alstory Simon. It was also key because Alstory Simon claimed Ciolino obtained a statement from him maliciously and illegally. If Simon's claims were true, it was possible other statements were also gathered dubiously. Such evidence could reveal not an investigation, but a modus operandi.

The story of how Protess and his investigators got Taylor to change his statement is illuminating and disturbing, a dark window into the wrongful conviction movement. In 1998, a few months before Protess and his students became officially involved in the Porter case, another investigator who worked for the state appeals division, Appolon Beaudoin, and Porter's original lawyer in the case, Dan Sanders, visited William Taylor at his North Side apartment. Exactly why this investigator and Porter's attorney suddenly showed up out of nowhere so long after the case has been tried was never explained. What is clear is that they were working closely with Northwestern students, providing them with key information about the case. Taylor himself had no idea what was coming his way. The Porter case had long since been buried. Taylor had moved on with his life. He was living on the North Side. It was only a matter of time before Porter was to be executed. Then Beaudoin and Sanders arrived at Taylor's apartment. After meeting with him, they said Taylor still insisted that Porter was the offender. This is a key fact. Fifteen years after the murders and Taylor was still insisting Porter was the shooter.

But Beaudoin did score one victory, one that became crucial for the Northwestern investigators. He came away from the meeting with an affidavit in which Taylor claimed he was threatened by the detectives during the investigation of the murders. Fifteen years after the murders, Beaudoin, who was working hand in hand with the Northwestern

investigators, decided to go visit Taylor and happened to come away
with an accusation of malfeasance by the detectives. Beaudoin presented the affidavit. In it, Taylor said that when Salvatore first encountered Taylor, Salvatore shook a large flashlight in front of Taylor then
slapped it against his own hand, asking Taylor who he was more afraid
of, the cops or Porter.

One aspect of the accusation in the affidavit that is particularly suspicious was the claim by Taylor that the detectives threatened him at the
first moment they encountered him. Before Salvatore even knew whether
Taylor was going to cooperate, before he even asked if Taylor was going
to make a statement, Salvatore began threatening Taylor? Why would
Salvatore do that? Wouldn't he wait to see what Taylor said first?
Another accusation in Taylor's retraction is equally dubious and suspicious. It was argued that the detectives coerced a statement out of Taylor
because they wanted to pin the murders on Porter. Here again is an
instance of activists employing the theme of what monsters the Chicago
Police Officers were. The accusation was that the detectives didn't even
care who truly killed Marilyn Green and Jerry Hillard. They were just
using this double homicide to get Porter convicted as a kind of revenge.
That's how evil the Chicago cops were. One wonders about all the cops
that rushed into the park that night in response to the shooting, having
no idea what they were heading into. They rendered aid to two dying
people, chased down witnesses, conducted a long investigation. And in
the end, a few detectives decided to just pin the murders on the wrong
guy? How did the detectives get to the officer who observed Porter running from the scene of the crime in the park? They would have had to
contact him, get him to join in their conspiracy. What about the two cops
who heard Taylor and Williams mention Porter's name as they were carrying the wounded Hillard down the bleacher steps? Salvatore and Gray
must have also gotten them to join in their conspiracy.

This affidavit is revealing in the intent of the Northwestern investigation. The corroborating witness statements already proved Taylor's
original eyewitness account to the police was sincere and exact. It was
already obvious that what Taylor initially told the police was true. How,
then, could it be argued that Taylor was coerced into making a false
statement against Porter? More so, if the detectives were coercing false
statements in an effort to frame Porter, why is it that none of the other
five witnesses claimed they were intimidated or bribed or coerced into
making similarly false statements? If the cops were up to no good, other

witnesses would surely claim some sort of abuse or coercion as well. The detectives wouldn't have just singled out Taylor and left the other witnesses alone.

The motives behind the making of this affidavit become even clearer. When Beaudoin and Sanders typed it up, they made no mention of the fact that Taylor still claimed Porter was the killer. Sanders and Beaudoin only mentioned the vague, impossible claim of intimidation. Why would the two men, working closely with the Northwestern investigators, ignore the central fact that Taylor still fingered Porter for the murders and instead focus only on some absurd claim of intimidation? This was another sign that investigators were only interested in dismantling the case, not getting at the truth of the murders. Once again, Taylor said he saw Porter kill the couple. Undaunted, the Northwestern students now took up their investigation. They made contact with Taylor, asking him yet again about his testimony. This time it was student investigator Tom McCann who talked Taylor. Here again is an instance of Protess letting a student get deeply involved in a dark, extremely disturbing move to undermine a murder case. The Northwestern student got Taylor's contact information from Beaudoin. McCann described this surreal communication with Taylor in the grand jury:

McCann: I said hello . . . My name is Tom McCann. I am a student just doing a project on the case of Anthony Porter. I found your name and I wanted to ask you a few questions. And he [Taylor] was taken aback. He didn't sound like he wanted to talk about it, he just wanted people to leave him alone.

Q: What did he say to you that made you think he just wanted to be left alone?

McCann: He told me he said all that he wanted to say, that some people came by his place not too long ago [Beaudoin and Sanders]. He talked to them, why does he have to talk anymore? His mother I believe or his—I think his mother was sick at the time and she just died. And he felt very full of stress and he made mention of saying, you know, I know beyond a doubt Anthony Porter is guilty, I just wish he were executed and I can get on with my life.

McCann's testimony gives one pause. Taylor was afraid to give a statement the night of the murders. He finally gave up Porter's name, then testified in the criminal trial. Fifteen years later, Beaudoin came to his door and asked about his testimony again. Taylor gave him a statement repeating the claim that Porter was guilty. A few months later, McCann called on Taylor asking about the statement. Taylor again repeated his claim that Porter was the shooter and said he was tired of being bothered about it. How many bites of the apple did Protess and his students want? How many times would they "interview" Taylor before they got an answer they would accept? How deeply would Protess push his students into this mess? Is this squeezing of Taylor by Northwestern investigators a revealing look at how wrongful conviction advocates obtain witness statements? The prosecutor saw it for what it was. He pounced on this harassment of Taylor.

Q: Okay. Did . . . Appolon [Beaudoin] tell you that . . . Taylor still maintained that Anthony Porter was the shooter?

McCann: Yes.

Q: That's what they told you?

McCann: Yes.

Q: That in August of 1998 William Taylor still maintained that Anthony Porter was the shooter?

McCann: Yes.

Q: Although there was nothing about it in the affidavit?

McCann: Right. And he [Taylor] maintained it when I called him.

Q: The first time you spoke to him he continued to maintain that Anthony Porter was the shooter?

McCann: Yes.

Q: And of course he told you how he knew Anthony Porter, right?

McCann: Yes.

Q: Tell the ladies and gentlemen of the Grand Jury how it is that William Taylor knew Anthony Porter?

McCann: William Taylor knew Anthony Porter in the neighborhood before 1982 because he knew him as a bad person, and he saw him mug two old people in front—I don't know if it is in front of his mother's house, but he saw Anthony Porter mug two old people on the street . . .

Q: And in the memorandum, did you say on Saturday, November 14, "I talked over the phone to William Taylor, the eyewitness on the Anthony Porter case"?

McCann: Yes . . .

Q: Did you then write in your memorandum "he sounded bothered and not happy to talk about the Porter case"?

McCann: Yes.

Q: Did you also write "but I agree with Appolon that he will talk if you keep pushing him"?

McCann: Yes.

Q: Did you write that?

McCann: Yes.

Q: Did you continue on "our talk was friendly though he sounded on guard throughout the call." Is that what you wrote?

McCann: Yes.

Q: He said "there is no doubt in my mind that this man is guilty"?

McCann: Yes.

Q: Is that what he said to you?

McCann: Yes.

Q: You put that in quotes, didn't you?

McCann: Yes.

Q: "He's had to live with this for 18 years and he wants to put it behind him"?

McCann: Yes.

Q: He said "he will not be happy until Porter is finally executed"?

McCann: Yes.

Q: Is that what the man told you?

McCann: Yes . . .

Q: After he had once been visited by an investigator [Beaudoin] in August and told them already that it was Anthony Porter who was the shooter; right?

McCann: Yes.

Q: You continued on in your memo "before hanging up, he told me he didn't want to talk about this case anymore" . . . ? You continued to make the plan after the man told you he didn't want to talk to you anymore about the case, right?

McCann: Yes . . .

Q: Did you read the transcript?

McCann: Yes.

Q: Did you see his sworn testimony?

McCann: Yes.

Q: You read his sworn testimony?

McCann: Yes.

Q: So you knew that at least on three occasions: once in 1982, once in August of 1998, and again with you in November of 1998, William Taylor was saying I saw Anthony Porter do the shooting?

McCann: Yes . . .

Despite Taylor's repeated statements that he saw Porter commit the homicides and that he didn't want to talk about it anymore, the Northwestern group keeps applying pressure. McCann testified to the grand jury that he still wanted to talk to Taylor. McCann said he wanted to clear up his "confusion," not seeing that part of his confusion arose simply from the fact that McCann hadn't spoken to all the witnesses, hadn't taken account of what every witness had seen. One has to look at the evidence and talk to the witnesses, as the detectives had. But clearly the prosecutor, who read all the statements and documents, wasn't confused. So once again McCann confronts Taylor, this time going to

Taylor's apartment with Private Investigator Paul Ciolino, this jaunt the third attempt to get a statement from Taylor. What is particularly disturbing about this in-person visit with Taylor is the fact that Protess did not go along. Shouldn't the professor of the class at least go to look out for his student? The entire investigation was part of a journalism class at Northwestern. Why would a student go with only a private investigator to gather such crucial information? One wonders if Northwestern would have sanctioned such activity, had they known about it. In any case, what followed was one of the strangest "retractions" ever to find its way into a courtroom. It is worth reading the entire account by McCann:

> **Q:** In the course of your class work with Professor Protess, he instructed you on an investigative technique known as good cop/bad cop?
>
> **McCann:** Yes.
>
> **Q:** What does that mean exactly to you?
>
> **McCann:** It means that two people go on an interview, one person plays the role of someone who is big and intimidating, kind of, and applies pressure, I guess, and another person who is just laid back and just a nice guy, sympathizer. And usually the person doesn't like the intimidating fellow and opens up to the nice guy.
>
> **Q:** And that indeed is the technique that you and Ciolino employed when you talked to Taylor that night, is that correct?
>
> **McCann:** Right.
>
> **Q:** What did Ciolino say to Taylor when you saw him play the bad cop?
>
> **McCann:** Well, he said basically could you please talk to us about the Porter case. And William said the same thing as he said before, I don't want to talk about it, I just want it to go away. And he [Ciolino] said well, I have something to tell you, William, it is not going to go away, we have to talk about this sooner or later. There is a competency hearing coming up and there are issues about his innocence, and he is going to be put to death pretty soon so whether you cooperate or not you are going to have to deal with this sometime. And then he introduced me, we shook hands, he already knew me. And I think for the first time I started asking him why your testimony says you saw this, but really there is this. You know, your testimony said that you saw Anthony Porter shoot with his left hand, even

though he was right-handed. Your testimony said that you stood on the south end of the pool along, long way away from the north end of the bleachers at 1:00 in the morning, how could you see a face from that far away. And from where you stood putting on your clothes from the testimony right next to the fence, how could you see anything through a wrought-iron fence that's an obstructed view completely. And he kind of went silent and, you know, it looked like he was thinking in his head. And then Paul, you know, started saying, you know, we read your affidavit about how the police treated you that night. And, you know, I have been doing this for thirty years, I know exactly what's going on, you know, how these police officers do these things to people. And he is really a victim here; if they did anything to him, please speak up. And you have a man's life who is about to die; if you have anything to say about what really happened that night or if you are not saying anything you should be saying, you know, please talk.

Who was intimidating whom? Ciolino's real intentions are clear. Ciolino jumped right to it, saying he read the strange affidavit about Taylor being intimidated by the detectives, but clearly, like the students and Protess, Ciolino had not read all the witness statements either. If he had, he would have already been aware that an independent witness had bolstered Taylor's original statement. In any case, Ciolino went right to the image of the police as torturers, abusers. Then Ciolino dropped the bomb. You know these cops: "How these police officers do these things to people." One wonders: Do what things? Find murderers and lock them up? Ciolino made this statement right in front of McCann. The student did not protest, made no statement to Ciolino like, "Hey, listen, Paul. Take it easy. Not all cops are bad." It's a moment that reveals the extraordinary bias, the extreme radicalism that permeates the Innocence Project's actions. And Protess was not there to explain his presence with a man engaged in such clear coercion. Instead he allowed a student to go.

Ciolino dropped another bomb. He called Porter a victim. A victim. One wonders if the bias and radicalism of the Innocence Project is so extreme that they somehow feel as if all criminals are somehow victims, even someone as clearly evil as Anthony Porter. Such a bias might explain some of the devious actions on their part in this investigation. One wonders: What about their other cases? Nevertheless, McCann testified that Taylor told him how Porter was known as a bad man in his neighborhood, a neighborhood already overwhelmed with gangs and violence. Taylor had told McCann that he saw Porter commit robberies against two elderly people. Taylor had already testified and repeated his claims that he saw Porter kill Hillard and Green in the park. Porter had shot a man in the head over a barking dog two weeks before the murder. He had brutally gunned down two people in a crowded park right after he robbed Henry Williams at gunpoint. He was a gang enforcer, a notorious stick-up man of elderly people. How could anyone then claim that Porter was a victim? The prosecutor knew Ciolino has crossed the line. He asked McCann:

Q: Did you ever complain to Professor Protess about Ciolino's investigative techniques?

McCann: No.

One has to ask: Why not?

One other fact comes to mind. The Northwestern investigation culminated in 1998/99. Detective Salvatore retired in 1998. The case was sixteen years old. Protess and his students could easily have contacted Salvatore and asked him about the case. Salvatore might have been willing to sit down with a group of students and point out how thorough the investigation was. An interview with the retired detective would likely have ended the whole affair right then. After all, Salvatore was used to working with students as a college teacher himself. He would have been happy to explain the investigation that night. But it was not in the interest of Protess to sit down and talk with investigating detectives, even though he was a professor at a journalism school. It was not in his nature to hear the police side of cases.

By the end of this meeting with Taylor at his apartment building in 1999, McCann and Ciolino came away with a handwritten affidavit saying that Taylor had retracted his original claims that he saw Porter commit the homicides. He now said he did not see Porter shoot Green and Hillard. The creation of this affidavit tied up one of Protess's students directly in the plot that was taking place. Not content with the first affidavit Taylor signed, Ciolino and Protess returned to Taylor's apartment a few days later and spent several hours with him, ending up at a North

Side restaurant where Taylor began drinking wine. In this conversation, no students were present. At this meeting they handed Taylor a typed affidavit repeating his earlier "retraction" that, suddenly, after sixteen years of insisting he saw Porter commit the killings, repeating the claim several times after the trial, Taylor now denies it. What one would give to hear a recording of this conversation between Ciolino, Protess, and the hapless Taylor, what tactics the Northwestern investigators used in this meeting to persuade a witness to change his statement. One wonders what promises were made. Was there further discussion about movie and book deals? A short time later, Protess picked up Taylor at his apartment and took him to a news studio, where Taylor repeated his retraction on camera for the world to see. But one thing Protess and Ciolino never did was explain how Taylor's original statements to police and his testimony in court matched in such detail the other witness statements. If they had, they would have known that Taylor's so-called retraction was on its face pure bullshit.

There is one more crucial detail in this affidavit Protess and Ciolino got from Taylor. The professor and his private investigator submitted it without mentioning the fact that even though Taylor was now changing his statement about seeing Porter shoot Hillard and Green, Taylor still maintained he saw Porter in the pool area at the time of the shooting. He still put Porter at the scene. This was crucial because the only alibi Porter ever presented was that he wasn't at the pool that night. Taylor still put Porter at the pool, despite his so-called "retraction." And then, of course, Kenneth Edwards still claimed he saw Porter kill Green and Hillard. The other witnesses still maintained in their original statements that they saw Porter at the pool. There was also the testimony of the now-deceased Williams, who said he was robbed at gunpoint by Porter shortly before the shooting, testimony that put Porter at the pool, armed, willing to commit armed robberies. There was also the testimony of an officer at the park that he stopped Porter fleeing from the scene, yet another witness putting him in the park. Even with this fraudulent retraction by Taylor, the case against Porter was still overwhelming. Nevertheless, one has to ask why Protess and Ciolino would neglect to mention in their affidavit the crucial fact that Taylor still maintained Porter was at the scene. In any case, the Northwestern investigation was revealed clearly in the grand jury hearing. Under the scrutiny of the prosecutor, it fell apart.

Six years later in the civil trial when Porter was suing for his "wrongful conviction" and trying to claim millions, the attorney for the detectives, Walter Jones, would rip apart Taylor's retraction in a deposition. Grilled by Jones, Taylor admitted he signed the affidavit only to get Ciolino to leave his house and because he was tired of being harassed by Northwestern investigators. He also stated that he did not provide the affidavit to Ciolino willingly, an open admission of coercion. Taylor further reaffirmed in the civil trial the fact that he told the prosecutor the night of the murders that he saw Porter shoot Green and Hillard in the bleachers. These admissions by Taylor in the civil trial showed once and for all that the retraction obtained by the Northwestern investigators was fraudulent and coerced. The irony is so thick. Here is a movement based upon claims that the police manufactured confessions through coercion and even torture. Yet there was clear evidence that they themselves were guilty of such devious tactics. But this irony was never acknowledged. Even after Taylor testified in the civil trial that his statements to Ciolino and Protess were coerced and false, many people in the media still maintained Taylor had retracted his eyewitness statement.

Salvatore and I went over other key claims of the Northwestern investigation that were false. Salvatore pointed out that Protess and the students altered the location of the shooting on the bleachers. Protess, Salvatore said, placed the crime scene in a corner where it did not occur and where the witnesses could not have a clear view. Protess's students made much about how the witnesses were blinded from this view and this fact undermined their statements. Strange, then, that two sets of witnesses encountered at different times, witnesses who had no reasonable chance to talk to one another, came up with identical accounts of the murders. Salvatore showed how in the crime scene photos and documents, the shooting occurred in a different location, where it could be seen clearly by all the witnesses. But just as important, the two detectives, the prosecutor, and the witnesses Taylor and Williams had already walked through the crime scene the day after the shootings. The detectives and prosecutors would have noticed the fact that the witnesses could not have seen the murders. But somehow the students, at their young age with so little experience in life, let alone in crime scene investigations, were filled with such youthful hubris, and without the proper guidance of the professor who should have been supervising their every move, these students believed the original investigators could not see something so obvious that they could, coming back to the park so many years after the murders. It's strange to imagine a group of Northwestern students wandering around the pool at Washington Park, measuring things, taking notes, drawing diagrams, and yet they didn't even have the correct location of the murders. But it was also becoming clearer that the Northwestern investigation was not geared toward finding the truth. It was aimed at undermining the police investigation, no matter what.

The absurdity of the Northwestern investigation would become even clearer in 2005, six years after Porter was released, when Porter's attorneys would sue the city, based on the claims that Salvatore and Gray framed Porter, for more than $20 million, and lose. The question after this trial became even more compelling: What was Porter doing out on the streets? Even after this trial, no one asked what was going on at the Innocence Project. No one connected the dots.

In Salvatore's era, there were sometimes nine hundred murders a year in the city. Each day he came to work, he was assigned another one and investigated it. He had an astute legal mind and was good at interviewing people. As we sat and talked about the case, I often wondered what would have happened if the city had settled the lawsuit Porter brought against the detectives after Porter was exonerated, after a governor, himself now sitting in prison, had freed Porter. It was a crucial question because there were many other wrongful conviction cases that the city settled, ones in which the detectives wanted to go to court and have their say. Unlike Salvatore and his partner Gray, these other detectives never had this opportunity to clear their names. They watched as men they had convicted of murder were set free, then became rich, and they never had their day in court. Many of these detectives believed they had been betrayed by the city. I often tried to imagine what it would be like, what would it have meant if the allegations made against Salvatore, that he had framed Porter, even those that the cops had tortured Porter, had remained unaddressed in court and the city had written a massive check to Porter, as they did in so many other cases. Porter would be driving around a multimillionaire, the media fawning all over him. Salvatore would have to live under those allegations the rest of his life. It would be unendurable. I thought about all the cops who told me the city settled their cases, how furious they were, how they said they could have easily won in court.

Salvatore told me, "Anthony Porter spent approximately nineteen years on death row, and when you're on death row, who are you living with day in and day out? Other prisoners on death row. It seems to me that the same accusations being made against me were being made against other detectives. Then I started talking to other people. The accusations were the same: intimidation, conspiracy, brutality, no probable cause. In my opinion, if anybody did the intimidation, it was Northwestern. The people who worked for Northwestern intimidated William Taylor into signing an affidavit saying he didn't witness the murders and that I intimidated him. If anyone did intimidate, they did, not me."

Salvatore told me about the time when Porter was released in 1999. He hadn't heard much about Porter up to that point, save the fact that Porter was spared the death penalty because of his supposedly low IQ. Then in 1999 Salvatore learned that another man confessed to the crime and Porter was about to be set free. Salvatore's reaction was illuminating. By 1999 the flood of wrongful conviction claims by Protess and other activists was overwhelming the justice system. These cases painted a picture of cops who didn't give a shit, who would pin a murder on anyone, who would go after someone simply because they were black. But Salvatore was destroyed when he heard the news that Porter had been wrongfully convicted. It was almost impossible for him to live with the fact that he had almost put an innocent man to death, even a guy as violent and criminal as Porter. He was in agony, unable to sleep, replaying his investigation over and over again in his mind, trying to figure out where he had gone wrong. Salvatore spoke with me about his religious convictions, how he felt that he had failed them. He collected all the documents of the investigation and pored over them as the allegations that he intentionally framed Porter, even tortured him, took shape and were repeated in the media. It's important to note that Porter was freed right around the time Salvatore retired. These were supposed to be Salvatore's years of rest and peace after thirty years of chasing criminals. The Porter release placed a great strain on Salvatore's family and his reputation. As he researched the case, he slowly began to see what happened, began to see how completely baseless were the claims of Protess, Ciolino, and the students, how they had manipulated and compromised the facts. His self-doubt turned to anger. He took specific aim at the civil trial, demanded that the city take it to trial. His attorney, Walter Jones, said that in preparing the case, all kinds of detectives volunteered their time and labor, even those who were retired, traveling from long distances to help prepare. These detectives walked Jones through the case, until Jones saw Porter was guilty and argued that theory in the civil trial, and won, vindicating Salvatore and Gray.

But were they vindicated? Did the civil trial really matter? Afterward, prominent journalists like *Chicago Tribune* columnist Eric Zorn, Professor Protess, and other wrongful conviction advocates still appeared on television and in the media sticking with the Northwestern narrative of the Porter case, no matter how much it had been refuted in court, no matter that witnesses had refuted Protess's version of the murders. No matter that one of the witnesses, Taylor, said he was coerced into testifying by Ciolino and Protess. No matter that many of us had brought the proof to members of Northwestern, to Zorn and other journalists and columnists. No matter that it meant an innocent man was in prison. They merely stuck with their claims, which continued to drown out the verdict in the civil trial and the other evidence that clearly showed Porter was guilty. Those who pointed out the meaning and significance of this civil trial, those who disagreed with the journalists and activists, were condemned by them. There is nothing the wrongful conviction advocates wouldn't do to push their agenda. Alstory Simon, and Detectives Gray and Salvatore are proof of that.

16. HIGH LIFE

There are no longer enough hours in the day. My phone goes off again on Lake Shore Drive, but I can't answer it because I'm on my scooter. I know it's Peter, and I know he's pissed. I'm running late for one of our biggest interviews. I can imagine Peter already waiting in the high-rise building downtown with the cameraman, along with the interviewee, Walter Jones. The problem is that every time I tried to leave my condo, the phone rang. They were calls about the documentary and my book. I couldn't ignore them. I thought there was still plenty of time to get downtown, but when I got to Sheridan and Granville, road construction backed up the road for half a mile. I did a U turn and cut through side streets until I made it onto Lake Shore. I turned the throttle up to sixty miles per hour. When I get to Randolph, I sneak the scooter between two cars. Again my phone goes off. As I run awkwardly across Randolph, still limping a little from my back surgery, the phone keeps ringing.

I find the address on Dearborn and run into the building. There are marble floors and shining brass. Everyone is dressed in expensive business suits. The security guard eyes me. I'm dressed in jeans and a T-shirt. I had thought about getting dressed up, but I figured the best thing to do with this interview was be myself as much as possible. Now I think twice about this decision. I look like a plainclothes cop, which is similar to a single guy sitting around his condo on football Sunday watching the games and drinking beer. I get an elevator to myself, push the button for the thirty-third floor, and come out onto the hallway of what feels like a palace. The marble floors shine and the wood on the walls gleams. A beautiful woman sits at the reception area. There is soft music, pleasant artwork. She looks at me suspiciously.

"I'm here to film an interview . . ."

There's Peter, waiting at the entrance of a conference room, giving me the evil eye and waving me over like his servant. I have been out to eat with him several times when he's made this same gesture to waiters, often when the waiters were swamped with other tables. The waiter would walk over and ask Peter what he needed, Peter oblivious to the venom in the waiter's eye. This gesture by Peter is revealing in what he thinks about me and it's a last straw. I walk past him without saying anything and shake hands with Walter Jones.

It's crucial for me to me to interview Jones because he was a lawyer at the center of the case whose opinion changed 180 degrees. I want to ask him about this evolution, how and why it changed, as well as how it guided his strategy in the trial. I also want to ask him about the pivotal moment after the verdict when he stated to the media that he believed Porter was guilty of the murders. As I sit down across from Jones at the large table in the conference room, I make sure I'm on the other side of the camera so it will be more difficult for Peter to hover over me. If I don't, Peter will stand next to me, often poking me in the shoulder and handing me a note with some questions on it.

Jones is an African American man whose father had been a Chicago Police Officer. He is warm but cautious as the interview begins. He looks at me with a gaze that seems to say, *Who the hell is this guy?* Here I am a patrolman dressed in jeans and a T-shirt, strolling into his office about a case from seven years ago. Jones is a colorful speaker, his language rich and pleasant. He's also shrewd in his answers. I have read the transcripts of the civil trial many times, seen how effectively Jones ripped apart several witnesses. I have to be careful.

After the cameraman nods that we're on, I ask Jones what he thought of the Porter civil case when he first got it. It was considered a "dog," he says, meaning a case that's not winnable.

"My initial impression was not good. I mean, here was a man who had served sixteen years on death row and had received a pardon from the governor, and I was being asked to exonerate a number of police officers in what I perceived to be a very nasty case," Jones says.

On top of that, another man, Alstory Simon, had confessed to the murders. Most people felt that the case would never go to court. Instead, they believed the central issue was how much money Porter's attorneys would get from the city in a settlement. Jones was leaning in this direction at first. But then he says that Detective Salvatore, who had retired from the department at the time of the trial, would not leave him alone.

Salvatore called Jones and demanded that he visit Washington Park where the murders occurred and go through the case step by step.

"I drove down to Washington Park and I met with Salvatore, and he took me through the entire thing," Jones says. "My mind started to change because he [Salvatore] was so energetic and so determined to show me that the police officers had been right many years ago."

Jones began to re-interview the witnesses himself. He says he found another witness who had never testified at the trial, another sign that the pool area was crowded with people who saw Porter murder Green and Hillard. This witness told Jones he was sitting in the pool and he watched Porter commit the murders, then saw Porter flee the scene.

Another factor that compelled Jones to take the case to trial was the character of the cops who had investigated the murder.

"It's clear that the investigation they ran [Salvatore and Gray] is as good as it gets," Jones says.

Jones says Salvatore assisted in the preparation of the case. This demand to take the case to trial and the willingness by the detectives to assist Jones was, to me, hardly the behavior of cops who had framed someone. If Salvatore and Gray had set Porter up, the last thing they would have wanted was a trial. Rather, they would have wanted the city to cut Porter a check and be done with it. After all, if they had framed Porter, the civil trial would likely only uncover more evidence of it, evidence that could lead to criminal charges afterward. Instead, Salvatore and Jones hunkered down for months, grateful for the opportunity to put their investigation, and their character, on the line.

"They [Salvatore and Gray] did everything. These guys are to be commended," Jones says.

It wasn't just Salvatore and Gray who worked so hard. All the cops associated with the murder case came forward and pitched in. "I thought they [the cops] were extraordinary. My father had been an old Chicago Police Officer. I thought that these police officers were just the best. They donated as much time as I wanted, and they lived in every different locale in the world. Some were in Georgia, some were in Kentucky. It didn't make any difference. They came to Chicago and donated their own time. They weren't getting paid for this to try and set this cart right," Jones says.

Jones was put in a tough spot. On the one hand, he could easily settle. But, on the other, he believed the detectives were right. In the end, he sided with the detectives, a bold, courageous move. In doing so, he contradicted the entire process that freed Porter, including the claims of Governor George Ryan. He was also contradicting the entire investigation by Protess and his Northwestern students, who were by now international celebrities. As Jones describes the evolution of his decision to take the case to trial, my respect for him grows. How easy it would have been for him to simply settle the case and move on with his career. He was taking on a tidal wave of public and journalistic opinion backing Porter's claims and the Northwestern investigation.

How then to present the case? Jones could simply argue that the detectives did nothing wrong. He could argue that their decisions were lawful. He could point out that all their actions were reasonable and guided by probable cause. But this strategy appeared hopeless so long as one believed Porter was innocent. If Porter were innocent, Porter's attorneys could argue, then something along the way that put him in prison must have been wrong. That logic pointed right back at the detectives. The public image of the police was at its lowest. The police, particularly Burge and his men, were taking a terrible beating, with almost daily accusations of torture and coerced confessions. Jones decided to put everything on the line.

"The only way we win this case is by retrying it and show the jury that Anthony Porter was guilty," Jones says.

Jones acknowledges that Porter's attorneys were likely shocked at his decision to go to trial.

"Do I think they [Porter's lawyers] ever thought we would go to trial on this case? Probably not," Jones says. "They did what any good lawyer would do. They thought that they had all the facts and they warned me. I think their initial settlement offer was something like fourteen million dollars, but if I had the audacity to take it to trial they were going to request that the jury return of verdict of twenty-four million."

The pressure on Jones was immense. If he lost the trial, he could cost the city another ten million dollars. It could be a devastating blow to his reputation.

Then something astonishing took place. As the reality of a trial approached, so, too, did the first claims of torture against the detectives, some twenty-one years after the murders. Out of nowhere, Porter suddenly claimed that the detectives had tried to beat a confession out of him. Porter said the detectives had smacked him in the back of his head with a phone book, placed a bag over his head—accusations eerily similar to the ones made against Burge and his men, though Burge and his men had nothing to do with the case. Porter claimed he wouldn't give in to the detectives' abuse, so there was no confession. They tortured him, then just threw in the towel, he said. Nevertheless, photos taken of Porter after he was processed showed no bruises of any kind. There was no physical evidence, no witnesses, nothing. Porter said nothing about torture to any state's attorney, nor during his criminal trial or in his appeal of his conviction.

For the detectives, the torture allegations were one more incredible turn in the case. Here they had successfully convinced their attorney that Porter was the killer. They had convinced Jones to take the civil case to trial. Then Porter claimed the detectives tortured him. It seemed obvious to the cops that Porter was merely tapping into the wave of torture claims arising from the Burge cases, tapping into what would certainly seem to them a vibrant mythology in the city, for the detectives had never laid a hand on Porter. In fact, they had never even met Porter in the course of their investigation. All Salvatore and Gray ever did was get a warrant issued for Porter's arrest based upon witness statements. Porter turned himself in to other detectives. How, then, could detectives torture a man they had never met? Porter had been on death row for many years, living among many inmates who also claimed torture against Burge. Many of these death-row inmates had been set free based on their accusations. Now that Porter saw his own case slipping away when Jones refused to settle, he seemed to grasp at these torture myths for his own financial salvation.

I bring up the torture allegations to Jones.

"Now that is something I had an opinion about. I thought he [Porter] totally fabricated those allegations," Jones says.

Jones likened Porter's claims of torture to accidents involving city buses. When the police first get dispatched to a call of a traffic crash involving a CTA bus, it may come out as ten people riding it, but by the time police get there, Jones tells me, the bus is often packed. This metaphorical bus that inmates were getting on, claiming torture, was a compelling acknowledgment that inmates were using this claim fraudulently, and frequently. Clearly, there were plenty of lawyers willing to use the allegations in court. The torture bus: I thought it was an apt description. How many inmates have been riding it? Who is driving it? Is there more than one bus? Is there a fleet? How bad was the original accident? Was it a fender bender or a head-on crash? In other words, had the original incident been an all-out torture involving electrocution and

burning of flesh, or had someone been smacked around by a few dis-
traught officers?

For Salvatore and Gray, it was one more outrage they had to deal
with. Now, not only were they accused of framing Porter; they were torturers as well. What next? It became even more crucial for them to win
the case, because with an allegation of torture, criminal charges might be
on the horizon. After the trial, would the People's Law Office and other
activist attorneys suddenly "discover" more inmates in the prisons willing to make the same claims against them?

Jones and I work our way to the point right after the verdict. This is perhaps the most illuminating and disturbing event, aside from the verdict
itself. I review with Jones the moments after the trial, when a collection
of stunned journalists lingered in the courtroom. A *Chicago Tribune*
reporter walked up to Jones after the jury ruled Porter would not get any
of the twenty-four million dollars he was demanding. Jones answered
the *Tribune* reporter honestly. He pointed at Porter and said, "The killer
has been sitting in that room right there all day." That is, after all, the
legal theory that had just won the trial. Among those standing within
earshot of Jones was *Tribune* columnist Eric Zorn, a vocal supporter of
wrongful conviction cases by Protess and his students, whom Zorn
would one day "toast" in one of his columns, calling Protess, Ciolino,
and the students "warriors": "To the Northwestern University journalism students who helped Protess dig into long-dead cases, and to the
investigators who did some of the most dangerous sleuthing, including
Paul Ciolino . . ." Zorn was also prolific in his support of wrongful conviction claims by other activists and law firms and joined in the condemnation of Jon Burge and his men.

In response to this statement by Jones alleging once again that Porter
was the killer, the *Tribune* published a column by Zorn. In it, Zorn
argued that the city owed Porter an apology because of Jones's statement. The reason the city owed the apology, Zorn claimed, was that
Porter was innocent. Zorn then reviewed much of the Northwestern
investigation in his column and cited the fact that the governor had pardoned Porter.

"We know, in short, that Porter's case was a flagrant and frightening
miscarriage of justice . . ." Zorn wrote, not mentioning any of the evidence in the civil trial or the grand jury that disputed Porter's innocence.

Zorn argued that the jury's verdict is not the equivalent of a guilty verdict, which is true; it was a civil trial. But the fact that Jones's legal strategy was to argue that Porter was guilty is one more compelling sign of Porter's guilt, one that Zorn refused to acknowledge. At the end of his column, Zorn described walking over to Porter's attorneys, asking them if they would file a defamation lawsuit against Jones for his claim that Porter was guilty.

Jones, who had once believed the case was unwinnable, had investigated it, re-interviewed the witnesses and concluded that Porter was guilty, and took it to trial. This transformation by Jones should have been compelling to anyone looking at the trial, particularly members of the media. Jones was no radical, no one with an ax to grind against anyone. He was not reflexively pro-police. There was no apparent agenda operating in his representation of the detectives. He never knew them before he met them. There was obviously no racial bias in favor of them, for Jones was black and the detectives were white. Yet, despite the evidence presented in the case, Zorn insisted Porter was still an innocent victim and deserved an apology from the city. Zorn made no mention of what the detectives had just been through for six years, the fact that they had endured the worst accusations of malfeasance and then they had won the trial that tested those allegations. He refused to acknowledge that the verdict in the trial was one more ominous sign that Anthony Porter did indeed murder Green and Hillard.

When, I wonder, did a columnist ever walk over to a losing lawyer in a case and suggest a lawsuit of defamation against an opposing attorney, simply because that attorney expressed his opinion based on the evidence? One glaring omission in Zorn's column was the fact that Jones uncovered so much testimony that eyewitness William Taylor had been coerced into retracting his original statements to the police and at the criminal trial. It's important to step back and look at the larger picture. Alstory Simon claimed he was coerced into confessing to the crime. Simon's allegation generated little interest by Zorn and other journalists writing about wrongful convictions. Now William Taylor was claiming he was coerced. Inez Jackson and Walter Jackson would also claim that they, too, conspired with Protess to falsely accuse Simon of being the killer in a ruse to get Porter out of jail. This was an overwhelming amount of evidence that the Northwestern investigation was completely fraudulent. But none of this clicked with any Chicago journalist, including Zorn. Instead, Zorn railed against Jones for merely asserting Porter was the killer.

There is, in my mind, a note of panic in Zorn's column. Many journalists like Zorn had embraced the Northwestern group, Zorn's "warriors," without checking the facts. In doing so, they had, in fact, helped a killer to get free and put an innocent man in prison. One wonders about Zorn's conception of "warriors." What would Zorn call the cops who rushed into the park the night of the shootings and found witnesses, carried bleeding victims into the wagons? What he would call the detectives who went to Porter's mother's apartment where Porter was possibly hiding in a bed with a shotgun? Did they not qualify as "warriors"?

To me there seems another looming panic in the wake of the civil verdict: Perhaps re-investigating the Porter case in response to the allegations that Jones had made both in the trial and right after might lead to what many city detectives had been claiming all along, that the Porter case was only the tip of the iceberg, that many other wrongful conviction cases were just as fraudulent.

As I mention Zorn's column to Jones, he sits up, clearly agitated.

"I have never been pleased by that column because that reporter [Zorn] had never even followed the case during the trial. He was astounded at the verdict. I'd like to see what he has to say today because in his column he said it would be overturned. I'd like for him to know this went all the way to the Supreme Court and was not overturned. I was very displeased with his column," Jones says.

The camera runs out of tape. I stretch my back in the hallway, walk out to the area by the elevators. I gather my thoughts for what will likely be the end of the interview. When we sit back down, the cameraman nods at me that we are rolling. I have grown to like and respect Jones. He stood by the detectives in the face of tough odds and against powerful public and media pressure. Now he's willing to talk to us. He has no obligation to put himself out there for a case long dead and buried. Clearly it's a moral conviction, a feeling that the detectives had been railroaded in the case and that a killer had been set free that compelled him to talk to me. But now I have to bring up a sore point. If Jones believes Porter is guilty, that means Alstory Simon, the man Protess and his cohorts claimed was the killer, is in fact innocent. Jones acknowledges that there was no evidence he could find indicating Simon was even in the park that night. I point out the irony that wrongful conviction advocates were themselves guilty of a wrongful conviction. Jones grudgingly admits the theory has merit.

Why then, I ask, is there no movement to get him out? Why has no one among the city attorneys or even the prosecutor's office who saw Jones argue that Porter was guilty, why has there been no movement to get Simon a hearing? I ask him then something I feel is the core of the issue: If someone had come to believe Porter was guilty and should not have been exonerated, wasn't it inevitable to uncover the investigation that led to Porter being freed? Wasn't it natural to review this investigation to find out what went wrong? Here Jones insists that it was his job to represent the detectives in the case, solely in regard to Porter. That's true, but after the ruling I wonder why the City of Chicago lawyers and the county prosecutors never took a second look at the Porter case. I wonder why there was no urgency to reconsider Alstory Simon's case. After all, here was an immense amount of evidence that a man was wrongfully convicted and that Chicago detectives had been railroaded. I can't understand why it is that once the Porter exoneration fell apart in a legal proceeding, no investigation into the Innocence Project investigation ever unfolded. Many detectives and lawyers were hoping for it. They wanted a review of many wrongful conviction cases in the city. From Jones's civil trial, it would be another six years before Protess would be fired from Northwestern, before his malfeasance would be revealed. For this, Jones has no answer.

I tell Peter I have to get going right after the interview, to avoid the long conversations afterward. Back out on the street, I find a parking ticket on my scooter, past the meter. I shove it in my pocket. I get on the scooter and head to work, taking State Street all the way down. After Roosevelt it's a pleasant ride, where, if you time it right, you can hit a long section of green lights. I'm thinking about the timeline. Porter got out in 1999. His civil trial was in 2005. Salvatore told me that as the civil trial approached and then concluded, no reporter ever called him up. By 2005 the allegations were endless that the cops were convicting the wrong man in dozens of cases. After the Porter case, Protess initiated many other wrongful conviction claims, and won. No one from the state's attorney's office launched an investigation based upon the ruling in the Porter civil trial. None of the lawyers for the city stepped out and called for an investigation. The repercussions of the civil trial, and Jones's argument that Porter was indeed the offender, faded away in an eerie silence.

17. DOWNSTATE

I eye Peter as he stands outside the Whitehall Hotel on the Near North Side, holding a tray with coffees and donuts on it. He's having trouble balancing them. I walk up from about a half block away where I got out of a taxi. It's very early in the morning, right before dawn on a summer day. Few people are out on the North Side. Peter doesn't recognize me until I'm right next to him. He offers a coffee but I show him the one in my hand.

"Where's Jim?" I ask.

"Around the corner. Be here in a second," he says.

There's something nervous in Peter's speech and manner. He seems a little too excited to see me. It's the first alarm about the day ahead. Of all our interviews, this is the one he set up, and it's crucial. But because he's so fidgety, I'm not sure everything is lined up the way it should be. I have taken several days off work this week. I only have a few vacation days left, and I'm worn out after so many days of shooting other interviews. If today's interview falls through, I will have to reassess working with Peter. If he can't handle simple things like setting up an interview, how can we shoot an entire documentary together?

"Listen, I talked to that guy at the studio and I think we're all set. This is gonna be great. I'm telling you we've really got something here. What I want to do with this . . ."

I tune Peter out. Rather than get things done on his own, I have to remind Peter over and over about them, then eventually do most of them myself anyway—letters, phone calls, lists, copies, transcripts. I suspect that Peter's sales pitch this morning is partly geared to avoid addressing crucial questions about the interview and whether he has set it up correctly. He will keep jabbering to prevent me from asking those questions. This strategy worked when I first became involved in the project, because I figured he knew what he was talking about. But now I have lost a lot of faith in him. He knows my trepidation about our plans today, my feeling that, despite his claims he has sorted everything out, the day will be a fiasco. I just cut him off.

"Do you have the paperwork we need to get into the prison?" I interrupt.

"Yes, I've got it. Calm down. I keep telling you. It's not going to be a problem. We'll get in," Peter says.

"You're sure we have permission to shoot the interview inside the prison?"

"For God's sake, what did I just say? I keep telling you. You're worrying about nothing."

"Don't worry about my worrying, Peter. I'm not wasting another day off for nothing."

"You're not wasting anything. It'll go fine. Believe me."

Peter seems to have forgotten all about the clusterfuck of the Shaw interview. His reassurances only make me more anxious. As I formulate a response and a warning that this day better be set up right, Jim's Lincoln Town Car pulls around the corner. I look at Jim in his car. Jim, the private investigator and retired DEA agent who has taught me much about the Porter case, always on time, always informed, always willing to do the extra work. Here he is getting up early in the morning, driving from the far western suburbs and picking us up and driving us downstate, all because he wants to get an innocent man out of prison. One reason Jim is picking us up is that Peter refused to rent a car and drive himself, so Jim had to drive almost two hours out of his way so Peter could save fifty bucks. Peter's cheapness, his willingness to let other people do the work and spend their own money, is another warning sign. Peter jumps in the front, of course. I take the back.

We're on our way to southern Illinois, to the state prison in Danville where Alstory Simon is housed. He's about thirteen years into his thirteen-year sentence for the homicides of Marilyn Green and Jerry Hillard, the murders Anthony Porter committed. Simon speaks to Jim on the phone regularly, Jim trying to keep Simon's spirits up. The news that people were getting involved gave Simon hope. It will be the first time he can tell his side of the story in the media. Today we are going to get a step-by-step account of how Simon "confessed" to the killings to private investigator Paul Ciolino. We also want to go over Simon's account of his actions on the night of the murder itself.

The narrative provided by the Northwestern investigators alleging Simon was the shooter held some peculiar details. It was posited by Protess and Ciolino that Alstory Simon shot Hillard and Green over a drug debt. Then there was the incredible claim that Simon and his wife, Inez Jackson, went out for ice cream after the shooting. The Bud Billiken Parade draws huge crowds, many from different gangs. Mix with it a lot of drinking and getting high, and there is almost always some kind of gang violence in or around the park. Seeing gangbangers loitering when he approached, Simon did not want to go in and warned Green and Hillard to do the same. Obviously, it turned out to be a wise decision by Simon. Simon's story was that after they turned away from the park, that's when he and Inez went out for ice cream, which they brought home for Inez's kids. They did not find out Jerry and Marilyn had been murdered until the next day.

Our goal for today is to get Alstory Simon's statement on tape. It will be several hours in the car each way. I have never even been to this part of the country before. It has taken a long time to set up the interview. First, Simon had to get us on a list to visit. We had written letters to Illinois Department of Corrections officials, the governor. A sticking point was the fact that cameras are not allowed in the prison systems. Peter said he had finally gotten approval, but I'm not so sure. Peter is always claiming people are his friends and that he has connections in high places, but he rarely comes through on anything. The sound of his bragging voice grates on me.

When there's finally a pause in Peter's speech, Jim suggests a different route.

"We can take the freeway, but I know a state road that is just as fast and is a much better drive," Jim says as we moved through the South Side. We're right on the expressway where the Robert Taylor Homes used to be, near where Anthony Porter lived. When people arrived or left the city, the reputation for violence that took place in these large buildings imposed a kind of anxiety on them. They often didn't even notice the slight pressure they placed on the accelerator, for no one ever wanted to break down along this stretch of the expressway. Now these projects are gone from the horizon. People are forgetting they existed. But the cops still talk about them. For a cop to have worked this area was a badge of honor. If he worked Porter's neighborhood for even just a year or so, he was a seasoned cop. He had seen it all.

Taking a country road is fine by me. I love country roads and I haven't been out of the city in a long time. Jim's Town Car is a great cruiser. It's peaceful to move off the interstate onto the state highway, then into the rural areas, corn farms everywhere. No longer in back pain, I put my feet up, stretch out on the backseat. This summer has been one of the worst droughts in the state's history, but today there are ominous signs of storms all across the horizon, layers and layers of dark clouds low to the ground. Soon there's lightning far off to the west. It's wonderful to imagine the parched ground getting soaked, wonderful to be moving through it all day, the earth taking a deep, satisfying drink. The first few drops hit the windshield. We're right on the edge of the front.

Jim announces we have to stop for gas. We pull into a small town with a gas pump and a little convenience store right off the road. Jim refuses to take any money from me. I go inside the old store, buy more coffee, then head outside and wait for Peter and Jim. I look around. We're on the edge of the town. To the north is the center of the little municipality, desolate, most buildings boarded up. There's farmland everywhere else, with large modern windmills on many of them, used to generate electricity. Darker clouds are rolling in. I walk out of the parking lot where the horizon is fully in view. I find myself wanting to wander down the road alongside the gas station and wait for the storm. I want the rain to fall on me. I can feel the drooping trees, the rows of corn all craving the water that's about to arrive, and I crave it too. It dawns on me that I'm approaching a state of mind I have not entered in decades, in which one finds some continuity with the life and place all around them. I feel the trees craving the water that's about to come, anticipated the cleansing it will give, like a kind of absolution. Trees blow gently as the rains approach, as if they're dancing in anticipation. I want to be a part of this cleansing. I walk a little more down the road. Memories stir. A great, fulfilling loneliness comes over me. I have always loved rainstorms, love to be stuck in them.

Once I was hitchhiking home from college in New Mexico where I had finished my freshman year of college in a Great Books program, right around twenty years old. I was just south of the Illinois border in Missouri. I had hoped to make it to Chicago that night, but I wasn't sure I could. A storm was chasing me all afternoon. It would be a long night if I didn't get to the city. I would turn to the left as I walked along the road, watching the storm approach, the lightning getting nearer. I figured if the rain came, it came. There was nothing I could do about it. I would try to find a large tree to stand under or some abandoned building, something. Perhaps up the road a little bit was a restaurant. I could

sit there for an hour, have some coffee and a sandwich. Part of me
wanted the rain to come on. It would be fine just to watch, to pour on
all the farms.

Just when the first drops started coming and the wind kicked up, a
pickup approached. I turned toward it, put out my thumb. It stopped.
There was a large dog in the cab, no room for me there. The driver
pointed to the back of the truck and said "use the plastic." I nodded and
jumped in. I sat against the cab of the truck with the plastic wrapped
around me. Little rain hit me, and it was warm. We passed along country roads for hours. I could hear some of the music he was playing in the
cab, felt the rocking back and forth as the truck moved through curves
on the highway. By the time he dropped me off about an hour from
Chicago, the rain had stopped. It was wet everywhere, and cool. We
shook hands. He handed me a couple of beers. I put them in my back-
pack and walked for a while until I came upon an old gas station, abandoned. I went to the side of it where it was dry, sat down on the cement,
and cracked open one of the beers. There was a steady breeze blowing
across the fields around the gas station, the sound of birds. After I drank
both beers, I walked back out to the road and began walking, singing out
loud.

In this peacefulness on the road next to the convenience store, this rec-
ollection of an earlier trip makes me think that nothing has changed in
my life, or that everything has. I can't be sure which one. Am I that same
person from back then, or am I completely different? Whichever I am, I
feel the ancient pull of the road. I consider the possibility of just contin-
uing to walk, not returning to Jim's car. I have a few hundred dollars in
my pocket, some credit cards and a debit card. Jim and Peter will get
along without me. I could call them on my cell phone while I'm hidden
in a row of corn, tell them something came up, to go on ahead without
me. It would be wonderful to walk through the green stalks, feel the soil
underneath my feet. Jim and Pete would be angry with me, but they
would get over it. Peter in particular would throw a big fit in the parking lot of the convenience store. I smile at the notion of him flinging his
Styrofoam coffee cup against the asphalt, saying I had betrayed him. I tell
myself I can last a few months with what I have on me until something
else comes along, and something else will surely come along. Otherwise,
there would be no road. Right?

Some drops fall on me. I spread out my arms to catch as many of them as I can. I begin to daydream. Perhaps I can get a job in one of these farm towns where not every decision I make could get me sued or indicted. I suddenly feel so much possibility. I want to wander cornfields and swim in midwestern lakes. I step off the road, a few feet into some farmland, my feet sinking into the dirt. I think about rolling around in it, playing with some caterpillars, climbing a nearby tree. Then I settle on the image of me stripping down naked, deep in the cornfield, and running through it—running so hard that I'm gasping for oxygen, right across the road into another cornfield. All the while the rain will wash over me.

How badly I want to move deeper into this communion with the rain and the road. It seems holy. I have always sought a similar communion in Chicago, but it's impossible. The city's mind is partitioned off into bellicose units, like the sociopath's mind, like the cells in the prison we're going to visit, each occupant mired in his own criminality. That's certainly me. Here I am a cop going to investigate what I believe is surely a wrongful conviction, and I feel more a criminal than I ever have in my life. I'm trapped in the city, within criminal walls I barely understand. They're isolating. They make the continuity I feel on this country road impossible, absurd. Away from the city, on this lonely road, I become aware of how much I crave the destruction of these walls. I have this sense that my life has been wasted, doomed because I have always been trapped behind them. I should have left the city years ago. I should never have come back to it. Never. I dread returning to it after the interview, dread even going to the prison downstate, for once I arrive at either destination, the walls reappear, and I'm criminal again.

A pickup truck drives past. I think about sticking my thumb out and leaving once and for all. But it's a sign of my maturity that I don't. In my younger years, I would have taken off in a moment. But what is the value of a life in flight, away from my walls? They will always pursue me, call out to me. There is something I have to figure out in Chicago, something I have to overcome. I work too hard not to be a refugee, so I let the truck pass. I know now I need my walls, because I need to find a way through them. This is why we're heading to interview Simon, isn't it, to sort things out?

Right?

I hear a car honk. I turn. Jim and Peter are waving their arms. I stare at them, then the lonely old farmhouse across the road, with the rows of corn next to it. Rain falls on my jacket. I like the sound of it as I walk back toward the car.

"Where are you going, you dizzy motherfucker?" Jim says as I got closer.

"Nowhere. I just like the rain."

When we arrive in Danville, the storms have not reached that part of the state. We pull into the parking lot of the prison. There are two deputies, a sergeant and a canine officer with his dog. They announce they're searching all cars that day for weapons and contraband. As we get out of the car, Jim tells the two officers he's a retired federal agent and has a pistol hidden in the door. The music stops. They ask our information, check our credentials, write up a report, then tell us we will have to leave the gun at the local police station, several miles away.

The rain starts as we head into town, torrential. Quickly the streets back up with water. Jim's windshield wipers are on full, so you can only catch a glimpse of what's outside. We drive into the parking lot of the police station debating what to do. We are three men sitting in the parking lot of a police station in the middle of a rainstorm. We all feel like outlaws. We decide to just leave the gun in Jim's car and take a cab back to the prison. I call a cab on my cell phone while we wait in Jim's car, the rain still falling heavily. A beat-up old minivan shows up about ten minutes later. I get out of the car and wave it over to us.

In the cab, Peter starts talking a lot. He's getting nervous, I can tell. The day is not living up to his promises. We drive through downtown Danville, a city reeling from the modern economy. There are boarded-up buildings, crappy roads. People are just getting by here. Certainly a prison job is one of the best in the area. The taxi rattles and thumps along the roads, then pulls back into the prison. The corrections officers are gone from the parking lot. If only we had come a little later.

I stand next to Peter as he approaches the sergeant about our visit. Peter has several pieces of paper in his hand, unfolded. Jim waits in the corner. While Peter is talking to the sergeant, other visitors begins showing up and walking right past us. The sergeant looks up our names, gives a confused look, and says he knows nothing about it. I smile and chuckle to myself. Peter becomes nervous, raises his voice a little too much to the guy, tells him to call the warden. *Not good, Peter. You don't tell these guys what to do,* I want to say. I withdraw and go over by Jim. The sergeant repeats his statement that we are not cleared to visit Simon and begins making phone calls. Peter keeps asking the sergeant questions, so I call him over to Jim and me as if I have to ask him a question, but I really just want to get him away from the sergeant. Part of me wants to grab him by the shirt collar and pull him toward me. I want to say to him, "I thought you had this all set up?" Then I want to remind him about the Ricky Shaw interview when no one could get ahold of him. But what purpose will it serve? I knew miles ago this would probably happen. Peter's Los Angeles shtick of everyone being his friend doesn't fly in Illinois. We need permission from higher-ups, signed letters.

I look out the window at the rain. Peter stands next to me, railing about the injustice of it, how he had it all set up, how he can't understand what has happened. Jim sits politely and listens. Nothing ever rattles this guy. I let Peter go on for a while, then can't take it anymore. I go outside under an awning, where I figure he won't follow me. It's nice out there, peaceful. I can watch the rain fall. Then there's a knock on the window. I turned around slowly and there's Peter on the other side of the glass panel, only inches from me, shaking his head and giving me a confused look. His arms are outstretched. He's mouthing some words to me. I turn back around, ignoring him.

After three hours of waiting, the sergeant tells us there's nothing he can do. Peter remains at his counter, arguing, asking that he call the warden again. The sergeant has had enough. I walk over and give it one last shot. Moving Peter aside, I appeal to him on the grounds that we are both in law enforcement. He looks down, remains silent. I can tell he wants to help me but he can't. I call the taxi back. It arrives in a few minutes. We run out to it in the downpour, then drive home from the police station downtown, the three of us not saying much.

18. SOUTH-BOUND

I'm driving south on I-55, over an industrial section of the city on my way to meet Bill Crawford, the journalist who introduced me to the Porter story, in a suburb called Stickney. I'm at a point now where the only thing that remains in the Porter case is Alstory Simon's confession to the double homicide. Simon stood up in court in September 1999 and confessed to the murders. The events that led up to Simon's confession, the manner in which he was duped and coerced by Protess and Ciolino, should have initiated an investigation, should have put a halt to the case. Nevertheless, Simon admitted at the sentencing to the murders. He turned and faced the mother of Marilyn Green and apologized. I turn this confession over and over in my mind as I drive south. In looking over the case, almost everything else had fallen through. The so-called witnesses had. Simon's wife, Inez, recanted her statement right before she died of AIDS, saying on the record that she lied about Simon being the killer. So did her nephew, Walter Jackson. William Taylor, an original witness, stated under oath he was coerced into changing his statement. The Northwestern investigators admitted they had not even interviewed a crucial group of four witnesses who put Porter at the scene. Porter's case had been dismantled in a grand jury hearing in 1999, then again in a civil trial in 2005, where Porter came away with no money. No witnesses every put Alstory Simon at the scene, and the police investigation showed clearly that the killer was Porter. But it was this confession, the fact that Alstory Simon would admit to the murders early in the morning in February 1999, that was so impossible to fathom.

Trucks pass me by. Some lights flash in my rearview mirror. It's a semi, right behind me. There are about ten cars behind him. I can tell they're pissed. In my rumination on this confession, I have slowed down while I'm in the left lane. I give the car some gas, move into a slower lane, and let them go by, ignoring their stares. There's one central point about the Simon confession. If one believes Porter was indeed the killer, as the detectives had, as the jury in the criminal trial did, if one rejects the Northwestern investigation as the grand jury had and the jury in the civil trial did, if one believes the numerous witnesses collected at the time of the murder, then one has to wonder: How did the Northwestern investigators get a confession from Alstory Simon? The confession itself is so bizarre. Why would a relatively street-smart man allow a stranger into his house and eventually allow himself to be taped giving a confession to a double homicide from sixteen years earlier? Simon's claims pass through my mind again: Ciolino flashing a gun, claiming to be a police officer, threatening Simon with the death penalty, affidavits claiming Simon was guilty that were later retracted, a fake tape of a man saying he saw Simon commit the murders, promises of a short prison sentence, then wealth afterward if Simon confessed, Ciolino obtaining a lawyer for Simon.

I begin to ruminate on the months between the time Simon turned himself in, in February 1999, and when he confessed in court, in September 1999, a seven-month period where he lingered in the county jail. Even if he was duped that one morning in February when he confessed to Paul Ciolino, didn't he wise up in the months afterward? After the debacle of not getting to film Simon at the prison with Peter, I got on Simon's phone list at the Danville prison and began talking to him frequently. Each day we went over his case. Simon told me he did have second thoughts about confessing. When Simon got up at his first hearing, he said he pleaded not guilty. He said he didn't want to go through with it. He said he called his attorney Jack Rimland and told him he couldn't go through with the plan, said he would not plead guilty at court. Rimland, Simon said, cursed him out and told him he had to or he would get the death penalty. Rimland said the Milwaukee police were looking for him in a murder there as well and that if he didn't confess they would pursue him on that murder. He would get the death penalty or another life sentence. This, Simon said, was why he stuck with the confession.

Simon's hopes of getting someone to listen to the story of his bizarre confession were slim until he obtained the grand jury materials. It was illuminating what he had to go through to get them. Simon told me that after he was sent to prison, he received a letter from Rimland stating that Rimland was no longer representing Simon. This was a shock to Simon, because he believed there was a deal to get him out of prison in just a few years. On his own, Simon demanded all the records for his case. Eventually, Simon sent Rimland a letter demanding them, but, Simon said, Rimland refused to send them. Simon was forced to file a complaint, at which time a judge ordered Rimland to send Simon the transcripts. Simon told me this order was on the record of his case, so one day I went down to the county court building and checked it out. There it was, an order from the judge demanding Rimland give up the materials to Simon. It was then that Simon, sitting in his cell, read the grand jury hearing in which the Northwestern investigation fell apart. Simon was furious when he read the transcripts. His attorney had never let him know how the Northwestern case had fallen apart under questioning. It was evidence Simon could have used in his own defense. Nevertheless, Simon now had some hope because the grand jury materials, then the civil trial afterward, begged one central question: If the Northwestern investigation was wrong, if Porter was clearly the murderer, how then did Ciolino, Rimland, and Protess get Simon, an innocent man, to confess?

Traffic slows down. I'm stuck between two huge semis, waiting for my exit. I get off and drive into Stickney, Illinois, turn right on a side street. Just as I do, Bill pulls up right behind me in front of Lisa Medonia's home. A few minutes later, Don the cameraman also pulls up. Peter is back in Los Angeles. I have never met this woman, only spoken to her on the phone a few times. She leads us into her home, where Don sets up the camera in the kitchen. She has two daughters at the house, both very poised, polite, and friendly. At this time, she's a single mother. We sit in the kitchen talking while Don tests for sounds. I have to turn off an air conditioner, unplug the refrigerator. A guy outside is trimming his bushes with a power trimmer. I go out and ask if he can turn it off for a little while. He hesitates, then agrees. Then Bill sits in the corner next to the camera with his notes. Lisa tells us her story.

A few months after Ciolino obtained a confession from Simon, Lisa was sitting in her living room, along with her three daughters and her then-husband, all of them watching television. At the time, Lisa's husband was injured and had initiated a lawsuit against a doctor. Suddenly there was a terrible pounding on the door that wouldn't let up. Lisa's husband went down to see who it was. Standing there was Paul Ciolino with an associate. Ciolino confronted the husband, identified himself as a former state trooper. He then told the husband that he was working on behalf of the doctor the husband was suing. Ciolino said that if the husband didn't withdraw the lawsuit, he could wind up with a "bullet in his head." The whole family could hear the exchange at the front door and the daughters became extremely alarmed. The husband didn't back down from Ciolino. Finally, after a long argument, Ciolino and his partner left. Lisa and her husband weren't sure what to do. The following day they went down to the police station and filed a police report against Ciolino. When the case came up for court, she and her husband talked with the prosecutor, who then talked with Ciolino's attorney: none other than Jack Rimland, the same lawyer who "represented" Alstory Simon.

The prosecutor came back and told them the case had been dismissed. While watching television one day, Lisa saw the Porter case covered on the news, saw Ciolino had extracted a confession from a man named Alstory Simon. She knew nothing about the Porter case, nothing about Alstory Simon. Immediately she suspected something was amiss, based upon the day Ciolino had come to her house and threatened her husband. She wrote a letter to Alstory Simon in prison, explained who she was and what Ciolino had done to her and her family. Simon wrote back, describing the confession he gave to Ciolino, how he was threatened and manipulated. Convinced something terribly crooked had taken place in the Porter case, Lisa eventually scheduled a visit to the prison and met Simon. It was a strange image: a suburban white woman looking up a black man from the South Side projects, now in a prison, a man she never knew anything about. The times I had spoken to her, she didn't strike me as a fool, not the kind of woman who flippantly makes friends with convicts through the mail. She was genuinely impressed that Simon was a decent man, so much so that she even brought her daughters to the prison to meet him. Simon never tried to hustle the family for money. Lisa and her family said Simon was a perfect gentleman. Lisa heard Simon's account of how Ciolino obtained a confession from him, and it struck her as exactly what Ciolino had done when he came to her home: barging into a home, armed, making claims of working for the police, threats of violence. Eventually she contacted private investigator and former DEA agent Jim Delorto and told him her story. She wrote out an affidavit for him as well. All this time, she kept in contact with Simon while he was in prison, exchanging letters and Christmas cards. After the interview, Lisa gets up and brings several of Simon's letters over to show us. We read them over at the kitchen table while Don packs up his gear.

Outside of Lisa's house, Bill and I lean against his car.

"Some kind of woman," I say.

"Yeah, and to think she went to bat for Simon so much, a man she didn't even know."

"Yeah."

It's a central theme by Protess and other wrongful conviction advocates that the police obtain confessions illegally, brutally, that they frame suspects. This was the argument made by Porter and his attorneys. But the magnitude of malfeasance in the Northwestern investigation, the cruelty and duplicity engaged in, is itself an epiphany. The fact that no wrongful conviction activists observed the fraudulence of the Northwestern claims, that none of them pointed out the obvious signs of coercion in the Simon confession, betrays evidence of their own crooked solidarity, their own malevolent hearts. In this regard, the Porter case is a kind of window. As I drive out of Stickney back onto Interstate 55, I recall how deeply the wrongful conviction lawyers would dig for evidence of malfeasance against the cops, with a kind of mania. Look at the frenzy with which they went after Salvatore and Gray. My mind goes back to a detail in the Burge saga. The activists called to the witness stand a woman who had been on a single blind date with Jon Burge. What could a woman who had been on one date with Burge reveal about how he did his job? What could she possibly contribute?

Traffic on I-55 begins to thin out. The sun is going down. I have the night to myself, no work. I decide to head downtown and get a nice meal with a couple of beers. I'll sit outside in the glow of a yellow summer evening, while the beers give me a slight buzz. This glow is already all around me as I drive. It resonates off the skyline. It always held me in awe the way it bathes the city.

19. OLD FRIENDS

I remember getting the phone message one morning that Wrigley had been shot. It was 2005, and I began researching wrongful convictions. I was standing motionless in my apartment with my cell phone to my ear. Everything suddenly turned white and I wanted to vomit, but I held it down. The call had come the night before but I hadn't heard it. I felt guilty that I had missed the call, that I had not rushed to the hospital like a good friend should have. Wrigley had helped me out so many times. I dialed various numbers of coworkers trying to get more information, wondering if Wrigley was dead or hooked up to a bunch of machines. Had he been shot in the head? Was he paralyzed? Where was his fiancée, his family? Then there was the child he was to have, a daughter. I sat down because the thoughts made me dizzy. Finally I got ahold of a fellow cop who told me Wrigley was all right. He had been shot twice, but the wounds were not serious. He had been saved from a probably fatal wound to his chest by his bullet-proof vest, which caught the bullet right on the edge of the vest. Two other cops had been shot along with Wrigley, I learned, on a traffic stop in the West Side that had gone all wrong. They were also okay. One of the cops was hit by a ricocheting bullet. The offender had been shot some eighteen times, but was still alive. Wrigley was out of the hospital, my friend told me. Just then, I saw Wrigley's number coming in and I pushed the answer button.

Wrigley and I had become close friends in the academy. The instructor asked the class on the first day—when we were still in civilian clothes—if everyone had their own car. I was one of only two people who didn't. Everyone stared at me when I raised my hand. *How could you not have a car*, their gaze seemed to ask. It was the first instance of me feeling completely out of place. Not only did I not own a car; I had never had one in the city. I had ridden the trains my whole life. The fact that I didn't have a car presented a daunting logistical problem. Without one I would have to haul with me on the train the immense amount of stuff needed for the academy every day: gym clothes, uniform changes, equipment for the range, books, notebooks, and folders. I would have to change trains twice, commuting at least an hour every day, then walk several blocks with my stuff from the train station to the academy. It would be obvious from what I carried on the train that I was in the police academy. This could be dangerous on a public conveyance, where any gangbanger could confront me. I also couldn't wear the academy uniform, so I would have to carry it as well, then change before class started. I didn't have the money to buy a car, and I wouldn't finance one because it wasn't a sure thing I would stay on the job. I wasn't sure I could make it through the academy. But as we introduced ourselves to our classmates, Wrigley let it slip he had just moved into an apartment a few blocks from me. It was almost impossible for him not to offer to drive me to the academy every day, though I could tell he didn't really want to. He was too polite and good-natured to turn me down.

I accepted the police job ambivalently. I had been taking care of my parents for several years prior to getting hired, an experience that had wiped me out physically and emotionally. It had also left me isolated, full of self-doubt. There was no money saved up, no other career I could fall back on. All the things I had to buy for the academy would be put on my credit card, which had only a five-hundred-dollar limit. My dreams of being a writer seemed almost entirely washed up. I was bitter and angry that my life had not gone the way I had hoped. I had grown used to not succeeding at things, so used to it that I almost expected to fail out of the academy. Plus, I had a strong rebellious streak and didn't know if I could thrive in a job that was part military. These were my thoughts as I stood outside the academy on my first day, wearing a dress shirt and tie that barely fit me, thirty-eight years old, the idea of a getting yelled at every day not appealing to me much at all. "Ah, fuck it," I could hear myself saying to an instructor as I slumped out of the position of being at attention and headed to my locker, then out the door. I would jump on the Blue Line el, transfer to the Red Line, and head back to my last doorman job and see if I could get it back. But the police job, I figured, would offer me a steady income and a pension. It would also allow me to wander the city every night. I still had hopes of writing about the city, and I would have a pension. A doorman no more, I could say.

Wrigley was the opposite of me. He was born to be a police officer. He had come to Chicago hoping to further his career after many years working as a cop in St. Louis. For him, law enforcement was a calling, something he had learned from his father, who had also been a police officer. You could tell the way he prepared for class every day, how organized he was, the way he sat and read through the Illinois Compiled Statutes before and after class, memorizing the elements of common crimes. In my manner, my native rebelliousness, I figured I made Wrigley a little uneasy. I thought he was too straight-laced, too by the book. But in our discussions to and from work, I found the opposite. He was willing to look at things on their own terms, no matter what they were. He never, for example, reflexively took the side of the police. He would point out how cops often made the wrong decisions. In our arguments, I often discovered that it was me who looked at the world through some ideological lens. I began to relax around him, and when I set out my doubts about the job, he was always encouraging, always offering to help me.

"What this job needs, the kind of cops that should be on the street, are smart people willing to think things through," he said.

So every morning I waited on the corner of Leavitt and Montrose with two cups of coffee, one of which was my lame contribution for the rides every day. Wrigley went over everything I would need for academy that day. Often we would have to drive back to my apartment so I could pick up what I had forgotten.

Every class elects a commander among their classmates after the first week, when the recruits have had a chance to get to know one another. This class commander is the liaison with all the instructors, all the bosses. It's his or her job to keep everyone in line and to keep things organized. It's a crucial position. A good commander can smooth out problems before the instructors ever learn of them. I quickly realized the only person who gave me a fighting chance was Wrigley. I could pepper him with questions to and from work, have him explain how things worked. He had already been to two other police academies, so he knew how to handle things. Plus, he had experience as a cop. He could diffuse any problems between instructors and me. It was obvious to me he wanted the position in the class. With his knowledge, he could make the experience at the academy as smooth as possible for all of us. I lobbied hard for him and he won by a few votes. His election to class commander was the first break I got. With Wrigley helping me, I might make it.

Wrigley and I were a study in contrasts in other ways. Wrigley was impeccably neat. I was unkempt, always forgetting some crucial part of my uniform like the pin for my name tag or a sweatshirt for the gym. Sometimes I left my coffee cup in his car and I could tell that drove him nuts. Wrigley was in top shape; I was overweight. Wrigley planned things out, was organized. I did everything off the cuff, making it up as I went along. I was politically left and Wrigley was far more right. Because of these contrasts, I kept expecting some dissension to arise between us. We did fall into many disagreements. In fact, as we got to know each other, the rides to and from the academy were often one long argument. But rather than get angry, we almost always ended up laughing. Our arguments were generally good-natured.

"The academy is different than the street. Just because a guy does well in the academy doesn't necessarily mean he'll do well on the street. You'll pick things up out there. This academy stuff is important, but a lot of it is bullshit, a lot of drama. It's just a façade," he said, keeping up my spirits when I got down about the job, when I felt that I just couldn't fit in.

One of my biggest concerns was the gun range. It loomed ahead of me the first few weeks. I had no experience with firearms at all, had never even fired a handgun. I was never a person for details and the gun range was nothing but. Everything had to be just right, and you better not come down there having forgotten something: There was the gun, the gun kit, rounds, the belt, the many rules on the range, the course of fire you had to remember. It was also very military. There was no joking around, no easy banter. If you made a mistake down there, it really counted against you. I remember the day at the academy when the gun retailers came and showed off their wares. They laid out all these different pistols, some American, some Italian, some Swedish. Many of my classmates had been in the military or grew up hunting or were the offspring of police officers. They picked up the various guns and slid them open, pushed buttons on them that made magazines fall out. The clicking and sliding was completely foreign to me. My classmates bantered with the salesmen about range, velocity, calibers, and handgrips. I stood like an idiot in the background, leery of even picking one up. Finally I picked the closest one to me and filled out the order form for it. Turns out it was most expensive one they sold, a Sig Sauer.

"What did you get?" a classmate asked me afterward as all the class-mates discussed why they had picked their gun.

"I got the Sig," I said, abbreviating its name to sound knowledgeable.

"Awesome, it has great action and balance," he said.

"You bet," I lied.

When it was time to go pick it up at the store on Devon Avenue a few days later, just across the city border, I was almost out of money, having run up my credit card for the endless uniforms, name tags, and shoes. What little savings I had was gone. I went into the store and asked them to cancel my order and show me the cheapest gun they had that I could use on the job. They brought out a Berretta 92-D. That night I took it out of its box, looked at my reflection in a full-length mirror pointing a gun at myself, one of those moments you barely recognize yourself or what you have become.

The first few weeks or so at the academy gun range, you don't get any real bullets. Instead, you use fake plastic ones. Our first test was to stand on a line while all the instructors, who were always shouting directives, ordered us to take the gun apart and put it back together. I had practiced this maneuver at home before I registered the gun at the range in the academy, keeping the instructions at my house and going over them. But that was several days earlier and my mind was a little foggy. Now, on the line, they told us to kneel on the floor and take the gun apart. I sprang into action, pulling the slide back, locking it, pulling out the spring, set-ting the parts out on the floor in front of me neatly. Perfect. I was feel-ing pretty good when the order came to reassemble. I put the pieces together and sat back, looking left and right. I was among the first done, so I relaxed. Then we stood in the line with our unloaded guns pointed forward. We were ordered to slide the lock forward. To do this, you push a lever on the side of the gun downward. The gun snaps back into its normal position, except that mine didn't. Instead, the lock slid forward and kept going all the way off the gun. The spring exploded, pushing all the central components up in the air, so high that one of them hit the ceiling. The shit had just hit the fan. Through my peripheral vision, I could see that no one else had encountered the same problem. I stood there with my partial gun pointed to the floor.

Two instructors charged at me, screaming insults and orders to fix the gun. I bent down and picked up the various pieces, trying to recall how they went together as the two instructors stood next to me letting me know what an imbecile I was. Finally I put the gun together but couldn't get it to work correctly, couldn't get the slide to come forward. I was doing something wrong, but I couldn't remember. There was another lever on the gun that I should have switched before sliding the lock forward, but had forgotten all about it. The range instructors were shouting more and more at me. Finally, unable to figure out what was wrong, I turned my head to one of them.

"I think it's broken," I said, hoping it was, hoping I could blame this complete clusterfuck on something else. But that was in vain.

"No, it's not fucking broken. Don't give me that bullshit. It's you. You are doing it wrong. You are not prepared. Why are you not prepared? Fix it, now," the instructor yelled. I could tell he had pizza for lunch. The other instructor stared at me and said in a calm voice, "You are not going to pass this class," a statement that hit me hard. I was thinking the same thing, but it infuriated me to hear him say it.

Finally one of the instructors showed me what I was doing wrong. The damage was done. They stopped the instruction and ordered all of us back into a classroom where an instructor called me out and made me stand in front of the class, my knees bent against the wall with a toy machine gun over my head while he berated me. Within seconds I could barely remain standing, my leg muscles were aching so much. The mixture of humiliation and rage that welled up in me was barely containable. I was thirty-eight, the third oldest guy in the class, and I was standing against a wall with a toy machine gun over my head. I turned and looked at the door, thinking that this would be as good a time as any to make my exit, but I needed the job badly, so I put up with it. But I really wanted to tell the guy to go fuck himself and get the hell out of there. I really wanted a piece of that instructor.

From this day at the range, I was a marked man. The instructors kept a close eye on me, looked for any mistakes. Many of my classmates later told me they thought it was only a matter of time before they ousted me. My spirits were so low the rest of the day, I couldn't focus on anything. This failure at the range brought to life so many others. On the road home that day, Wrigley gave me a pep talk, told me this kind of thing happened all the time and it would fade away. I gave voice again to my doubts about taking the job, and he countered them one by one. From that day forward, I really began to lean on Wrigley, knowing that without his knowledge and advice I had little chance of surviving. He gave it freely, helped me out every step of the way. Without it, I could never have become a cop. He was a really great friend.

One thing that stuck in my head was the statement by the instructor that he didn't think I would make it through the range curriculum. This kind of lit a fire under me. When I was a kid, I took archery lessons. At first, my arrows always went exactly two whole targets to the left, wildly off target but consistent. I couldn't figure it out. I checked and rechecked the sights on it, the way I was holding it. Then the teacher approached me and pointed out the manner in which I released the arrow. I was pulling the string back right before I shot, yanking it backward. The instructor showed how you important it was to just let the arrow go without any last-second jerking motions. Remembering this, my next shot hit the middle of the right target. With that one tip, I became one of the best archery students in the class. One of the instructors at the gun range talked much about squeezing the trigger, not pulling it. As soon as he said this I felt as if I knew what he meant. It was just like archery, how you release the arrow. This lesson hit me and I kept it in mind. Nevertheless, when the first day to shoot approached, I feared yet another screw-up. If I fucked up again, that would probably be it. I had rung up over two thousand dollars in bills buying uniforms, guns, et cetera.

My nerves got the best of me so much that, just before they were about to march us into the range, I began to have a stomachache. I had to use the bathroom. The request to go to the restroom did not endear me any further to the range instructors, who were already eyeing me closely. They had pegged me as the class screw-up, but what could they say? Going to the bathroom at the range was difficult because you had to take off your belt, all the snaps, and set the gun down. There was no convenient place to put them, so you kind of hung them over the wall of the toilet stall. I had to quickly reassemble everything and put it back on before I got back to the range, where everyone would be waiting. There was too great a chance I had forgotten something crucial, like a magazine, so I checked and rechecked the bathroom floor. As I ran back into line, I could see everyone looking at me. *Jesus Christ, Preib again*, was the look on their faces. Then the instructors led us out to the range, where we each took a booth, put on our ear covers, and faced the targets. Instructions came over a loudspeaker from an instructor in the booth. All of a sudden on the line, I felt myself relax, everything become quite simple. The order was given to draw and fire. My arm went down smoothly, the gun came out. I had a good grip on it. As it rose my eye found the sight, aligned it easily, and my finger put pressure on the trigger, not a pull but a squeeze, the lesson from archery as a kid still in my mind, and whammo the gun went off. The kick was slight, almost pleasant. I could see a hole in the target, right down the middle after I re-holstered. With each call to draw and fire, I felt the same confidence and ease. Sometimes we fired twice before re-holstering, sometimes more. Sometimes you ran out of bullets, the gun went into slide lock. You kept it pointed down-range, released the magazine, and reached for a full one from your belt, slid it in, tapped, then released the lock forward and kept firing. I counted the shots, one, two, re-holster, fired one, two, dropped the magazine. All my shots hit. One moment I glanced at other targets and saw that some classmates had missed wildly.

I found myself completely enjoying it, felt relaxed and in control. I felt every shot was going to hit right before I fired. When the shooting was completed, we took our targets and stood in line to have them graded. In mine there was a cluster of shots all in the center, only slightly left. They all scored except one, just outside the target. I went out of my way to walk my target over to the instructor who had berated me the most when I fucked up assembling the gun. I could tell he was eager to see my target, eager to fail me. His look showed he was confident I had probably shot badly. I acted sheepish, reticent to confirm his suspicions. I laid it down. He silently looked it over, counted the holes all clustered in the center by pointing at them with the pen in his hand and counting them up. He paused then wrote 24/25 at the top. As he did so, I resisted the strong impulse to tell him: "Guess you were wrong about me, mother-fucker."

Instead, I looked at him, nodded, and said as innocently as I could, "Wow, looks like I got them all but one," then walked away as he scowled at me.

I eventually won the top gun award for best shooter. Wrigley came in second, right behind me. As a prize, I got a plaque and a meeting with Mayor Daley at his downtown office. But I never would have made it through the course, or the academy for the matter, without Wrigley's help.

The night Wrigley was shot, he and his partner were just dropping off a curfew violator at his home when they heard loud reports, a police phrase for possible gunshots. It was shortly before they were done for the night. Many cops would ignore these loud reports because they wanted to get home. Gunshots were nothing unusual on the West Side. But Wrigley wasn't that kind of cop. Because he was class commander, he got to choose where he went after the academy. He could have taken a cozy North Side district, but he chose the busiest, most dangerous part of the city, the West Side. He and his partner got in their squad car and headed in the direction where they heard the shots. As they got closer, they observed a minivan driving down a one-way street the wrong way with the lights turned off. They pulled behind it and ran the plates. They followed the vehicle while the computer spit out the information. Nothing came out irregular, so they activated their lights and pulled it over for the traffic violations. Just as they did so, another squad car pulled up to assist them, two officers from another unit. As they all approached the car, the driver exited the car, shouting that they were harassing him because he was black. It's always an alarm when someone exits the car on a traffic stop. They placed him against the van to frisk him, trying to calm the man down. At first he complied, but then he began wrestling with them. One of the cops saw he was reaching for a pistol and shouted, "Gun, gun," but the driver got to it, pulled it out, and began shooting. Three officers pulled their guns and fired as they took cover, hearing the rounds fly by their heads. Even though their rounds struck the driver, he continued shooting at them. The gunfight went on so long, Wrigley dropped his magazine and put in a fresh one. Finally the offender ran out of ammunition. The cops stopped firing in return.

Wrigley realized he had been shot twice, once in the arm and once in his chest. Two other cops had been struck, one by ricocheted bullet. Wrigley yelled into the microphone, "Officer down, officer down!" Then Wrigley grabbed the first cop he could and told him to take him to the hospital. One of Wrigley's most harrowing descriptions was, apart from the rounds flying by his ear, the drive to the hospital in the back of a squad car. He did not know if he was about to die. In the car, Wrigley felt his arms, legs, torso for any fatal wounds, checking his pulse, making sure he was breathing okay, since he had no idea where the bullets finally landed or what damage they had done. He prayed and called his girlfriend to tell her what had happened. Cops blocked off intersections as he was rushed to the county hospital. The other two wounded officers were taken to other hospitals. The offender went in an ambulance. It turns out the offender, Howard Morgan, was an off-duty railroad cop. He had also once been a Chicago cop, but, strangely, he quit the job after less than ten years. According to the terms of his current employment with the railroad, he was not allowed to carry his gun unless he was on his way to or from work. Morgan was doing neither when Wrigley and his partner stopped him. What he was really up to, no one ever found out. Wrigley was shot once in the chest, but that round had been blocked by his bullet-proof vest. He was also shot once in the lower arm. That bullet traveled up his arm and exited his shoulder, doing little internal damage.

From the beginning, Morgan's attorney and his supporters tried to make the incident a racial issue because all the cops were white and Morgan was black. Their theories suggested the cops gunned down Morgan simply because of his race. It was one thing to read about detectives from thirty years ago being accused of racial violence, but to have someone you knew and knew well, someone who had taught you much about the art of policing, to see him transformed into a racist killer was an entirely different thing, particularly when there was no evidence whatsoever to pose such a theory. The fact that Wrigley and his coworkers had almost been killed only added to my anger. Here they were pursuing gunshots, fighting to improve the quality of the neighborhood, and this was the thanks they got. Many people from the community rushed to support Morgan.

The theories of racial antipathy guiding the officers began to take absurd and obscene forms. It was suggested that the four officers, who barely even knew one another, somehow conspired to murder Morgan that night. It's impossible to wrap one's mind around. The theory was that they somehow devised a plan to gun Morgan down, then did so, but failed to kill him. Rather than keep shooting until he was dead, the officers stopped for some reason. Morgan remained on the ground, the theory went, wounded some eighteen times. The officers then decided to make their attempted execution look like a bona fide shooting. They did so by deciding to shoot and wound each other. One has to keep in mind that two of the officers were from different units and barely knew each other. There was no way they could have formed this plan ahead of time. That meant the officers conspired to unlawfully stop Morgan, then decided to shoot him, all within a matter of moments. It meant that the four officers agreed to this insane plot even though they were largely strangers to one another. According to the paranoid theories submitted by defense supporters, the cops then shot each other, somehow knowing the shots wouldn't be fatal, including the one right to Wrigley's heart, which just caught his vest. Afterward, as three of them lay wounded in the street, not knowing if they would live, they put their complex alibi story together about the offender shooting them during a traffic stop, an alibi that just happened to match exactly the immense amount of forensic evidence at the crime scene. Then they stuck to this story as they were rushed to different hospitals and gave their accounts to various detectives. It's incredible to imagine, lying on the street, bleeding, after dozens and dozens of shots were fired, three of them wounded, the four officers risking prison, the ruin of their careers, the loss of their homes and pension, and they organized an alibi that they all stuck to.

These were the theories about the shooting that took shape not only in the courtroom but in the community, as several religious organizations banded together and began advocating on behalf of Howard Morgan. They were very effective. They got Morgan out on bond, despite him being charged with four counts of attempted murder. What a bitter pill for Wrigley and the other officers, for any cop, to see that a guy is charged with four counts of attempted murder of the police and he gets out on bond.

The truth is that much of what happened in the case did not surprise me. Having read about James Ealy, Andrew Wilson, and Anthony Porter, I knew that any kind of hysteria, of race-baiting high jinks, infected police shootings. But now it was touching my life more directly. In the tactics to turn the tables on the cops and free Morgan, I was starting to sense that the wrongful conviction advocates were involved, either directly or merely in the strategies used to get Morgan off the hook: charges of racism, police cover-up, turning the tables on the cops, ignoring the massive amount of evidence. Wrigley and I spent hours and hours going over the case, often in his backyard on a summer afternoon over a beer. I also wrote many bitter letters to the editor, letters to the reporters on the case, those who gave voice to the insane claims by Morgan's defenders. As the trial approached, the religious groups backing Morgan began a smear campaign against Wrigley and his fellow cops. Once again I saw the wrongful conviction strategies at work—a media disinformation campaign aimed, in my mind, at infecting the jury pool. The groups backing Morgan made a documentary echoing their claims. I watched it at Wrigley's house, the two of us dumbfounded. Wrigley found out these groups had made inquiries into his entire work record, not simply in Chicago but since the first time he ever took a job. He suspected they were tapping into his Facebook account, looking for any piece of information, any image, that they could use to transform Wrigley and his colleagues into racist monsters.

The absurdity of the defense claims in Wrigley's first trial didn't matter. There were a few jurors who bought into it, and ended in a hung jury. Tensions were obviously very high among the jurors. The majority of them were clearly furious at the few who sided with the defense. The vote split mostly on racial lines, though some African American jury members voted for the cops. Morgan would remain free until the next trial. Wrigley and the other cops would have to go through an entirely new trial. In the years between the first trial and the second trial, the religious organizations backing Morgan pushed their case of a racist execution even more. They claimed there was a vast cover-up, that even the highest-ranking members of the police department were involved.

By the time of the second trial in 2012, seven years after the shooting, much had changed in Wrigley's life. He had broken up with his fiancée, married another woman, and they had their first child together. Wrigley's father had also died from cancer, a devastating blow. The two were very close. His father, a retired police chief, often went over Wrigley's case with him. Wrigley was awarded the medal of valor for his actions that night, one of the highest awards a police officer can win. At his father's funeral, he placed the medal in the casket and it was buried with his father. It would be much harder to endure the trial and the accusations without his father's support, without his father sitting in the courtroom, especially when the verdict came in. For Wrigley's father to die before the second trial imposed a terrible loneliness. It would be that much harder to bear the disgusting theatrics of the defense in the second trial without his father there.

In the second trial, the Morgan side of the courtroom was packed with activists, many of whom stared at me or any other cop when we walked in and sat on the other side. When the jury recessed and everyone walked out of the room, many of the supporters for the defendant would hold the door open for their fellow supporters, then let it shut on any of the supporters of the cops. They clapped when the defense attorney made accusations against the cops, and then were thrown out of the court. They prayed loudly in the courtroom before the proceedings began, prayers that baited the cops and accused them of being thugs. During testimony of the cops or their witnesses, they made noises in the gallery to distract the jury. They came over to our side of the courtroom and banged on the wooden seats with their feet. They whispered amongst themselves so the jury could hear. The judge was too meek to do anything about it.

"Shush," I finally told one of the noisemakers, after I saw a jury member looking over, distracted.

"Don't you shush me," he said back.

"I already did."

"You motherfucker."

"Fuck you, asshole," I said. I was off duty.

At the next recess, I stood up and turned. The man was standing in the aisle staring at me.

"C'mon on with it," I said, facing him, "you fucking clown."

I recognized the wrongful conviction movement all over the case. Their ability to turn the tables on the cops, no matter how clear the evidence, was unfolding right in front of us. Wrigley and I had spent many evenings talking about how it would end up. For a long time we figured Morgan would get off. There would be more hung trials until the prosecutor finally gave up, or there would be a jury with enough members on it to believe the defense. They would dig in. We had to prepare for the fact that Morgan might get off. And what if he did? After the shooting, Morgan's attorneys had filed a civil lawsuit against the cops. These lawsuits were pretty much routine anytime someone was shot by the police, no matter how clearly justified the actions of the officers. If Morgan beat the criminal case, this civil lawsuit would quickly gather momentum. Would Wrigley be like so many detectives in the city seeing a shooter set free, then made rich off a lawsuit? We turned these possibilities over and over during the seven years of the case. During this time, Wrigley had to endure the allegations that his actions were racially motivated as the second trial approached, that he wasn't a victim, but a cold-blooded killer.

But this time, the prosecutor was so well prepared that he could shoot down any claim of conspiracy from the defense with simple facts and argument. The forensic evidence was vast, the witnesses all solid. One of the most compelling pieces of evidence was the bullet that fell out of Wrigley's clothing when he was at the hospital. It matched the caliber of Morgan's pistol. One question the defense could never answer was: How did that bullet get in Wrigley's clothing? Clearly he was shot at. By the time of closing arguments, the defense attorneys were stammering witlessly and incoherently various contradictory claims of malfeasance by the cops, and the prosecutor was shooting them down easily. The defense attorneys looked like buffoons. When the jury went to deliberate, several of us went to an Italian restaurant a few miles from the courthouse, wondering if the defense had sold their racist hysteria to any of the jurors. You never could tell about a jury in Cook County. In a few hours, the jury came back with a verdict of guilty on all counts of attempted murder. The long nightmare seemed to be over. Morgan was sentenced to forty years. When asked if he had a statement to make, he told the judge, "I am a child of God."

Aren't we all, I wondered to myself.

One thing was clear by the time of Morgan's conviction. Trials didn't matter much in the city anymore. Look at the Porter case. Porter was found guilty in a criminal case. He appealed through all the courts and lost. His claims of innocence were destroyed in a grand jury hearing. His guilt was reaffirmed in a civil trial. Every legal proceeding that looked into his case revealed he was the killer, yet he eventually walked free. The same force took shape in Wrigley's case. Despite the fact that a jury heard all the overwhelming evidence that Morgan had shot three cops, journalists in the city disregarded their verdict and sided with Morgan. *Sun-Times* columnist Mary Mitchell wrote about the case, likening Wrigley and the other cops to the Trayvon Martin shooting and the Jon Burge scandal:

> At a time when the shooting in Florida of Trayvon Martin is drawing supporters from across the country, Chicago has its own shooting scandal.
>
> Like the Trayvon case, nothing about the 2005 shooting of Howard Morgan makes sense. Chicago police officers shot Morgan 28 times during an alleged traffic stop. However, it was Morgan who was charged with attempted murder, among other offenses.
>
> But unlike the Trayvon case, Morgan's wife and supporters have had a difficult time getting the media to pay attention to the case even though it involved a volatile mixture of cops and race.
>
> Morgan is African-American. All of the police officers involved in the shooting are white.
>
> "This man is the only man in the world who was shot 28 times and still alive to tell the truth about what happened," Rosalind Morgan told me during a telephone interview on Monday. "This is crazy. There's been a news blackout. I had to go outside to get someone to help."
>
> After a second trial, Morgan was convicted of attempted murder and is scheduled to be sentenced at 26th and California at 8 a.m. Thursday amid protests that the second trial amounted to double jeopardy.

"He should have been acquitted of the remaining charges," Rosalind Morgan argued. "His constitutional rights were violated. He did not have a fair trial."

Occupy Chicago protesters are planning to demonstrate in front of the Cook County Courthouse Thursday, although uniformed police officers are expected to pack the courtroom. Morgan faces up to 80 years in prison.

Morgan, a former Chicago police officer, was working as a policeman for the Burlington Northern Santa Fe Line in 2005 when he was shot 28 times by four white police officers during a traffic stop.

Although the police officers alleged Morgan opened fire when they tried to arrest him, the fusillade of bullets turned Morgan into a human sieve and put him in the hospital for seven months.

He was later charged with four counts of attempted murder; three counts of aggravated battery and one count of aggravated discharge of a firearm at a police officer.

Morgan languished in jail until an anonymous donor put up the $2 million bond.

In 2007, a jury acquitted Morgan of aggravated battery and discharging a weapon at a police officer. They deadlocked on attempted murder charges.

Prosecutors retried the case and in January, and a second jury found Morgan guilty on the attempted murder counts. Morgan's supporters argue that the verdict subjected him to double jeopardy because he was acquitted in the first trial of discharging a weapon.

"It's just wrong. They want to sweep this under the carpet and don't want to take the blame," the wife said.

"All of the young people who were victims of police shootings are dead. They can't tell their side of the story. Mr. Morgan was shot 28 times—21 in the back of his body and seven times in the front. The man deserves to be treated fairly," she said.

This controversial police shooting occurred around the same time the cover was being pulled on police torture and corruption in Chicago.

Yet similar to the public's initial nonchalance with respect to the Jon Burge torture victims, the Morgan case hasn't sparked any protests.

"None of the big ministers have gotten involved. Jesse Jackson hasn't stepped in," Morgan told me.

I caught up to Jackson in Memphis where he is taking part in observances marking the anniversary of the assassination of Martin Luther King Jr. Jackson's been all over the Trayvon Martin shooting. But he agreed that it has been difficult for the public to sustain outrage over the Morgan shooting.

"When he first got shot, we visited him in the hospital," Jackson said. "After the first trial, we thought we won the case, but this has gone up and down. We intend to go to court with him on April 5th, and a number of our people intend to be in the courtroom," he said.

"This [police-involved shootings] is pervasive."

Meanwhile, the Morgans are pursuing a civil suit in federal court against the police officers.

"It's horrible, but I have to take up the mantle of justice for my husband," the wife said. "If they can get away with double jeopardy, they can get away with anything."

Mitchell never bothered to get any facts straight. She never bothered to observe that Morgan was not shot twenty-eight times. He had twenty-eight holes in him because several of the bullets were through and through. So much for her claims that Morgan was shot in the back so many times. She also ignored the fact that Morgan was twisting and turning when he shot and the officers were spread out, accounting for some shots in his back. In any case, when an offender is shooting at cops, the cops have every right to shoot back at any part of his body. Mitchell downplayed the fact that Morgan fired seventeen shots at the officers. Three of the officers returned fire, the number of their shots entirely reasonable, especially since Morgan kept firing at them. She also neglected to mention that officers stopped firing while Morgan was still alive. When Morgan ran out of bullets and no longer posed a risk, the officers also ceased fire, absolutely correct police use of force guidelines, a tremendous sign of their self-control and professionalism under fire. If their racial hatred was so intense that they were willing to fire indiscriminately at Morgan, they could have easily popped one more shot into his head and avoided a trial altogether. But they didn't. Mitchell also ignored the central fact that undermines any claim that Morgan was a victim. A bullet was recovered off Wrigley. That bullet likely came from Morgan's gun. Unable to contain my rage at Mitchell's column, I fired off a letter to her.

I am a writer and Chicago Police Officer currently working on a book about several murders in 1982. I have also followed closely the Howard Morgan case, sitting through much of both trials.

I have read many articles from journalists about controversial cases, but I do not think I have read any as depraved and morally bankrupt as your column today. Your overwhelming bias should banish you from serious journalism.

The reason Howard Morgan was found guilty was that there was overwhelming evidence that he pulled a gun on the officers and fired at them 17 times from a short distance for no reason. Naturally, you don't mention in your tripe that three of the officers were wounded as a result of Morgan's firing at them, one saved from a probably fatal wound to his chest by his vest. Nor do you mention the changing statements of Morgan and his wife throughout his case, the complete and total breakdown of his case during the trial, leaving his attorneys with no argument whatsoever to posit in Morgan's defense. You don't mention the fact that at one point the defense claimed that Morgan never even fired his gun, a claim devoid of reality given the immense amount of forensic evidence.

Then there are the connections you make from this case to Jon Burge and the shooting in Florida. There is nothing even remotely similar in these cases. Nothing. That you would tie them together reveals nothing about the Morgan case save your own despicable bias and racism.

The tide is turning in Chicago. The wrongful conviction movement is collapsing. Journalists, attorneys, cops, and civilians are seeing clearly the abuses of the justice system that have taken place in Chicago, particularly in the Anthony Porter case, where wrongful conviction zealots knowingly freed a cold-blooded killer for their own profit and celebrity. The most striking feature of this collapse will be the total negligence of the journalists in Chicago. You will be among the worst of them.

If you are seriously interested in rooting out corruption and racism in Chicago, you would do well to start by looking in the mirror.

See you at the sentencing hearing on Thursday.

I never heard back from her.

At the sentencing hearing, Wrigley was finally allowed to speak directly to Morgan so that all could hear:

In preparation for today, I carefully thought about what I would say in regards to a man who intentionally almost ended my life. The truth is, it's extremely difficult to put into words, my emotions and my thoughts, of not only that night, but also the effect the last several years have had on me, my family, and my friends.

On February 21, 2005, a Chicago Police Officer went to work that night, as a man with 11 years of Law Enforcement experience. In those 11 years, he served as a Police Officer in multiple jurisdictions, and served communities of people from different races, cultures, religions, and backgrounds. He always strived to maintain a good reputation within those communities, including Chicago, because he believed in the trust that should exist between the Police and the people they serve. And, he always strived to do his job with fairness and compassion. That was one of the Police Officers you encountered that night, Mr. Morgan. That was me.

The night I crossed your path, I was only doing what I have done a thousand times before as a Police Officer. Then you made a choice . . . You shot me, Mr. Morgan, and came very close to taking my life. I don't think we will ever know how you came to that choice, but you have shown me what type of person you are in the events following that night.

What is so reprehensible, Mr. Morgan, is you have shown no remorse or accountability in regards to your actions and choices that night. In fact, you have done exactly the opposite. You attempted to lead, and you have allowed people to believe, you did nothing wrong. That somehow, you were the victim in this case. You attempted to hide behind the racial fears of our community, and you manipulated organizations into believing that Police misconduct and corruption were the cause of me, and another officer, being shot that night with your firearm. The very idea goes beyond reason and logic. You preyed upon the emotions and sympathetic intentions of others. In doing so, you allowed these same people and organizations to slander our reputations as Police Officers, and as members of this community. Lastly, and more importantly, you allowed further damage to the trust between our community and the Police. You orchestrated and allowed all of this to occur, knowing it to be untrue, with the only intention of fulfilling your own self-serving agenda.

But you couldn't hide from the facts and the truth of this case. After all the evidence and testimony was heard, you were rightfully convicted. You are a fraud, Mr. Morgan . . . that's also the truth. I will leave here today with my head held high, knowing the truth of this case. Knowing that justice was served fairly upon you, Mr. Morgan. After this day, I will continue to serve with pride and diligence as a Chicago Police Officer. But above all else, I will continue and will always serve the people of this community with fairness and compassion.

The Morgan side of the gallery was completely silent.

Morgan had one last court appearance before he was shipped off to prison. This was a routine appearance that should have had little bearing on the case. At the sentencing hearing, when Wrigley made this speech, the court was packed with other police officers, members of the union, so many they spilled out into a hallway. The media was also there. But this hearing after the sentencing, few of us bothered to go, including me. Wrigley called me that morning. He told me that out of nowhere David Protess and Jesse Jackson appeared at the hearing. My suspicions that wrongful conviction radicals were somehow involved in the protests to get Morgan off this conviction proved true. Jackson was called by the defense and sworn in. Morgan's attorneys asked that Morgan be granted bond pending his appeal, and Jackson testified on behalf of this request. Jackson made positive remarks about Morgan's character as grounds that he should be released. Freed on bond after being convicted of attempted murder? After shooting three people? After he testified, Jackson walked over to the cops and shook their hands, knowing that if they refused, it would make them look bad. It was a disgusting gesture, a blatant "in your face" to the cops. One moment Jackson is calling for a man who tried to murder the three cops to be freed, then he walks over to the cops and shakes their hands.

"There is no way I would have shaken his hand. No fucking way," I fumed as Wrigley told me about the proceeding.

"What else could we do?" he said.

I just simmered silently as he recalled what happened. After the hearing, Protess had the attention of the defense supporters. He began telling them loudly he would show them how to turn this case into a wrongful conviction. He spoke within earshot of the four officers, almost taunting them. A wrongful conviction? Wrigley and the other cops in the shooting thought their ordeal was finally over when the jury came back guilty on all counts, seven years after they were shot, but it wasn't to be. It was just like when Salvatore and Gray had thought the Porter case was over after Porter was sentenced to death and all his appeals were exhausted. With Protess involved, who knew where Wrigley's case would go now? It might never end. It might go on the rest of their lives.

The group of supporters for the defendant cheered Protess and warmly embraced him as he breathed new life into their insane, racist worldview. Yet how the disgraced professor concluded that this was a wrongful conviction case he did not explain to the crowd. No one had seen him show up for one day of the trial. No one had seen him listening to any of the testimony. But that didn't matter. The Porter case already showed that Protess and his acolytes never really bothered to look at the facts of a case. Their forte was merely undermining cases, with the aid of journalists like Eric Zorn and Mary Mitchell. Wrigley and the three other cops were forced to remain silent while Protess carried on, but of course they were furious, and seething with rage. First Jackson gets up and asks for Morgan to be freed on bond, then he shakes their hand. Now Protess indicates that he is going to try to get Morgan off his conviction. Who the hell would want to be a cop in a town like this?

There was a glimmer of hope. All the time Wrigley was going through the shooting and the court cases after it, he was following closely my investigation into the wrongful conviction movement. Now suddenly with Protess emerging at his trial, Wrigley and I seemed to be meeting at a common point from two very different paths. Our friendship seemed to have a fatefulness about it, for now I was able to fill Wrigley in on the wrongful conviction methods and show how it was working in his trial. By the time Protess showed up at his trial, Wrigley knew all about the man because I had kept him apprised as I wrote my book and worked on the documentary. Wrigley was well aware of how Protess had been fired from Northwestern, the accusations that he had lied on his cases. Wrigley also knew about the malfeasance in the Porter case. Wrigley told me that Protess came off looking desperate and obsequious to the crowd. There was no fawning press reflexively echoing Protess's claims of wrongful conviction in Wrigley's case. No one outside the cabal of the most radical journalists like Mitchell would take up his claims, now that he had been fired from Northwestern and the school admitted he was a liar. There were no journalists hanging on his every word, no collection of ambitious young students hoping to make a name for themselves with his techniques. For the first time, the emperor had no clothes, and Wrigley said he looked like a complete fool talking to the crowd.

"Well, I suppose it's a good thing I wasn't there," I said to Wrigley on the phone. "I am not sure I could have restrained myself."

20. UP NORTH

Michigan looms in my mind, the shores of Lake Michigan. I can see the endless dunes that you can walk for miles with no one in sight. I can see myself strolling along the beach in ankle-deep water until I get too warm, then diving into the waves. These swims in the deep blue waters of Lake Michigan always feel like a kind of baptism. In the northern part of the Lower Peninsula of Michigan, dozens of smaller lakes are connected to Lake Michigan. I would swim in these smaller lakes as well. In the evenings I would watch the sunsets and the yellow light across the miles of forest off the shore. This light has always seemed sacred to me. My family had been vacationing in the northern part of lower Michigan ever since I was child. When my parents retired, they built a home there. A friend of mine had once pointed out that the power of the beaches on the Michigan side of Lake Michigan is that they ease all burdens, all antipathy fades.

This is what I need because the murders of 1982 have taken a toll on me. I have been living in them for five years and through three back surgeries. My attempt to capture them in some medium, a documentary, has failed. Peter and I cannot work together. He had taken all the footage of our interviews and gone back to LA to make what is called a sizzle reel, a short version of the documentary that can be used to garner attention for the project and some investors. What he came back with was ten minutes of interviews and images that make no sense whatsoever, that tell no story. He even had the date of the Porter murders wrong, off by a year. This was two years' labor with the guy shot to hell. My apartment is stacked with court transcripts and documents, different versions of the Ealy murder piled on my desk. I need to stop thinking about the Ealy case, about Alstory Simon lingering in prison. I need to get to northern Michigan, so I put in a request to use a baby furlough in July. There is a campground in Frankfort, Michigan, and I have all new camping equipment. It's a Saturday morning and I'm all set. All I have to do is get some clothes out of the laundry, pack up the car, and I'm gone. I head out the back door of my condo with the laundry basket where my neighbor is standing.

"Did you talk to Susan?" she asks. Susan lives above me.

"No, why?"

"She's got bedbugs really bad," she says.

I freeze. The papers have been running stories about bedbugs invading the city. There have been reports of a few units on the other side of the building having them, but I had forgotten all about it. I turn around and go back into my condo, set down the laundry basket, and walk into the bedroom. I turn on the light, pull the top mattress off. There is a dark stain along the ridge of the mattress underneath the sheet. I yank off the sheet. There are about a dozen small bugs. My heart races. I look deeper into the mattress. There are bugs everywhere. Taking a flashlight out, I look along the base boards, finding dozens more. I sit down in front of my computer and type "bedbug infestation" into a search engine. An Internet article says I have to throw out everything, the mattresses, the frame, the bedding. My vacation is slipping away. Even if I went to Michigan, how could I relax knowing about the bug invasion? I pull the mattresses and box springs out into the alley, along with all my sheets and bedding. I don't know it, but this is the wrong thing to do. I risk shaking them off and spreading them to other parts of my condo and to the building.

This is going to be very expensive, a new bed, new sheets. The management company says I will have to pay for half the extermination and it will take three sprays, the cost of which will surpass the money I have saved up for the vacation. I also have to make sure the bugs are not in my clothes. To do so, I have to put all of them in plastic garbage bags, then take them out to my car. Leaving the car in the sun with the windows rolled up will roast any bugs or eggs. The article says I need to find out how far they have infested my unit, so I pull furniture in the living room out from the wall, lift cushions off the coach and inspect them carefully. I can find nothing outside the bedroom, so perhaps they won't spread elsewhere. I call the campground in Michigan and cancel my reservation, my spirits plummeting.

What I also learn about bedbugs is that they crawl onto your body and infuse some kind of anesthetic that prevents you from feeling their bite.

They feed off your blood, then crawl back from where they came. There's a valuable metaphor here, but I am too stressed out to sit down and flush it out. The bugs have been feeding off me for months. I suddenly recall swatting things off me late at night, but had dismissed it as one of the cats sleeping next to me. The bedbugs, the article says, can go a year without feeding and reproduce rapidly, like roaches. They hide but can tell when you are asleep by the steady release of carbon dioxide when you breathe. That's when they make their move.

All day long I roast clothes, search my apartment, and spray pesticide in my now-empty bedroom. As evening approaches, I realize I can't sleep in my bedroom. I dread sleeping in the living room and drawing them out there with my steady breathing. But what choice do I have? I blow up my camping mattress and put it on the living room floor. It's a hot summer night. All my windows are open. All the time I lie there, I think about the bugs sensing my breath and slowly creeping my way, infesting the rest of the condo. Sleep is impossible. I pick up my mattress and a sheet and head outside to my backyard, which is a private lawn on the shore of Lake Michigan. I put the mattress down and lie on top of it. The stars are out, and there are large waves crashing the beach. There are hundreds of lights from the boats cruising up and down the shore. There's an occasional breeze. Our private yard is fenced in, but anyone can walk up from the beach. Bushes will block the view of me sleeping in the grass, but I worry about some gangbanger seeing me and sensing opportunity. I also know that rats scurry to the lake at night to drink water, so they are all around me. My cats have caught plenty of mice. They are out here, too. I think about setting up my tent, but that would be too conspicuous. Best to just shut my eyes and hope sleep comes.

But sleep does not come. Every time I hear a car starting or a distant voice, I am startled. I find myself finally sitting up. It's so hot out I'm dripping sweat into the mattress. It dawns on me nothing has changed. I have been in the city for two decades and never found a place to call home. Now I'm kicked out by bedbugs, much as the roaches had once chased me out of another apartment not far from where I am now. That was what, two decades ago? I want to leave the city, never to return. I'm thinking about buying a farm in Michigan, near the shore of a little lake, close to Lake Michigan. It would be fine to live in a place where people do not hate one another with such intensity, such violence, a place where the killers aren't in charge. I look at the lake. Michigan is just across it, but it may as well have been another universe. I am trapped,

trapped in these murders, trapped as a cop, trapped in the city's imagination.

Without even formally deciding to do so, I find myself standing up and walking to the basement storage area of my condo. Some people keep kayaks there, paddles, a windsurfer. I had an old inner tube there that I had purchased several years earlier outside a tire store in northern Michigan. The tire store took them off old tractors, patched them up, and left them outside with a little box where you left five dollars for them. Kids used them to float down rivers and on the lakes. I bought this one because it was the largest I had ever seen. I had floated on the lake outside my condo one day until a lifeguard came and told me they were prohibited, and that was the end of that.

Now I unfold the tube in the basement, plugging in the same pump I had used for the mattress. It spreads out before me as the air goes in, almost pinning me in the corner. Also in the basement is my neighbor's waterproof carrying bag, sitting in his kayak. I borrow it, along with a paddle. Next I go into the back door of my kitchen, fill the bag with two water bottles, three beers, some granola bars, a sweatshirt, a kitchen knife, my cell phone and wallet. I reach into a drawer where I keep some rope and take a roll of it. Returning to the basement, I carefully push the inner tube through the door, carrying the bag, the paddle, and the rope, and roll the tube down the alley to the beach. I have to carry it across the sand because it won't roll. I place it in the water, the needle facing down, and tie the bag tightly to it. Then I connect a length of rope to a hole in the top of the paddle and secure the other end to the tube. If I drop the paddle, I can retrieve it with the rope.

A warm wind is blowing. The waves are noisy. I push the inner tube out a little way, until I'm up to my knees. A scan up and down the shore reveals no one watching me. I jump and turn at the same time, falling into the center of the tube, which sinks a ways under my weight, then rises up, only a small section of my ass touching the water. With my arms I feel for the rope holding the paddle, find it, and pull it toward me. I paddle deeper into the lake, one stroke on my left, another on my right. Once I clear the crashing waves, it's easier. There seems to be a small current pushing me out, so I set the paddle down across my body and stare up at the stars. To my astonishment, I become drowsy, the stress and labor of the day taking their toll on me.

When I awake the water is still. I'm only a little chilly from partially sitting in it. I have no idea how long I've been sleeping. Part of me knows

I should be alarmed at my condition, but I'm not. It's so peaceful on the lake. I can follow the Big Dipper to the North Star. From there I can figure where east and west are. There's no land in sight, nor any light on either side. Nor are there any boats to be seen. I reach for the bag, pull it toward me, and take out a beer and a granola bar. The beer tastes good, so I open another. What should I do? Where should I go? I could try calling 911 on my cell phone and explain my situation.

"Hi, I'm an off-duty police officer floating on an inner tube in the middle of Lake Michigan, not sure how far off the city of Chicago. Can you send the Coast Guard? Also, I'm a writer."

"You're who in a what, where?"

"Never mind."

The beer fills me up and I need to urinate. There's only one thing to do. I pull my shorts down and hold my cock in my hand. The spray rises up in the air in a long arch, just over the inner tube into the water, making a loud, steady sound. It's actually quite graceful. Of course some doesn't clear the tube, so I reach out and cup some water, splashing it on myself and the tube. Just then I see a light spreading out across the lake, coming closer to me. With the paddle I turn the inner tube in its direction, in time to see a huge ship bearing down on me. It's so close I can't decide which direction I should paddle to avoid it, so I just hold the paddle in front of me, waiting. Someone once told me that these huge cargo ships never run into smaller boats because they put out such a large wake. This wake will push away a lighter watercraft before it can strike the vessel. Sure enough, a large wave in front of the ship comes toward me. I lean in one direction on the inner tube so it don't flip over, staring up as the monster vessel goes by me. It raises me up, turns me hard to the left. I grab tightly on to the tube, lean right to stay on. Then it sinks down on the other side, and I lean the other way. I can see sailors on the ship looking over the side and smoking, but they don't see me. Diminishing waves rock me as I watch the ship fade into the lake. Then it is quiet again, and I fall back to sleep.

When I awake, I again don't know how much time has passed, but I turn in the water with the paddle and see artificial light in the distance. It must be the city, I figure. Lifting the paddle from my chest, I begin slowly paddling toward it, hoping I will come out close to my beach in Rogers Park, and no one will be the wiser about what I have done. I will never tell a soul. What's so strange is that there are very few lights from the banks, a sign that I have drifted into a remote area. Then the first rays of morning light arise, but it's in the same direction as the artificial light. I pause, remind myself that the sun rises in the east and sets in the west. Right? If that's true, then I have crossed the entire lake. I'm headed for Michigan, not Chicago. Over and over I review the simple fact of the sunrise and the sunset, and each time I confirm the truth of it: rises in the east, sets in the west. There's nothing to do but paddle toward the shore. When I get close, I will know for sure, since the shore of Michigan is endless dunes while the western shore has rocks and crags.

Soon a current catches me and pushes me toward the shore. The waves pick up and rock me a little bit. I can make out some dunes and trees. They are lovely in the morning light. Seagulls are talking above me. The sun will rise above the horizon soon. In the water next to me, I see a school of salmon slowly swim by. A few of them look to be over thirty pounds. A huge fish with a pointed snout swims near me, then glides underneath my inner tube. I reach to touch it, but it moves slowly out of my reach and goes on its way. It must have been a sturgeon.

When I reach a sandbar near the shore, I jump out of the inner tube, stiff and sore from the night of sitting in one position. The water is cold and I shiver. The sun will be up and warm me soon. My toes curl into the gentle, smooth sand on the bottom of the lake. There is no one on shore. The dunes spread out for miles, sometimes rising high above the lake. The morning light on them is breathtaking. I walk toward the shore, pulling my inner tube along with me by the rope attached to the paddle. As I get onto the shore, the sun comes up above the trees, warming me, bathing everything in a yellow light. I am suddenly so alive. The world is beautiful, and there are sacred things in it. To be alive is to be sad and joyful at the same time, like this light off the water. I walk onto the shore and lift my legs high, jog a little up a dune to get my blood flowing and warm myself, then I just stand on the beach for a while taking in the lake, the dunes, and my own loneliness. It could be miles of walking before I hit a town, but I know I will find one. Every seven to ten miles there's another small city along the lake. Either direction I will run across one.

The question eventually arises of what direction to walk—north or south? South would be logical because that's the way to Chicago, but to the north I can see dozens of seagulls on the beach, a sign perhaps that a river empties into the lake. Wherever there are rivers, there will be little towns close by, or at least some cottages whose residents might provide me with some information, or I will find a road. North it is, then. I walk along the shore, towing the inner tube with the string in the shallow water. My feet sink into the sand and water. The light becomes more intense. I carry the bag over my shoulder, the paddle in my left hand. As I walk, the place suddenly becomes familiar to me. This little river is called the inlet, a small stream that feeds water from a smaller lake called Lower Herring into Lake Michigan. I have been coming here since I was a boy, have fished for salmon here. When my parents retired, they built a house on this smaller lake. It's difficult to deny that I am trapped in something fateful, the fact that I could float across the lake and end up here, and I begin to sense a purpose in the bedbugs, for they had been the catalyst for this trip.

As I approach the inlet, the seagulls take flight. I wade into its shallow water. It's warmer than the water in Lake Michigan. Memories come back to me in the form of clear, authentic voices, mostly the voices of loved ones. In them there is the tone of forgiveness and understanding, as if all antipathy, all hatred is merely misunderstanding. This possibility stirs me, because the antipathy in the city comes from something evil, beyond understanding, from something rooted in the inexplicable mind of a sociopath. I welcome the voices, let them have their say. My parents are deceased, but the memory of them comes flooding back to me here, especially the years of my mother's declining health, her slow descent into the horrors of dementia. This inlet is where I often came when I could arrange some time away from her. Now I can hear her voice, gentle, even as it was on the days we went to see the doctor and knew we were going to hear something devastating, the days when they explained the results of a brain scan, for example. I can also hear my father's voice, no longer disapproving of me, and I feel no antagonism toward him. I feel as if we forgive each other, as if everything is forgiven. We just hadn't understood where each other was coming from. In these waters, I can perceive he suddenly sees that perhaps there is logic in my chaos, and he wishes me well. It was all just a misunderstanding, but it's all right now. The sun warms me. I can feel its intensity. Soon tourists from a nearby resort will come out to the beach and wonder who or what I am. I have to push on.

I walk into the middle of the inlet. There's an old dam there we used to dive off. Fish would collect on one side of it, where the rushing water created a deeper pool. I can't help it. I dive into it with my eyes open. Little fish move just beyond my grasp. A few larger ones stare at me. I climb over the dam, pull the inner tube toward me, then climb aboard when the water becomes too deep. I paddle against a gentle current for a hundred yards or so until I emerge onto Lower Herring Lake, still hugging the western shore, close to Lake Michigan. Across the lake to the east is a public access, a boat ramp and a road. That roads leads to the highway, which will take me wherever I need to go. I lift the paddle, then put it back into the water. Already I have developed a good technique with it. The lake is calm and I stay near the shore as much as I can. When I get to what seems the shortest distance, I will have to launch out across the lake to get to the public access and the road. There will be watercraft on the lake, some fishing, some early morning skiers. They may think I'm in distress and approach me. Some, as they got closer, may recognize me. Everyone knows our family and me from the years we spent up here. I don't want to explain myself, don't want to give an account of myself.

"Well, you see, yesterday in Chicago, I found out I had bedbugs . . ."

I move out into the lake, exposed. The paddle moves me steadily, as the water is still quiet. A few boats come close to me, but I give them a thumbs-up, as if I do this every day. They move away. I mark myself as being about halfway across, my arms a little weary, but I keep on. Around the lake are signs of people starting their day. There are some runners and bikers on the shore, a few boats pulling up to a launch. Soon I am getting close enough to shore that I can jump off the inner tube and walk in, so I do, sinking in the water up to my neck, my feet on the sandy bottom. I gently push the inner tube ahead of me. Somewhat noisily I emerge from the water, wet, chilly and tired. I stand on the grass, dripping and shivering. There's morning dew on the grass. The inner tube floats just off the shore. I pull it to me with the string, then set it down on the ground. I take off my shirt, wring the water of it, then grab the dry sweatshirt from the bag and put it on, pushing up the sleeves.

I hide the paddle and the tube in some deep grass, the waterproof bag hanging on my shoulder. The way things are going, I may have to float back. It's a short, familiar walk to Highway M-22. To get there I will walk by my parents' old house. Here my mother had suffered through several strokes; my father and I had engaged in a bitter feud. This was the house my parents had built, that they had planned on leaving to their children. The house had been purchased by another family when my parents were ill. The patriarch of this family pestered my parents to sell. He was pushing the deal onto two people facing the terror of old age and dementia. My mother would call me and tell me about these offers, unable to process them, to make a decision. I would instruct her to tell him to stay away. It had infuriated me. But I could never get around to confronting the man. There was always some other medical emergency to deal with. As I walk by, there's some woman hanging clothes out to dry, much as my mother used to do. The woman looks at me, but I don't make eye contact. I'm barefoot, my shorts are wet, and I am carrying everything I have in a bag. I turn back and steal a glance at the house, re-creating in my mind the image of my mother on the porch reading the paper, my father getting ready for a day of working in the yard. How did things end up this way, I wonder.

Out on Highway M-22, I have to decide north or south again. Standing on the side of the road is hard on my bare feet. There are rocks and other sharp objects, likely broken glass in some spots. At the intersection I look both ways. Best to just see where the first car comes by, I figure. I want to get out of there before someone recognizes me. I hear a car coming. It's a pickup truck, going south toward Arcadia. As it comes closer, it strikes me how easily one can return to some long-forgotten ritual. I haven't hitchhiked for years, but I remember to face the vehicle as it approaches, look toward the driver even though I can't see him. I put out my thumb high in the air as the truck nears, and just like that he stops. He looks like a farmer, sunburned with a baseball cap on. The pickup is at least fifteen years old. That's good because the interior is all torn up and my shorts are still wet.

"I'm just going into Arcadia to get some gas. I can get you that far," he says after I close the door.

"That's fine."

"Did you run out of gas or something?" he asks.

"Yeah, something like that. Car wouldn't start. Got someone coming for it, but I had to get into town first. I really appreciate the lift," I say.

"Where are your shoes?"

"Covered in oil and anti-freeze. Got to get a new pair," I lie.

He nods.

Arcadia is only seven miles down the road. There's a gas station/convenience store and a restaurant. The pickup begins a long ascent before we get to town. We come around a curve, and there's Lake Michigan and miles of endless dunes, an image that arrests anyone traveling this road. You drive through a forest, take the curve, and suddenly, there it is, like a revelation. Afterward, we begin a steep descent into the town, and the man pulls into the gas station. There are a few cars on M-22, a few more at the gas station. People are getting up now, starting their day. I figure it to be around 8:00 a.m. Inside, as I had hoped, there's a rack of cheap flip-flop sandals and another of T-shirts. I buy both, along with copies of the local papers, the *Manistee News Advocate* and the *Traverse City Record Eagle*, then walk down the street to the only restaurant in the town.

There's the smell of fresh coffee when I walk in, not the cheap stuff, but gourmet coffee, and it smells freshly ground. It makes me want to cry, because I don't know what it would forebode if, after all I have been through, I had walked into the only restaurant in town and they had shitty coffee. I take a two-top in the corner, spread the papers before me. A young woman, plump and sunburn, walks over with a coffeepot and menu. I nod as she approaches, letting her know I want coffee. The aroma rises. I put a dash of cream in and take a sip, then another. I close my eyes for a second, then look out the window across a large meadow, with a farm beyond that. I scan the menu as more customers come in, then set it down. The waitress sees me and starts walking over. She's good.

"Have you decided what you want?"

"Yes, I have. Thank you. Can I have some fresh-squeezed orange juice and some fresh melon, and then after that I'd like the Denver omelet with rye toast, a side of bacon, and also an order of blueberry pancakes."

She raises her eyebrows.

"Somebody has quite the appetite this morning," she says.

"I surely do. I feel as if I just crossed Lake Michigan on an inner tube," I say.

"Well, that surely would work up an appetite," she says, smiling, then walks away after refilling my coffee.

I drink the orange juice in one shot and eat a few chunks of the melon before the omelet and pancakes come. So many times omelets are too dry in little towns like this one, but this is moist and has a heap of hash browns with it, and I put lots of pepper on them. The bacon strips are thick and wide. Each mouthful is washed down with more coffee and, just as I realize I was probably badly dehydrated, the waitress brings over an ice water. Halfway through the omelet, I push it aside and draw the blueberry pancakes toward me, still very warm, dousing them with some maple syrup and butter and attacking them with my fork and knife, dividing and conquering them, rubbing in their defeat with another swipe of sweet syrup. The blueberries are in season. Blueberry pie crosses my mind, blueberry cobbler. Blueberries are so fucking great. Back and forth I go from the omelet to the pancakes, oblivious to anything else save the police blotter in the paper, which I read while chewing my food: DUIs, domestics, small stuff. Everyone in town knows when you get locked up. It's right there in the paper. And then I sit back at the table, my belly plump like a watermelon, washing the last of my breakfast down with more coffee. There are a lot of decisions waiting for me, like where and how I am going to live, but I don't really care, not then. I can't help but watch the waitress as she glides from table to table.

Outside the restaurant it's sunny and the heat is bearing down. I had put the newspapers in my waterproof bag. I'm growing sleepy, despite the coffee, and I want to lie down somewhere, so I walk back to the gas station, use the bathroom, then buy a beach towel and a quart of water, and walk down the road to the public beach access. There are already several cars there, and I can hear the sound of children playing. I walk up the sand dune, then down the beach, the dunes and then the blue lake spread out before me. The back of the beach is shaded by trees, and will remain so for several hours. It's here I put down the towel and my bag, sensing there's too much wind for mosquitoes, and I don't see many flies about. I lie down in the sand. It welcomes me by shaping itself against me. I turn to my right side, and I sleep.

It's the sun on my feet that wakes me. They're burning. I'm stiff in all my joints, a sign of a deep and fulfilling slumber. The beach has many more people on it, mostly families. I must have been sleeping for around two hours. I stand up, take off my shirt, and walk to the water. The first five yards or so are covered with rocks, which makes it difficult to walk, but after that there's only rippled sand. I walk up to my knees in the water, then up to my waist. Medium-size waves pick me up and set me down. Fathers are tossing their kids into the air, letting them fall into the water, the kids screaming with delight. A couple tosses a stick from the beach, and their Labrador retriever is obsessively and joyfully chasing it down. Deeper in I go, until I spot a sandbar about thirty yards out. Taking a deep breath, I slip underwater, toward the bottom, where I push myself steadily toward the sandbar, my body just over the ripples of the sand until I can't hold my breath anymore. I come up and touch the bottom, the water up to my neck. It's perfect. I let the waves come in, pick me up, and set me down again. Every now and then I go back to the bottom holding my breath. The blue-and-green light breaks through the water in prisms.

I must have been in the water for about an hour when I decide to head back to shore, swimming back from the sandbar until I can touch the bottom with my feet. I emerge from the water and head back to my spot on the beach, pick up the towel, shake it, then wrap myself in it and dry myself. Spreading it out again, I sit and pull the newspapers from my bag, mulling over an idea. I open each one to the classified section and begin looking at the job opportunities. The notion is that I will move to Michigan permanently, find a new life here. At first there seem to be many possibilities: bartending jobs, hotel work, waiter. I have done them all. I have saved enough money that I could buy a small house with a few acres. But then I think about my back. Could I really do this work anymore? Many of these jobs don't have medical care. What if I got sick, needed another back surgeon? Where would I find a good back surgeon up here? I think about walking away from the police pension. Doubts come on. I gather up my stuff into the waterproof bag and walk back into town. In northern Michigan, the jobs are seasonal. Much of the winter there is little work. What would I do for money in the winter?

There's only one motel in town. I walk in, but don't see anyone. I hit a bell after waiting a minute. A woman calls out to me, then emerges from a back door, behind which is the kitchen to her home. I haven't given much thought to lodging for the night, but I should have. This is high season. I guess part of me figures I can hitchhike to the next town, buy a sleeping bag from a sporting goods store, and find a place to sleep on the beach. If I were younger, I might have done it and saved the eighty dollars for the hotel room. My former vagabond life still appeals to me. But I'm almost fifty now, and I need a place to sleep, a hot shower with clean towels, and I like the notion of watching the local news on TV. It's too late for me to radically change my life. There's one room left, the lady says, available for only one night.

I sit on the bed of my room after a shower, wrapped in a clean white towel, the local news on. After I had checked in, I went back to the convenience store and bought a fifth of Irish whiskey. I hold a glass of it with two ice cubes and think about what to do with my life. It's late in the afternoon. I know—but I won't admit it just yet—I have to return to Chicago, to a city that has perfected its own evil. It does so by capturing people's imagination. The paranoia inherent in such a crooked city comes back to me. Alstory Simon is still in prison. There are dozens of wrongful conviction cases pending. Porter is walking around on the South Side. James Ealy's trial for murder will begin soon. As I realize I have to return to the city, the feeling of my own essential criminality returns as well. The suffocating feeling of prison emerges again, that for all my efforts to capture the city in some story or narrative, a prosecution waits for me. I grow more and more anxious in the hotel room, begin pacing back and forth in my towel. Reflexively, I stop and check the window through the curtain. As if in response to my fears, I see red and blue lights. It's a blue squad car heading south on M-22 toward the hotel. It keeps coming, then swerves into the hotel parking lot, gravel flying up as it stops right near my door. In the backseat I can see my inner tube and the paddle. *What the fuck*, I wonder.

Two uniformed cops jump out, both young and strong-looking, one pulling out his pistol. *What the fuck*, I wonder again. Was it the paddle I stole? Was it illegal to cross Lake Michigan in an inner tube? Had the wrongful conviction advocates turned the tables on me, the way they had on so many other detectives? Had they gotten a warrant out on me for something? There's pounding on my door, shouts that I should come out with my hands up. I freeze. A moment of silence follows, and I think maybe they aren't coming after me, but the guy in the next room. But what about the paddle and inner tube in their car? Had someone else crossed the lake the same night I did? No, it can't be. That's when the door is kicked open and the two cops come lunging toward me. I put my hands up. Doing so, the towel falls to the ground and I am naked. They throw me down, and one of their knees goes into my back, choking me.

I feel myself unable to breathe under their weight, and I begin writhing to get free. Sweating and clammy, I sit up, gasping for air, not in the hotel room, but in the backyard of my condo building, the first light of the morning coming from the east. Sweating and exhausted, I gather up the mattress and head inside. Exterminators are coming soon.

ACKNOWLEDGEMENTS

I would like to thank Rob Keast, an editor and friend. Also, I would like to thank the many detectives who sat down and told me their account of several pivotal murders in Chicago. This book could not be possible without the assistance of Bill Crawford, an old school journalist. His research into the Porter case was a great aid and a splendid piece of investigative journalism. Jim Delorto, a retired federal agent, was also a great friend and advisor.

27978251R00138

Made in the USA
Middletown, DE
28 December 2015